THE EIGH[...]
A DECADE WHEN [...]

"Losers are boring."

—Producers [...] Bruckheimer
(*Flashdance* and *Beverly Hills Cop*)

"Rules are for fools."

—Wall Street Wunderkind Charles Atkins
(before his arrest)

"One picture is worth a thousand bucks."

—Artist Mark Kostabi

AND WE SAID...
"Yuppie," "Insider Trading," "Hostile Takeovers,"
"Reaganomics," "Irangate," and "Fax it"
NOW JOHN TAYLOR SHEDS LIGHT ON
ONE OF THE MOST PERPLEXING DECADES
OF THE CENTURY IN...

<u>CIRCUS OF AMBITION</u>

THE CULTURE
OF WEALTH AND POWER
IN THE EIGHTIES

"[An] exuberant anthropological adventure through the
decade."

—*Business Week*

"Entertaining . . . riveting."

—*Chicago Enterprise*

"Entertaining . . . controversial."

—*Publishers Weekly*

"A provocative collection of tales about modern money
players that commands interest."

—*Vance Packard*

"An engaging rundown on the high-profile *arrivistes*. . . .
Diverting socioeconomic reportage and commentary from
an observer with his wits about him."

—*Kirkus Reviews*

CIRCUS OF
AMBITION

◆

THE CULTURE
OF WEALTH AND POWER
IN THE EIGHTIES

◆

JOHN TAYLOR

WARNER BOOKS

A Warner Communications Company

A portion of Chapter 2 first appeared, in substantially different form,
in *Manhattan,inc.* magazine.
Chapter 4 and Chapter 6 originally appeared, again in substantially
altered form, in *New York* magazine.
The author is grateful for the permission to reprint.

Warner Books, Inc., 666 Fifth Avenue, New York, NY 10103

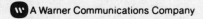 A Warner Communications Company

Printed in the United States of America
First trade printing: June 1990
10 9 8 7 6 5 4 3 2 1

Library of Congress Cataloging-in-Publication Data

Taylor, John, 1955–
  Circus of ambition: the culture of wealth and power in the
eighties / John Taylor.
    p.   cm.
  ISBN 0-446-39157-3 (pbk.)
  I. Title.
PS3570.A9413C5   1989
813'.54—dc20   89-40365
                                                                   CIP

Book designed by Giorgetta Bell McRee
Cover designed by Jackie Merri Meyer
Cover illustration by Brian Ajhar
Marbleized paper by Katherine Radcliffe

For Maureen

ACKNOWLEDGMENTS

More than one hundred people agreed to be interviewed or otherwise provided me with information for this book. I would particularly like to thank Stuart Abrams, Bill Agee, Kent Barwick, Julie Baumgold, Pat Buckley, Jerry Bruckheimer, Mario Buatta, Robert Downing, Michael Eisner, John Fairchild, Richard Feigen, Robert Felner, Ashton Hawkins, Walter Keichel, Mark Kostabi, Hilton Kramer, Hope Lampert, William Leurs, Harry Macklowe, Robert Prechter, Robert Rubin, Steven Shepard, William Simon, Don Simpson, Carl Spielvogel, Martha Stewart, Michael Stone, Arthur Sulzberger, Michael Thomas, Robert Towbin. Many others provided me with recollections and insights but asked not to be quoted.

I would also like to thank Ed Kosner, the editor and publisher of *New York* magazine, for encouraging me to explore a number of the topics in this book.

Finally I would like to thank David Denby, Susan Stein, Jeannette Walls, and lastly my father, Jay Taylor, for reading the manuscript, or portions of it, and for providing many useful suggestions.

CONTENTS

CIRCUS OF
AMBITION

1

THE MONEY CULTURE

MONEY IS GOOD

By the summer of 1980, the Reverend Jerry Falwell could feel that he had really arrived. During the week, his private jet logged as many as 5,000 miles as he flew back and forth across the country making speeches, holding rallies, attending board meetings, conducting prayer services, and giving interview after interview.

Journalists were morbidly fascinated by Falwell. He seemed to distill the sense of impending apocalypse that possessed so many of them at the end of the seventies, the feeling that the moral center was collapsing and that an age of hysteria and intolerance had begun. Falwell also made great copy. He denounced homosexuals as moral perverts. He discouraged his followers from watching "Charlie's Angels" on television. He prophesied a nuclear holocaust in which blood would flow in the streets "up to the bridles of the horses." His influence over his followers was so strong that he was believed to be personally delivering some 25-million votes to the Republicans in the upcoming national election.

While journalists no doubt exaggerated Falwell's power, the appetite for his message was genuine. Such large numbers of people—sometimes as many as 17,000—flocked to hear Falwell preach at the Thomas Road Baptist Church in Lynchburg, Virginia, that he had to conduct up to five services each Sunday. On top of that "The Old Time Gospel Hour," the televised broadcast of those services, was carried by around 370 television stations in the United States and abroad, and that was, as Falwell was fond of pointing out, one hundred stations more than carried "The Lawrence Welk Show."

"The Old Time Gospel Hour" was merely the cornerstone of a gigantic religious empire that included Liberty Baptist College, a seminary, a Bible institute, a summer camp, a private school, a merchandising operation, and a treatment center for alcoholics, as well as Moral Majority, Inc. By the end of 1980, the revenues from all these operations would reach $51 million. That translated into an extraordinary financial success on anyone's terms. Despite the pessimism of his message, Falwell did not live as if he thought the world was coming to an end. Self-denial—sackcloth and sandals—was not his style. He conducted himself very much like a resourceful entrepreneur on the way up.

In fact, that very summer of 1980, when he was appearing on national magazine covers and causing such alarm to the Eastern establishment, Falwell, his wife, and their three children moved out of the rather modest house they had lived in for years and into a twelve-room mansion on six acres of land bought by a wealthy admirer and donated to the Thomas Road Baptist Church. Painted white, the old Southern house had towering columns, balustrades, a portico, and a curving drive. It had a swimming pool, long expanses of green lawn, tall graceful trees, and a high wall. At night it was bathed in floodlights. It stood on the top of a hill, from where it could be seen by many of the citizens of

Lynchburg, who began referring to it as the local White House.

A short time after moving into the house, Falwell allowed himself to be photographed by *Newsweek*, reading the Bible while stretched out in red shorts on a chaise lounge next to the pool, the grand house standing majestically in the background. When the photograph was published, it caused something of a stir, as did the disclosure that Falwell indulged in certain other extravagances, such as flying off with his children in the jet to watch World Series games while ostensibly on church business. To some, such lavish living appeared unseemly, even un-Christian. After all, wasn't the life of a man of the cloth supposed to testify to the futility of material acquisitions? Wasn't the accumulation of worldly riches a vain and selfish attempt to compete with the glory of God? Hadn't Christ Himself said it was easier for a camel to pass through the eye of a needle than for a wealthy man to enter the kingdom of God?

Falwell clearly had not anticipated any adverse reaction to the pictures of his grand house. He hadn't imagined that anyone would be offended by displays of wealth on the part of a servant of the Lord. Falwell had written an entire pamphlet explaining the Christian foundations of capitalism. It was all right there in the Book of Proverbs, he had observed, the religious premises for free enterprise, for the ownership of private property, for economic incentives, for ambition and competition, for rewarding success. Didn't these people know? Money is the way God blesses those who put Him first. Money is a sign of God's grace. Money is good.

While none of Falwell's dire prophecies had come true by the end of the eighties, the notion that money is good did emerge as a central tenet of the culture. If culture can be described as the accumulation of images, associations, and ideas that express a society's values and sensibility at a given time, the United States in the eighties produced a genuine money culture.* At its center was the belief that the accumulation of wealth is morally and even spiritually virtuous, though not everyone subscribed to the specifically religious connection Falwell made. And if the pursuit of wealth is virtuous, then so, too, is the display of wealth, since, to follow Falwell's logic, it demonstrates God's generosity to those who worship Him.

This shameless veneration of wealth ran counter to the attitude toward money that the Eastern establishment had long decreed to be socially correct. Since the twenties in the East, the establishment's attitude was one that had been defined by people of inherited wealth. The Kennedys and the Astors and, most supremely, the Rockefellers maintained (at least this was the official position) that wealth was a public trust, a burden to be borne dutifully rather than a source of pleasure or fun, much less of moral redemption. Describing the attitude of John D. Rockefeller, Jr., toward his inheritance, Peter Collier and David Horowitz wrote in *The Rockefellers: An American Dynasty*, "Instead of wealth coming, however obliquely, as a reward for individual effort, the individual would pay a life-time debt of service to the wealth itself and thus earn it after the fact."

Many Rockefellers have said they felt imprisoned by their wealth. By stripping them of the need to work, inherited wealth encouraged idleness and engendered feelings of worthlessness. Heirs to other great East Coast fortunes, such as the children of J. Seward Johnson of Johnson & Johnson, actually felt degraded by their money. Wealth, they came to believe, created a corrosive mistrust of others. "Yes, there is always the question," Mary Lea Johnson once

---

*This useful and resonant phrase first appeared in the pages of the *New Republic* as the heading for an occasional column on Wall Street.

said. "You wonder if people like you for you—or the inevitable disturbing question: 'Are they after something?'" And then she asked earnestly, "Did you know the wealthy have few friends?"

But for the most part that sort of ambivalence about wealth disappeared in the eighties. A new group appeared on the scene with a new attitude toward money. Their numbers were so large that they eclipsed the older families and their inherited wealth and overbred manners, their snobbery and insecurities. This new group had, by contrast, the triumphant energy and self-congratulatory manner of people who had *earned* their money, and they spent it on a scale unseen on the East Coast in at least half a century. In doing so, they established a new attitude toward wealth that was embraced throughout the country. Money came to be regarded unabashedly as an emblem of accomplishment and prowess, and even, to some, a sign of God's blessing. Money was good.

APOLOGIZE LATER

On June 5, 1980—not long after the Falwell family moved into their new home—a New York art gallery owner named Robert Miller looked out the window of his eleventh-floor office on Fifth Avenue at 56th Street. Across the street from him stood the Bonwit Teller Building. A handsome Beaux Arts structure completed in 1929, it had been designed by Warren & Wetmore, the distinguished firm that had created Grand Central Terminal. Bonwit Teller had sold the building the previous year to a then relatively unknown thirty-three-year-old real estate developer named Donald Trump, who was razing it in order to put up Trump Tower, a sixty-eight-story brown tinted glass building that was to cost

$190 million and, when it was finished, would become *the* symbol of New York in the 1980s.

A scaffolding surrounded part of the Bonwit Teller Building, but Miller could still see the two bas-relief sculptures embedded in the facade between the eighth and the ninth floors. Made of limestone, the gracious Art Deco sculptures were each fifteen feet high. Both depicted partially clad females. Their value had been appraised at several hundred thousand dollars. Miller thought they were as beautiful and as important as the famous architectural sculptures in Rockefeller Center, six blocks south. Der Scutt, the architect who designed Trump Tower, also considered them magnificent. He had actually suggested placing them in the wall of the Trump Tower lobby, but Trump, who wanted a thoroughly contemporary look, had rejected that idea.

The city had never designated the Bonwit Teller Building a landmark. When Trump bought it and announced his intention to demolish it, members of New York preservation groups expressed their dismay over the fate that was to befall the sculptures. Officials of the Metropolitan Museum, however, intervened. The sculptures had such artistic merit, they said, that they would install them in the museum's department of twentieth-century art. One of the museum's patrons even offered a gift to pay for their display. Trump agreed to give the sculptures to the museum if the cost of their removal was not prohibitive. Since Trump told the City Planning Department that he was donating the panels to the Met, officials did not think to take steps to require him to save them.

But as Robert Miller watched on June 5, workmen on the scaffolding began to shatter the sculptures with jackhammers. They chopped horizontally across first the left panel, then the right. The handsome, fifty-one-year-old bas reliefs splintered into pieces. Miller was astounded. So was his associate, Nathan Kernan, who began to photograph the action. Within no time, it seemed, the sculptures were totally destroyed.

The destruction of the Bonwit Teller bas reliefs made the front page of the *New York Times* the following day, alongside stories on the disastrous attempt to rescue the American hostages in Teheran, a United Nations resolution condemning Israel for the car bombs that maimed Palestinian mayors in Nablus and Ramallah, and Senator Edward Kennedy's declaration, after meeting with Jimmy Carter, that he was still a candidate for President.

Trump himself was conveniently out of town at the time. One of his vice-presidents explained that the sculptures had been destroyed because they were "without artistic merit." Their "resale value," he added, was only $9,000, and it would have cost Trump $32,000 to remove them properly. New Yorkers were galled by the hubris of all of this. The scandal intensified the following day when it was learned that a rare nickel grillwork that had been built into the main entrance of the Bonwit Teller Building—which Trump had also promised to donate to the Metropolitan Museum—had disappeared. The same Trump vice-president told reporters that no one in the organization knew what had happened to the grillwork, which was twenty-five feet wide and so heavy that cranes were required to move it.

When Trump finally surfaced several days later, he explained that he had ordered the destruction of the sculptures for altruistic humanitarian reasons. His "biggest concern," he said, was for pedestrians on the street who might have been hurt or killed if the panels had fallen while being removed. Furthermore, he and his people had recalculated the cost of removing the sculptures. It would actually have cost as much as $600,000. Had it cost a mere $32,000, he would, of course, have removed the panels—$32,000, he said, was nothing to him. "I contribute that much every month to painters and artists," he told a reporter.

When Trump spoke to Kent Barwick, then the city landmarks commissioner, he offered a different explanation. According to Barwick, Trump said it was a regrettable error that had happened only because he had been out of town. The contractors had misinterpreted his instructions. Had he been present, he would not have allowed the sculptures to be destroyed. By the time he learned of what happened it was, of course, too late. The destruction of the sculptures was unfortunate, he said, and filled him with regret.

To some of the more cynical observers of the affair, the explanations, the regret, the expressions of concern for pedestrians were transparently self-serving. To these cynics, it seemed clear that Trump had arranged the whole operation. Unwilling to delay his demolition plans long enough to remove the sculptures, they argued, he simply ordered their destruction and arranged to be away when the workmen carried out his command.

Real estate developers, financiers, and captains of industry have always been a ruthless lot. But fear of ostracism traditionally exerted some restraining force. In the eighties, however, there was so much money to be made that the lure of wealth overpowered conventional restraints. Like a sort of magnetic field, it literally altered behavior. As a result, the prospect of social stigma became more or less irrelevant. People destroyed art, betrayed friends, broke laws. There was too much money out there. They couldn't resist temptation. Anyway, as Trump demonstrated, most of the time you could go ahead and do it and just apologize later. In the end it wouldn't really matter. Because, if money was good, it seemed to follow that the behavior necessary to accumulate money was good too.

THE REVIVAL
OF SOCIAL DISTINCTIONS

The nouveau riche speculators, financiers, entrepreneurs, and corporate chieftains who were to capture national attention in the eighties and create the forms that gave shape to the money culture had their first national tribal gathering at Ronald Reagan's 1981 inauguration. Hotels in Washington, D.C., began to receive room reservations for the week of the inauguration immediately after Jimmy Carter conceded victory. By the next day many hotels—not only the most prestigious ones—were completely booked. Members of the victorious party always gather in Washington to celebrate during the inaugural week, but this was different. Reagan had received 43.9 million votes. Conservatives across the country believed a momentous shift in popular values had taken place, and they all wanted to be in Washington to participate in the official birth of what would turn out to be not only a new national mood but a whole new national style.

The shift was in part a reaction to the year-long humiliation of the Iran hostage crisis, as well as to the Soviet invasion of Afghanistan. Part of it also had to do with Carter's inability to tame the inflation rate, which at 13 percent (the prime interest rate had reached 20 percent), was the worst since the Civil War. But it ultimately represented something larger than mere dissatisfaction with Democratic policies. It was more than the combination of conservative direct-mail tactics and fundamentalist voter mobilization campaigns. It had to do with political aura. For the first time since the twenties, Republicans had shed the image of cautious sober bores and had assumed an aura of excitement and glamour.

From the early sixties up to the late seventies, glamour

had by and large accrued to liberals and their causes. It was the glamour of idealism, and it was embodied, of course, in John F. Kennedy. Liberalism represented virility and prowess in the service of egalitarian enterprises. Liberals were glamorous and sexy. They had all the fun. "Liberals get laid," young political activists used to tell each other.

But by the late seventies, liberalism had been drained of the last vestiges of Kennedyesque virility. Liberals, Carter made clear in the "malaise" speech that formed one of the most telling moments of his presidency, had lost confidence in their own ability to solve problems. They came to be seen not as virile conquerers of social and political ills, but as priggish scolds, as whiners and complainers.

Carter's particular lack of charisma aside, the Democratic agenda, with its emphasis on the redistribution of wealth, was losing its appeal. That appeal was based on the belief in "class convergence" that had prevailed in the country since World War II. As Paul Blumberg wrote in *Inequality in an Age of Decline*: "The basic premise of convergence theory is that a combination of economic, social, and political forces in the postwar world has increased the affluence of huge sectors of the population, reduced poverty, diffused education, and expanded citizenship and thus substantially reduced the importance of social class in American society."

The economic calamities of the seventies played havoc with the notion of class convergence. Instead of all sectors of the economy cooperating to produce an uplift that benefitted everyone, individuals began to compete—to fight—with each other for their share of the shrinking national wealth. The productive members of society began to feel annoyance with, rather than pity for, the nonproductive members whom their tax dollars supported. By the end of the seventies, the well of popular generosity was running dry. New York City, for example, carried almost a million people on its welfare rolls. They used more of the city's services than any other group but paid no taxes. The redistribution of wealth, the middle class began to feel, had gone far enough.

Simultaneously, the economic turmoil of the seventies had directed public attention toward the accumulation of wealth. A society reveals its aspirations in the occupations it celebrates, and by the time the decade wound down the public was transferring glamour from activists who redistributed wealth to entrepreneurs who created it. This shift had a cathartic effect. After some twenty frustrating years of being, at best, neglected and, at worst, scorned, those who created the nation's wealth were finally to get their due. *They* were to be recognized, to have *their* values accepted as the standards for the nation and *their* accomplishments held up as the national models. Their time had come. "Yes, I'm a Republican," Norman Comins, a Massachusetts businessman, said during Reagan's inauguration. "But somehow it feels different to say that now. It feels good."

Joseph Coors was also there. The Colorado beer baron was ecstatic at the prospect of the radical new era the Reagan presidency announced. "I've been waiting a long time for this," he told just about everyone he ran into. "I've been waiting a long time for this."

Individuals preoccupied with the distribution of wealth are usually also intent on eradicating social distinctions (or at least those based on wealth). That explained the embrace of working class fashions and behavior in the sixties. Individuals concerned with creating wealth, on the other hand, usually also set out to devise social distinctions that testify to that wealth. Nothing announced this new priority so clearly as the events surrounding Reagan's first inauguration. The men and women on the Inaugural Committee managed to create social distinctions in the most imaginative—and even diabolical—ways.

In the second week of January 1981, approximately 70,000 Republicans descended on the nation's capital. So many arrived by private jet that Washington's National Airport reported it was handling double its normal number of small planes. Others came by car. Pat Buckley, the wife of columnist William F. Buckley, drove down from New York with designer Bill Blass—not because she couldn't afford to fly, but because she needed a car to carry all her clothes. After all, ostentatious display had brazenly been declared to be the purpose of the festivities. The head of the Inaugural Committee actually promised Republicans an evening in which "every woman will be able to show off her dress."

Unlike the balls at the Carter inauguration, which were open to the public, the nine Reagan balls were by invitation only. Some events were more exclusive than others, and seating arrangements within events provided opportunities to establish further distinctions. Tickets to most of the balls started at $100. Boxes at the most select cost $10,000. The Inaugural Committee's computer debacle, which left thousands of people stranded without tickets, inadvertently served to further the cause of social distinctions, since it provided the ticketless with the opportunity to display clout and power in getting into events. For the elite, however, the crucial social distinctions were established not at any of the official functions, but with invitations to the dozens of private parties held the weekend before the inauguration.

When Marion and Earle Jorgensen—old friends of the Reagans—arrived from Los Angeles for the festivities, she carried with her a typed seven-page list of the events she and her husband were to attend. These included such exclusive and desirable private parties as the dinner Nancy Dickerson and her husband were throwing at Merrywood, their Virginia estate. To be among the hundred or so guests, which included the Reagans, at this party was to feel truly part of the elect. But even within this group social distinctions existed. The Dickersons could fit only forty-eight people into their dining room; the other sixty had to eat at a Washington club and travel out to Merrywood after the meal. Mrs. Dickerson insisted that the forty-eight people she selected to dine at her home were simply the first forty-eight to respond to her invitation, but one couldn't help feeling that yet another delicious social distinction had been drawn.

What a triumph it was to be among the first forty-eight— *the first forty-eight*, it had such a ring—to be sitting with Charlotte Ford and Jerry Zipkin and Bill Blass and Pat Buckley and, of course, Ronald and Nancy Reagan at the onset of an age where self-definition would come through the names of people whose acquaintance one could claim. For the eighties were to mark the blossoming of what Thorstein Veblen might have called the Conspicuous Friendship: a relationship or bond pursued not because of the psychological rewards it offered but because of the opportunity it provided individuals for enhanced status through mutual association.

Indeed, the inaugural parties became one long exercise devoted to status-enhancing associations. As the select few made the rounds and ran into one another again and again, each meeting reaffirmed their exclusivity, their sense of belonging to an elite group of initiates. At a lamb chop buffet at the Fairfax Hotel hosted by Earl Blackwell, editor-in-chief of the Celebrity Register, the nascent conservative chic even received the blessing of the avant-garde when Andy Warhol appeared and announced, "I'm a Republican."

At times the intensity of the desire to participate in these events, to *belong*, created a press of humanity that was frightening. In Georgetown, the wife of Senator Mark Hatfield and Nancy Reynolds, a close friend of Nancy Reagan, gave a party for Michael Deaver. The affair was so overattended that it became impossible to move from room to room. The concentration of human flesh literally rendered people immobile, and bartenders had to climb through windows to replenish their supplies.

THE HOLY ECONOMY
AND THE REBIRTH OF OPTIMISM

Reagan took the oath of office shortly before noon on January 20, 1981. The announcement that the American hostages had finally left Teheran would not come for another 25 minutes, and his speech was subdued. After dwelling at length on his determination to reduce the size of the government—it would, of course, grow larger than it had ever been in history—he eventually struck what would come to be the central thematic note of the eighties:

"Those who say that we're in a time when there are no heroes—they just don't know where to look.... There are entrepreneurs with faith in themselves and faith in an idea who create new jobs, new wealth, and new opportunities.... It is a time to realize we are too great a nation to limit ourselves to small dreams. We're not, as some would have us believe, doomed to an inevitable decline. I do not believe in a fate that will fall on us no matter what we do. I do believe in a fate that will fall on us if we do nothing."

The historian Debora Silverman and others have dismissed this rhetoric as the cynical "politics of symbolism," noting that the careers of Reagan and a number of his close friends did not exactly fit the pattern of entrepreneurial individualism that the President held up as a model for the country. The assumption of Silverman and similar pessimistic social critics like Christopher Lasch seems to be that the United States is in decline from an earlier period of superior moral integrity. But in many respects, Reagan's ideology represented a return to the traditions on which the nation was founded. It was Benjamin Franklin, for example, who first talked of worshipping the "holy economy." Even Reagan's rhetoric harkened back to an earlier time. In *The Americans: The National Experience*, Daniel Boorstin described the patriotic speeches of the early nineteenth century, noting that across the country "the essentials of the spirit were the same—the optimism, the enthusiasm, the vagueness of the line between fact and hope, between what had actually happened and what ought to have happened."

It has also frequently been argued that the apparent reinvigoration of the country that took place during Reagan's tenure was a charade, acquired by accumulating a huge and debilitating national debt that will haunt the nation through the nineties. That argument will continue for years. The point to be made here is that Reagan's rhetoric unleashed the greatest celebration of wealth—wealth as a virtue, as a good in itself—that the country has experienced at any time in the twentieth century.

It coincided with an extraordinary expansion of the power and wealth of the wealthy. Between 1977 and 1988, the wealthiest 1 percent of the people in the country enjoyed an increase in after-tax income of 74 percent. This was not a case of a rising tide lifting all boats, to use John Kennedy's formulation of the class convergence theory. During that same period, the poorest 10 percent of the country saw their income decline by more than 10 percent. But even the poor were drawn into the money culture. Rather than resenting the rich, they identified with them and fantasized about joining their ranks. State-run lotteries grew explosively during the eighties. Donald Trump emerged as a hero and role model for working class Americans, who eagerly bought his autobiography, *The Art of the Deal*.

It has become something of a cliche to compare the eighties with the twenties, to talk of the "Roaring Eighties," as the financial writer Adam Smith and others have done.

But the comparison is inapt. Although both eras were characterized by great bull markets, the more appropriate comparison with the twenties is the sixties. The sixties also enjoyed a powerful bull market; in fact, it persisted so long that it was referred to, awkwardly but in the fashion of the times, as the "topless market."

But the financiers who grew rich in the twenties, like Joseph Kennedy, and in the sixties, like Gerry Tsai, did not set the tone for the country the way the money people did in the eighties. Both the twenties and the sixties were dominated instead by the spirit of emancipation, by feminist movements, sexual freedom, intoxication, innovative music (jazz and rock), radical political groups, even—in Charles Lindbergh and John Glenn—aviation heroes. Most importantly, the two decades were dominated by the young and their anger and disenchantment.

"A first class revolt against the accepted American order was certainly taking place during those early years of the post-war decade, but it was one with which Nikolai Lenin had absolutely nothing to do," wrote Frederick Lewis Allen in *Only Yesterday*, a history of the twenties. "The shock troops of the rebellion were not alien agitators, but the sons and daughters of well-to-do American families, who knew little about Bolshevism and cared less, and their defiance was expressed not in obscure radical publications or in soap-box speeches, but right across the breakfast table into the horrified ears of conservative fathers and mothers. Men and women were still shivering at the Red Menace when they awoke to the no less alarming Problem of the Younger Generation, and realized that if the Constitution were not in danger, the moral code of the country certainly was."

Equally inapt is the comparison that has been made at times between the eighties and the fifties. Although both decades experienced the ascendancy of conservative family values, and although detached Republican Presidents ran the country during each period, the fifties, as Blumberg noted, were a time of class convergence. Furthermore, the general social and cultural program of the fifties was set by the middle class rather than, as was the case in the eighties, by the upper class. The representative television show of the fifties was "Father Knows Best." In the eighties it was "Dynasty."

A much more revealing comparison for the eighties is the one that has been made with the Gilded Age. During the years after the Civil War, men like Jay Gould, John D. Rockefeller, Andrew Carnegie, Cornelius Vanderbilt, his son William, and others all sought to take advantage of the westward expansion by creating corporate monopolies, and in doing so reshaped the country's business structure.

In the 1980s, a similar sort of expansion took place. America's economic boundaries were pushed out, and new sources of wealth created, as the Japanese and Europeans consumed the corporate and government debt that made the country's economic boom possible. At the same time, corporate raiders like Sid Bass, T. Boone Pickens, Saul Steinberg, Carl Icahn, and Irwin Jacobs carried out their assaults on companies as varied and as well known as Gulf Oil, the Walt Disney Company, and Trans World Airlines. In doing so, they had a more profound impact on the structure of corporate America than any group of financiers since the robber barons of the nineteenth century. As had been the case with the robber barons, their assaults on corporate America were violent and theatrical, involving stealth, ruthlessness, intimidation, and the dismemberment of corporate victims. As the robber barons had before them, the corporate raiders captured headlines.

The most towering among them was Michael Milken, who almost single-handedly created the market for junk bonds in the 1980s. By making it possible for his clients to raise money to finance takeovers, he gave rise to a set of circumstances in which virtually every publicly held company became a potential takeover target. In doing so he permanently altered the face of corporate America. Whatever the outcome of the insider-trading charges brought against him in 1989, his place in history is assured.

There was one significant factor that contributed to the preoccupation with finance during the Gilded Age and the 1980s. Both periods came after wars—the Civil War and the war in Vietnam—had divided the country ideologically. As a result, the nation's reserves of altruism had been exhausted. The one ideology that could still appeal to everyone was self-interest. Optimism and patriotism were rekindled when Americans had the promise of material wealth dangled in front of them.

Thorstein Veblen was actually referring to the latter part of the nineteenth century, but he could just as easily have been describing the current age when he wrote in *The Theory of the Leisure Class*, "The generation which follows a season of war is apt to witness a rehabilitation of the element of status, both in its social life, and in its scheme of devout observances and other symbolic or ceremonial forms. Throughout the eighties, and less plainly traceable through the seventies also, there was perceptible a gradually advancing wave of sentiment favoring quasi-predatory business habits, insistence on status, anthropomorphism, and conservatism generally."

The most vivid description of the spirit of the Gilded Age, however, can be found in Vernon Parrington's *Main Currents in American Thought*. And he, too, could be describing the 1980s. "Freedom had become individualism and individualism had become the inalienable right to pre-empt, to exploit, to squander. Gone were the old ideals along with the old restraints. The idealism of the forties, the romanticism of the fifties—all the heritage of Jeffersonianism and the French Enlightenment—were put thoughtlessly away, and with no social conscience, no concern for civilization, no heed for the democracy it talked so much about, the Gilded Age threw itself into the business of money-getting. From the sober restraints of aristocracy, the old inhibitions of Puritanism, the niggardliness of an exacting economy, it swung far back in reaction, and with the discovery of limitless opportunities for exploitation, it allowed itself to get drunk. Figures of earth, they followed after their own dreams. Some were builders with grandiose plans in their heads; others were wreckers with no plans at all. It was an anarchistic world of strong, capable men, selfish, unenlightened, amoral—an excellent example of what human nature will do with undisciplined freedom. In the Gilded Age, freedom was the freedom of buccaneers preying on the argosies of Spain."

Arthur Schlesinger, Jr., has established himself as the leading proponent of the cyclical theory of American history. In his view, the country has swung between periods where it was preoccupied with "public purpose" and periods where "private interest" was the prevailing force. "Public purpose" represents the democratic spirit, in Schlesinger's view. It emphasizes social responsibility and the welfare of the community over individual freedoms. It is embodied in the regulator, the labor organizer, the reformer, the demagogue. "Private interest," on the other hand, encourages the individual's unencumbered pursuit of his own goals. It stresses individualism, self-sufficiency, private ownership, and is embodied in the figures of the pioneer, the entrepreneur, the gambler.

While the inclinations toward both public purpose and private interest are present at all times, Schlesinger argues that at most times one or the other governs the national mood. Public purpose prevailed, to give the most clear-cut

example, during the thirties under Roosevelt, private interest during the twenties under Coolidge.

An occasionally overlapping theory of the national mood
has been worked out by stock market analyst Robert Prechter.
Prechter, who has tracked the national mood through the
twentieth century as it has revealed itself in the stock market
and in popular culture, maintains that the cycles of the
country's history reflect swings between optimistic and pessimistic moods. During optimistic periods, which of course
correspond to bull markets, individuals play down the plight
of the unfortunate (or deny their existence altogether) and
instead focus on themselves and on improving productivity.
They accumulate wealth and pursue personal gratification
through consumption.*

In pessimistic times, by contrast, self-centered behavior
wanes. Community spirit becomes more pronounced as
people rally together to ward off perceived threats to the
group as a whole. Individuals tend to focus on moral and
spiritual values instead of on materialism as the means to
self-fulfillment. But pessimistic moods, which naturally correspond to bear markets, can also give rise to mysticism,
intolerance, and the politics of hatred that brought Hitler's
popularity to its peak in July 1933, the very month, as
Prechter has noted, that all the major markets bottomed out
in the great global depression.

The theories of both Prechter and Schlesinger are interesting if somewhat unsatisfying. They fail to resolve the fact
that almost all periods are chaotic combinations of both
public purpose and private interest, both pessimism and

---

*Reagan, the quintessential optimist, loved to tell the story of two boys: One, a
pessimist, received a roomful of toys and immediately suspected a trick; the other,
an optimist, was given a roomful of manure, which he took as evidence he was
being given a pony. The flip side of optimism, of course, is the refusal to
acknowledge suffering. In one of his final interviews as President, Reagan was
asked about the homeless people sleeping on the grates outside the White House.
He insisted that the homeless were on the streets either out of choice or because
misguided liberals had released insane patients from mental institutions.

optimism: that the McCarthy hysteria occurred during the supposedly somnolent fifties; that the bull market of the sixties continued through the civil rights upheaval, the assassination of John Kennedy, and the deepening involvement in Vietnam.

The eighties, however, *were* shaped by a single overriding mood more clearly than any decade in at least fifty years. The renewal of optimism had been the primary thematic note of Reagan's campaign, and the creation of an optimistic spirit in the country may well have been his greatest accomplishment. The true success of his economic, military, and social policies will be debated for years—as will be the degree to which he deserves credit for developments in the economy and in international affairs. But it was undoubtedly Reagan's personality—in all its Panglossian blindness—that led the revival of optimism in the country.

That optimistic spirit would not take hold for two years; the country would first have to experience the most wrenching recession since the thirties. Then, too, sectors of the country such as farmers, the urban underclass, and steel workers in the Monongahela Valley of Pennsylvania, among others, would not participate in the optimistic uplift. Nonetheless, the eighties were shaped by the doctrine of optimism to an extent no one could have foreseen when Reagan made his inaugural address. Optimism was responsible for the perceived spiritual virtue of wealth, for the worship of power and status, for the cults of success and ruthlessness, for the theater of the deal, for the creation of staggering fortunes and new social hierarchies, and for the decade's giddy and unregenerate self-confidence, all of which together made up the money culture of the eighties.

2

CHARLIE ATKINS AND THE GLAMOUR OF INVESTMENT BANKING

A PRINCE ON WALL STREET

In 1981, when he was a mere twenty-seven years old, Charlie Atkins owned one of the most opulent apartments in New York. It was, to begin with, at One Sutton Place, that most prestigious of prestigious addresses, with a stone-arched driveway and a vast private garden overlooking the East River. The apartment's interior—all 5,000 square feet of it—was a flawlessly executed example of the High Establishment style. The rooms were adorned with rare books and rarer prints and paintings by Cavallino and Preti. There were little knickknacks like Fabergé matchboxes lying around. There were Tabriz rugs and George II giltwood tables and Louis XVI bureaus.

Now, none of these items were heirlooms. Charlie Atkins did not live on trust income. Charlie Atkins was a self-made man who ran his own investment and trading firm, which had a securities portfolio said to be worth $21 billion. Charlie Atkins was a Prince on Wall Street.

There are countless stories in New York about brilliant young men who become dazzling successes virtually overnight. But in the eighties, no one, it seemed, was quite as promising or quite as ambitious as Charlie Atkins. He had been called the smartest person to come out of the London School of Economics in twenty years. Newspapers like the *New York Times* and the *Wall Street Journal* referred to him as the "instant legend" and the "boy wonder." Certainly no one in the eighties became so successful, in both the social and the professional spheres, as rapidly and at such a tender age as Atkins.

Atkins could be said to be *the* prototype for the young professional of the eighties. He was one of the first of his generation to realize the great eighties fantasy of wealth, power, and status in investment banking. In fact, in his aspirations and values, in his self-definition, in the astonishing acceleration that his career enjoyed, he mapped out virtually the entire formal structure of the money culture.

He was, to begin with, possessed with the entrepreneurial spirit of the age. Atkins was not intent just on a career in investment banking. He wanted to start his own investment bank. He did, at the age of twenty-four. Its breathtaking success enabled Atkins, whose friends described him as a "Renaissance man," to live a contemporary version of the Medici life. Like one of those Florentine princes, he spent money on a scale inconceivable to most people. At his peak he was going through upwards of $18 million a year.

Other young men, such as the investment swindler Barry Minkow, amassed astonishing fortunes at an early age in the eighties. But even before their indictments they were regarded as somewhat unsavory. Atkins' unique feat was to translate so swiftly his financial success into a genuine position in the upper reaches of New York society.

It was a heady experience while it lasted. But just as New York is full of astounding success stories, it is also replete with cautionary tales of the ruin awaiting brilliant young men who fly too high too fast. And in the eighties, no one, it seemed, self-destructed as quickly and with as glorious a blaze as Charlie Atkins. His firm, the Securities Groups, which functioned primarily as a tax shelter, was so successful that it spawned a series of imitators. This proliferation of shelters provoked Congress into revising the tax laws permitting write-offs from losses in the type of securities trading in which Atkins specialized. At the same time, the Federal Reserve Bank began to crack down on highly leveraged trading firms, of which Atkins' was one of the most prominent. Consequently, less than six years after it opened for business, his firm collapsed. After that happened the "instant legend" decamped to Florida, where he filed for personal bankruptcy. He was then thirty. At an age when many of his contemporaries were only just discovering their true vocations, he had already, in a sense, gone into retirement.

That, however, was only the beginning of his legal troubles, which foreshadowed the troubles of similar young professionals enthralled by the mystique of investment banking. In April 1987 he and two others involved with the Securities Groups were indicted by Rudolph Giuliani, the U.S. Attorney for the Southern District of New York, on some thirty-one counts for creating "bogus securities transactions" that generated about $1.3 billion in "false and fraudulent tax losses," and for filing false tax returns. The trial commenced that October—it was held at the same time and in the same building as the trial for David Clark, an attorney charged with participating in the Foster Wynans *Wall Street Journal* insider trading scandal—and in December the jury returned a verdict of guilty against Atkins on every count. Vigorously asserting his innocence, Atkins appealed the verdict. By the spring of 1989, the appellate court had yet to issue an opinion. It was an ignominious end to a brief but remarkable career in the speculative markets.

THE IDEOLOGY
OF WEALTH CREATION

One of the remarkable phenomena of the eighties was the transformation of investment banking into a glamorous, even sexy profession. Investment banking used to be considered a rather unexciting job that involved courting corporate officers socially and analyzing reams of statistics. The social duties aside, it was seen, in many respects, as little more than glorified accounting and salesmanship. For business school graduates in other times, the excitement lay in corporate management, in running large, publicly held companies. The executives of major corporations were considered to be the ones who wielded the real power. Even within the business of providing corporations with advice, management consultants enjoyed more cachet than investment bankers. To many people, the transformation of investment banking into a glamorous profession in the eighties was baffling.

The explanation is to be found in the economic forces that have shaped the lives of the postwar generation. That generation can loosely be divided into those who came of age before 1970 and those who came of age after 1970.*

For the first group, economic prosperity was a given. The United States during the fifties and sixties was unquestionably the greatest economic power in the world. Its technology and manufacturing were unrivaled and its economy was robust, with low rates of inflation and unemployment. Year after year, particularly in the sixties, the stock market surged ahead and the standards of living climbed.

Americans coming of age during that period felt secure

---

*Credit for this distinction should go to Walter Keichel, an editor at *Fortune* magazine, who pointed it out to me in a conversation in 1988.

about their country's economic preeminence. They took it for granted. Surrounded by a surfeit of affluence, they saw little challenge or reward in creating additional wealth. This antipathy toward making money was reinforced by the fact that, as has often been pointed out, so many members of the postwar generation were raised according to the precepts of Benjamin Spock. Repeatedly informed at an early age of their uniqueness and gifts, they became as young adults unwilling to suppress their egos to the degree they believed was required in corporate life. And anyway, the great excitement of the day, the great challenge, was to redistribute wealth through social and political activism.

The members of the postwar generation who came of age in the seventies, like Charlie Atkins, had a somewhat different experience. The country fell into recession in 1972, which was deepened by the oil embargo the following year. In 1975, New York City almost went bankrupt. Cleveland actually defaulted on bond payments. The economic ascendancy of Japan forced the United States to face up to the fact of its industrial decline. Each year seemed to bring a fresh economic horror, and by the mid-seventies the country's economy was so beleaguered, and in such a puzzling fashion, that the word *stagflation* had to be coined to describe the predicament.

Young middle class Americans stopped taking money for granted. To cite one example, a generally ignored course on the basics of business that Steven Shepard (later the editor of *Business Week* magazine) was then teaching at Columbia University's School of Journalism suddenly became oversubscribed. To stay ahead of inflation, Americans across the country became speculators. They borrowed funds at fixed rates from savings and loan institutions and then invested in money market funds with higher returns. Real estate was also a popular inflation hedge. In fact, it became so popular it developed its own speculative upswing. Prices rose at such giddy rates that the writer Sara Davidson remarked that "real estate is the marijuana of the seventies."

Consequently, in a few short years the values of industrious labor and thrift—the values of the Protestant work ethic celebrated by Benjamin Franklin and accepted as the key to success by the American middle class for generations—were replaced with what Paul Blumberg called the Las Vegas Syndrome. Life had become a gamble; success went to the lucky speculators. Most people, of course, including many who had worked hard and grown up expecting to be rewarded for it, were not lucky. They experienced "downward mobility," the perceived and in many cases actual decline in living standards. Their disappointed expectations spread the belief that, as Jimmy Carter once remarked in another telling moment of his presidency, "life is unfair."

The numerous policy setbacks of the Carter Administration exacerbated the frustration and futility that many Americans felt. Carter himself, with his depressing world view and bleak pronouncements, seemed to personify failure. His persistent inability to inspire fueled the notion that while the heroes of the sixties may have all been martyred, the seventies had no heroes at all. The national psyche craved images of genuine success, of individual effort rewarded.

In the late seventies, authentic American heroes began to appear in what to the postwar generation was the most unlikely place: business. The conventional wisdom of the day held that the country would never again see the likes of Thomas Edison or Henry Ford. Corporate capitalism was in an advanced state; power was concentrated in the hands of conglomerates that crushed the entrepreneurs and inventors whose original ideas might threaten their hegemony. When Steve Jobs and Steve Wozniak built a personal computer in 1977 in the garage of Wozniak's parents' house and then subsequently founded Apple Computer, they destroyed that assumption. But they did more than that, and they did more than create a new industry. They rekindled the myth of individual triumph for the entire country.

Steve Jobs, it could even be said, was the man who made the creation of wealth socially acceptable to the idealistic camp of the postwar generation. One didn't have to go to work for a stultifying corporation that made deadly insecticides or perverse infant formula or, as Jobs himself once remarked with a sneer, "sugared water." Creating products and services could be exciting, noble, and even, as Jobs showed, romantic. Jobs' rapid success also reinforced the postwar generation's sense of entitlement and desire for immediate gratification. It wasn't necessary to toil for years in frustrating inconsequential positions or even to wear a suit and tie. One could become an entrepreneur and, if successful, achieve influence immediately, while still carrying on in as unorthodox a fashion as one wanted. (Jobs was a vegetarian Buddhist; Wozniak underwrote an exorbitant rock festival.)

By the end of the seventies, entrepreneurial fever was sweeping the country. That lent an aura of chic to venture capitalists. Those existentially intriguing figures, whose financing could convert dreams into realities, seemed to carry an idealistic charge: Just as Peace Corps volunteers had in the sixties, venture capitalists could "make a difference." The financing needs of entrepreneurs and the new profile of venture capitalists focused attention on Wall Street itself, which traditionally was an entrepreneurial place, a collection of one-man firms, small boutiques and fluctuating partnerships rather than rigid corporate hierarchies. In fact, for every executive who managed a financial behemoth from a suite high in a tower, there were hundreds, if not thousands, of smaller hustlers who inhabited cramped dark offices deep in the narrow canyons of Wall Street. They ran tiny mutual funds or acquired Milwaukee bowling alley chains or peddled over-the-counter stocks in weird companies no one had ever heard of.

Like the mavericks who had wandered through the Wild West, the men and women of this Runyonesque world roamed restlessly from firm to firm in search of the chemistry that would enable them to persuade others to entrust them with their money or to pull off a string of lucrative deals, and as those deals either succeeded or failed, the firms themselves merged, collapsed, and reproduced in a pattern as chaotic and inevitable as the natural order. On Wall Street, just as in Silicon Valley, and just as in the Wild West of the nineteenth century, it was possible to start a small operation on the basis of little more than an idea and within a very short period become phenomenally wealthy—as Charlie Atkins would.

During this same period Wall Street was witnessing the revolutionary creation of what became known as "the market for corporate control." High interest rates had depressed the stock market for most of the seventies. At the same time, inflation had greatly increased the cash value of corporate assets, which eventually became worth much more than the price of their stock. When interest rates fell in the early eighties, it suddenly became possible to acquire these companies and then sell off their assets for enormous profits.

The resulting takeover battles, and the much greater number of friendly deals, turned mergers and acquisitions from a sideline of investment banking into one of its most prestigious and profitable enterprises. At the same time, the deregulation of the financial markets in the seventies was leading to extraordinary new opportunities for trading. Options, futures, stock index futures, mortgage-backed securities, program trading, zero coupon bonds—within a matter of years a host of "financial instruments" and trading techniques so arcane that they seemed positively metaphysical had been created.

The Las Vegas Syndrome, the entrepreneurial successes, the rise of the corporate raiders, and the explosion in trading all contributed to the fascination with investment banking—and with The Deal—that was to be a hallmark of the eighties money culture. Each of the great bull markets have been accompanied by the emergence of new industries. In the Gilded Age it was the transcontinental railroads. In the twenties it was the automobile and radio industries. In the sixties it was high technology. No particular manufacturing sector drove the nation forward in the eighties, however. Instead, as Robert Sobel noted in *Panic on Wall Street*, "the new glamour industry was Wall Street and investments themselves."

When asked why they were interested in investment banking, new converts to the profession almost invariably replied that it was not just the money (though compensation of $200,000 and up was considerable inducement); it was, rather, the satisfaction of acquiring power and influence quickly. It was also, quite simply, where the action was. "What I'm doing at Merrill Lynch is like rock and roll was in 1968," said Jonathan Taplin, a former stage manager for Bob Dylan who had also produced movies such as *Mean Streets* before going into investment banking in 1984. "It's the highest adrenaline rush anybody could ever have."

All of these factors made Wall Street, despite the rhetorical venom it endured during the sixties, an ideal arena for the assertion of the baby boom ego. It attracted many people like Jonathan Taplin, people who in one fashion or another had passed through the counterculture of the sixties. Bruce Wasserstein was another example. Born in 1947, Wasserstein had covered the Free Speech movement for the University of Michigan's daily paper, become a poverty worker, and then was associated with Ralph Nader before winding up in the late seventies in the mergers and acquisitions department of the investment bank First Boston. By the end of 1984, Wasserstein personally had been involved in more than $30 billion worth of mergers, including Texaco's acquisition of Getty Oil for $10 billion and E. I. Du Pont's purchase of Conoco for $8 billion. Negotiating such deals turned Wasserstein, a portly, balding fellow, into a figure of glamour in the eighties. In 1985 approximately one-third— *one-third*—of the senior class of Yale applied for jobs as financial analysts at First Boston alone.

It has become almost obligatory to complain about the sort of values held by the young professionals described in *Newsweek*'s 1984 cover story, "The Year of the Yuppie." But these people did not have some spontaneously generated genetic deficiency that made them selfish, grasping, and insensitive to the impoverished. The values of the young professionals of the eighties were just as much a product of their circumstances as were those of the self-proclaimed idealists of the sixties.

In fact, for the postwar generation, investment banking had many of the same attractions as the war on poverty had in the sixties. In both it was possible to gratify quickly a sense of self-importance, to feel needed, to *make a difference*. What distinguished the two was that, because of the nation's economic slide, the ideology of wealth redistribution had been replaced with the ideology of wealth creation. And no one was more wholeheartedly dedicated to wealth creation than Charlie Atkins. Unconnected to manufacturing, to production, to anything concrete or real, he created, through acts of pure abstraction, nothing but money itself.

RULES ARE FOR FOOLS

Charlie Atkins was one of those unusual individuals who, though barely out of adolescence, display the self-confidence and social poise of someone much older. He was not conventionally handsome. He had a plump physique and a swarthy complexion. His black hair, which began to recede slightly while he was still quite young, was slicked back. His heavy curving eyebrows made him look a little suspicious. But there was nothing oily or insincere about Atkins. He had an immensely engaging personality. He was intelligent without appearing arrogant. He was polite and respectful. He was deferential when the circumstances required deference. In fact, with his aristocratic Virginia drawl he was the incarnation of the well-bred Southern boy, the old-fashioned courtly kind who ran around the car to open the lady's door and who addressed men as "sir." His friends called him "Charming Charlie."

Atkins was born on April 25, 1954, in Ashland, Kentucky. A small town on the banks of the Ohio River, Ashland is dominated by Ashland Oil, which Charlie's father, Orin Atkins, ran from 1964 to 1981. Charlie Atkins hardly spent any time in Ashland, however. He attended the elite Woodberry Forest prep school in Virginia. A good athlete, with a talent for golf, he also revealed exceptional determination and a particular aptitude for finance.

As if impatient to assume his position in the world, Atkins graduated summa cum laude from the University of North Carolina after just three years, even though a serious automobile accident incapacitated him for several months. In quick succession he was made a George C. Marshall scholar and attended the London School of Economics, then went on to Washington, D.C., where he studied international monetary policy at Brookings, concentrating on foreign exchange rates.

Atkins had started playing the stock market at a comparatively early age, and when he arrived in Washington to study at Brookings he began to cast around for a good broker. The manager of the Connecticut Avenue office of

Merrill Lynch introduced him to Edward Markowitz, a large and bearded twenty-seven-year-old commodities trader. Markowitz, who had earned undergraduate and master's degrees from MIT, had previously worked as an economic consultant for the Ford Administration, joining Merrill Lynch when Jimmy Carter took office.

Atkins, who had a weakness for the prestigious credential, admired Markowitz's MIT diplomas. He began trading through Markowitz and soon became so taken with the broker that he brought him additional clients. Because of Ashland's oil business, the Atkins family had extensive and affectionate ties with a variety of wealthy Middle Eastern businessmen. On Charlie Atkins' recommendation, a rich Iranian began trading in the currency market through Markowitz. For a while the Iranian was Markowitz's biggest client, but he dropped the broker after suffering heavy losses.

Whatever that may have revealed about Markowitz's real skills as a trader (Atkins was to complain a great deal about them later), it certainly didn't hamper their budding relationship. In 1977 Markowitz received a proposal to invest in a tax shelter that created paper losses for its investors by using a complicated technique known as a "straddle." In a straddle an investor hedged his portfolio, then generated tax losses by closing out the losing position just before the end of the year. Firms like Salomon Brothers and Goldman Sachs had been doing it for years for their own accounts.

The straddle looked interesting to Markowitz, not so much as a personal investment but as a business enterprise that could be duplicated and sold to others. He and Atkins, who turned down a job offer from Lehman Brothers because he wanted to work for himself, decided to form what Markowitz called a "clone" of the tax shelter.

In March of 1978 Atkins, who was twenty-four, and Markowitz, who was twenty-nine, began to put together the first of the limited partnerships that were to become known collectively as the Securities Groups. Markowitz was to execute the straddles, Atkins was to raise the money; they would split the income evenly.

Atkins began approaching potential investors. "I said, 'I don't have a lot of experience in business, but I have a concept that I think will be successful for you and will offer you potential tax advantages as well,'" he recalled in an interview several years later. The Atkins name did provide him with a certain degree of entrée. "A lot of people will see you because you're someone's son," he admitted. "But they won't invest money on that basis."

Atkins' task, however, was eased considerably by the fact that his father had become very interested in the project. Orin Atkins was a colorful buccaneer sort of character who had been involved in some of the biggest corporate scandals of the preceding twenty years and who seemed to operate on the premise that rules were for fools. In the summer of 1988, he was arrested by federal agents and charged with transporting stolen Ashland Oil documents, which he was trying to sell to Iran.* But that merely capped a long career of questionable behavior. In 1972, while he was the chairman of Ashland, the company made an illegal $100,000 contribution to Richard Nixon's re-election campaign. After confessing to the gift, he said, "I felt I was doing what was being done generally." A few years later Orin and Ashland admitted to making payments to foreign officials. Ashland also acknowledged participating in covert CIA activities overseas. In 1981 a dispute erupted within the Ashland board after Orin Atkins paid $1.3 million to a Libyan businessman who claimed to have arranged oil contracts for Ashland with the Sultan of Oman. Although the businessman returned the money, Ashland launched an internal

---

*This charge was subsequently dropped.

investigation. It decided that Orin had done nothing illegal but nevertheless forced him to resign.

Orin was a tall man with curly white hair and a bearish physique. He had a forceful personality and hard-living habits. He loved the bright lights of the big cities. During his heyday at Ashland he could be seen regularly in Washington, D.C., dining at the Jockey Club, and he was often in London. But his favorite city was New York. He loved the "21" Club. He loved the Sherry Netherland Hotel. He loved limousines and champagne. And like a true Southerner, he loved the Grand Gesture. Nothing thrilled him so much as to stride imposingly into the bar at the Sherry Netherland, order a bottle of Dom Perignon, drink one glass, and stride imposingly out. He was a man with an iron constitution, the sort who could stay up drinking until three o'clock then appear alert and decisive at an eight o'clock board meeting the next morning.

Orin Atkins apparently had a powerful influence on his son. Charlie acquired many of his father's values and aspirations, and even adopted some of his father's style, though adding a more refined, cosmopolitan twist. Orin was very proud of his son and quite naturally wanted to see Charlie's tax shelter succeed. To get the ball rolling, he put up $150,000 of his own money for three partnership units. And he made cold calls to potential investors in places like Palm Beach and Beverly Hills. Executives at Ashland were also steered toward the partnership. One perk for top Ashland executives was free advice on their personal finances from an outside consultant. The Ashland consultant at the time was Hamilton Gregg III, who later worked with Charlie Atkins and after that helped start Lion Capital, a tax shelter that went bankrupt amid much controversy in 1984.

According to a former Ashland employee, Gregg recommended Charlie's tax shelter to Ashland's executives. Not surprisingly, a number of executives chose to invest. For example, John Hall, who was then Ashland's president and later succeeded Orin Atkins as chairman, kicked in $25,000. Why not? It made Orin happy, but with four-to-one write-offs it seemed like a hell of a shelter, too.

Their confidence bolstered by such investments, Charlie Atkins and Markowitz moved to New York, rented a corner office in the landmark Seagram Building on Park Avenue, and opened for business.

One characteristic of individuals inclined toward what Schlesinger called "private interest" has always been a dislike for regulation. It is a great American tradition and, indeed, was one of the impulses for the founding of the country. It was an emanating source of the pioneer spirit, which survives in the entrepreneur. But only a thin line divides a dislike for regulation from contempt for it. During the eight years of the Reagan Administration, which treated the pursuit of private interest as an enshrined dogma, some 240 government officials were investigated for either illegal activities or conflicts of interest or ethical improprieties, according to the Democratic National Committee. Many of the bright young stars of Wall Street—from Martin Siegel, to Dennis Levine, to the Yuppie Five—found themselves crossing the line in order to fulfill the fantasy of investment banking wealth and glamour. Charlie Atkins anticipated them all.

No sooner had he and Markowitz opened for business than problems appeared. First they were "bawled out," as Markowitz put it later, by their lawyer for blatantly promoting their operation as a tax shelter. Tax shelters, strictly speaking, were illegal. Anyone operating a tax shelter had to pretend it was a legitimate business enterprise, and that while there *might* be tax write-offs due to losses, they were *not* the object of the investment.

Simultaneous with this chastening experience, Atkins and Markowitz began to realize that executing straddles was more difficult than it had looked. They had begun operating in December, just before the close of the tax year, having raised slightly less than $4 million in capital. To procure the four-to-one write-offs they had promised their investors, they needed to generate approximately $15 million worth of losses in three weeks. They had planned to do this by investing their capital equally in "short" and "long" positions in international currency futures—the short positions gambling that the currency would decrease in value, the long positions that it would rise. At the end of the tax year, they would close out the losing position, show a loss, then early the following year close out the winning position and thereby recover that loss.

It sounded so simple. It sounded so easy. But they found out to their dismay that the markets weren't really quite that symmetrical; the long and short positions didn't always balance each other out. That meant it was possible to have a real gain or a real loss, thereby spoiling the painless tax advantages for investors and possibly consuming the firm's capital.

With the end of the tax year rapidly approaching, a sort of panic overtook the young firm. How were they going to create $15 million worth of trading losses? To prevent disaster, a junior member of the firm named Steven Hageman arranged to have a friend at another firm concoct phony paperwork pretending to show that trades had been carried out and $8.5 million in losses incurred in certain government securities. The friend charged the firm $300,000. While steep, it was worth the price. It worked so well that Atkins himself, according to associates who later testified at his trial, then arranged for a family friend to fake some paperwork showing another $3.5 million in losses. This *was* easy. They were off and running.*

---

*Atkins, who declined to be interviewed for this book, maintained throughout his trial and after his conviction that he had been unaware of the fraudulent trades and the false nature of the paperwork. He testified that he had always thought the trades were legitimate.

But Atkins was furious with Markowitz. The man had claimed to be a sophisticated trader, to know currency futures inside and out, but he had been unable to set up the straddles as planned. On top of that, Markowitz had actually lost $330,000 of the firm's money on real trades that went bad. Upon returning from a vacation in April of 1979, Markowitz was summoned to a meeting the following day at the New York office of Ashland Oil. It was a Sunday and, except for Charlie Atkins and two lawyers, the place was deserted. When Markowitz arrived, the lawyers handed him a resignation letter and then, he later claimed, threatened to spread word through Wall Street of what they said was his abysmal trading record if he didn't sign. "I was accused by Charlie of not having produced the losses I was supposed to produce, of not having raised sufficient capital for the firm, and of generally being a bad trader, and I was to sign my resignation letter then and there or my name would be smeared," Markowitz testified at the trial. "I'd never work on Wall Street again."

Markowitz refused to resign. The next day, Atkins barred him from the office and instructed the other members of the firm to ignore his trading orders. The following month Markowitz sued Atkins, claiming, among other things, that Atkins was telling people Markowitz had "stolen" and "embezzled" money from the firm.

The suit was settled out of court, and Markowitz returned to Washington to set up a similar tax shelter of his own— only Markowitz offered write-offs of up to ten to one of his investors. Within a couple of years, he was claiming he had a trading portfolio of $6.9 billion. But not long after that, in one of the biggest tax shelter frauds on record, Markowitz admitted that most of the trades he had supposedly done to create the tax losses were totally fictitious.

THE MATERIAL FANTASY

By creating the fraudulent paperwork, the Securities Groups had easily been able to provide investors with the tax losses promised. As word of those write-offs got around, an ever greater number of investors clamored to get in under the shelter. Those who signed on with Atkins included Andy Warhol, Sidney Poitier, and Nancy Sinatra. Estée Lauder and her son invested $2.8 million. But the partnership list was not limited to celebrities. Some of Wall Street's most astute financiers found Atkins' proposition attractive. Michel David-Weill, the senior partner of the investment bank Lazard Frères, invested. So did William Salomon, the former managing partner of Salomon Brothers. Laurence Tisch, now the chief executive officer of CBS, and his brother Robert Preston Tisch, the former Postmaster General, put up $1.5 million. "Everything I heard about him was that he was a very intelligent young man," Larry Tisch would later say of Atkins. "He came with high references and the people who were associated with him were top flight."

It was easy to see what attracted those investors. The television producer Norman Lear and his wife, Frances, for example, invested $450,000 in the firm. According to their 1981 tax returns, the write-offs produced by their investment that year reduced their gross income from $3.1 million to $1.6 million and cut their tax bill from $1.06 million to $318,756.

Atkins' firm was successful beyond his wildest dreams, and it reached its peak in the early eighties. Each year Atkins created additional limited partnerships, which he operated through his umbrella organization, the Securities Groups. He also used the promissory notes of the limited partners to borrow more money. By the end of 1982 he had raised a total of $100 million in cash.

The firm naturally required new offices commensurate with its success. It moved from the Seagram Building into space in the aluminum-banded Olivetti Building at 59th Street and Park Avenue in midtown Manhattan. Atkins, the "Renaissance man," spent hundreds of thousands of dollars creating a sumptuous environment replete with European antiques, hunting prints, marble floors, and Oriental rugs. The place resembled nothing so much as an Italian *palazzo*, according to one visitor, who half-expected to see someone in a turban come through the doors.

The quantity of cash pouring into the Securities Groups enabled Atkins to hire experienced traders from firms like Lehman Brothers and Blyth Eastman Dillon by offering salaries that were huge even by Wall Street's inflated standards. According to an accounting report that the firm itself commissioned, salaries at the Securities Groups were 25 percent higher than the Wall Street norm.

No one's pay approached what Charlie Atkins awarded himself. His salary was in the mere $300,000-a-year range; however, he gave himself staggering bonuses. In 1980 he received a $2.18-million bonus. The following year his bonus came to $5.6 million. Also, as the managing partner, he could draw virtually unlimited amounts of money from the firm. And he did. In 1980 he borrowed $12 million, and in 1981 he borrowed $13 million.

What did the budding tycoon do with so much money? Inevitably, he sank much of it into art. His purchases included, for example, a pair of Van Kessel flower paintings ($532,183), *The Annointment of David by Samuel* by Preti ($349,325), and *The Witch of Endor* by Cavallino ($223,125). At times it seemed as if Atkins would buy whatever he could get his hands on. At Christie's one day, he acquired a George II giltwood side table ($107,220) and a brace of twelve-bore Purdey shotguns ($11,841). Entire rooms of his Sutton Place co-op were paneled with interiors taken from period houses in Britain and Provence. So profligate was Atkins' spending that someone once even thought to offer him a copy of the Magna Carta; he turned it down. By the end of 1982, however, when he was twenty-seven, Atkins valued his collection of art and antiques at $5.1 million.

Many of these acquisitions were financed with money borrowed from the firm. Atkins also borrowed from the firm to make more businesslike investments. For example, he borrowed $3 million to make a personal investment in an oil and gas drilling venture. According to his partners, Atkins also borrowed $2 million from the firm to buy 374 acres of virgin Colorado land that he intended to turn into a ski resort. And, they claim, he took money from the firm for a multi-million dollar estate and 117 acres of adjoining land in Southampton, the exclusive beach resort on eastern Long Island. He even borrowed the $1 million he needed to pay for a nonrefundable option to buy his and his father's favorite restaurant, "21."

Atkins paid this money back. What rankled the other general partners in the firm, some of whom subsequently sued him, was that he was using the firm's capital to make immensely profitable deals for himself. But, according to Atkins, it was all perfectly legal. The firm's bylaws—the writing of which Atkins had, of course, overseen—allowed Atkins to borrow millions of dollars with very few restrictions.

The most egregious illustration of this was the purchase of 500 Park Avenue by Atkins, his father, and his brother, Randall. In late 1979 the Atkinses formed a partnership, called 500 Park Avenue Associates, to acquire a ninety-nine-year lease on the Olivetti Building at 500 Park Avenue and the adjacent Nassau Hotel. The property cost $26 million.

"When we first learned of this real estate acquisition, we

were told that the Atkins family was purchasing the building with their own funds for their own investment purposes," some of the former general partners of the Securities Groups stated in a deposition filed in the suit.

According to the deposition, the Atkinses had put up $10,000 of their own money. But that left them a bit shy of the $26-million price tag. So, according to the partners, Charlie Atkins transferred $5 million worth of government securities from the portfolio of the Securities Groups to the portfolio of 500 Park Avenue Associates. The partners claim that the securities were then used as collateral to arrange a $30-million bank loan to pay for the building and related expenses. Once the deal was negotiated, Atkins moved the Securities Groups into the building, where it paid him, his father, and his brother rent of $1.3 million a year. The partners claim that when they learned the details of the arrangement, they went to Atkins to argue that the building rightly belonged to the firm, since its assets had been used as collateral. "He told us to 'mind our own business,'" the partners said, "that 'if the limited partners had wanted to invest in real estate they could have invested elsewhere....'"

In late 1981 the Atkinses sold their 95 percent interest in 500 Park Avenue Associates to the Equitable Life Assurance Society for slightly more than $54 million in cash. It was a stunning illustration of pure wealth creation. In less than two years, Charlie, Orin, and Randy—three "good ol' boys" from Kentucky, as their friends called them—had made a $27-million profit on a cash investment of $10,000. The Atkinses, as they say in the South, knew how to cut a fat hog.

While accomplishing all this, Atkins was also able quickly to insinuate himself into New York society. His first friends in the city were drawn from what was known as the "Southern network." But with his charm and his immensely lucrative business, Atkins soon graduated into full-fledged membership in the Park Avenue establishment. Through his father he had been able to get in to see such people as Samuel Butler, the managing partner of the distinguished law firm of Cravath, Swaine & Moore, and Pete Peterson, the former Secretary of Commerce who ran the investment bank then known as Lehman Brothers. He joined the Council on Foreign Relations and became a patron of the Metropolitan Museum. He sought out America's corporate elite and could be seen watching Yankee games with Lee Iacocca in George Steinbrenner's private box.

Atkins even made his presence felt in the inner chambers of the national government. He became a member of the Republican Senatorial Trust and had his firm start up and sponsor the International Monetary Advisory Board, whose members, including economists Arthur Laffer and Martin Feldstein, met to ponder the weighty issues of the day.

As early as 1979, Atkins had become sufficiently prominent to get Paul Volcker to give one of his first speeches to a board dinner shortly after Volcker became chairman of the Federal Reserve Bank. When Volcker tightened monetary policy a few months later, Atkins, who liked to refer to himself as his firm's chief economist, had the audacity to claim a measure of credit for that shift. "I'm very glad to see that Paul Volcker has acknowledged our suggestions and raised the discount rate," Atkins wrote to some potential investors. "I'm not sure that these steps will be totally successful, but at least they're a step in the right direction."

Charlie Atkins had acquired wealth and social status, aristocratic trappings, and even (he believed) political influence. Furthermore, he had acquired them without sacrificing independence and entrepreneurial self-determination. He was living out the primary material fantasy of his generation. And he had done it all by the age of twenty-seven. He had not had to wait.

BANKRUPTCY AND RUIN

There was, however, something frantic about the pace of Charlie Atkins' pursuit of the material fantasy. He seemed to know that he could not sustain his success, to realize that though he had not had to wait for it, neither had he truly earned it. Success, he seemed to sense, was temporary, and he had only a temporary period to enjoy its rewards. In fact, in 1980, when the firm had been open for less than two years, Congress began to consider eliminating tax deductions for losses created by straddles. Randy Atkins, who was also a general partner in the firm, wrote his brother a memo saying, "It is obvious that the IRS may be beginning to 'sniff around' some areas which may be of interest to us." He added that he was going to contact a lobbyist to promote their cause. Kenneth Kaltman, one of the firm's partners, who was sent a copy of the memo, wrote Randy back: "Remember, when you are up to your neck in shit, it is proper not to make waves."

It had never been Charlie Atkins' intention to remain a mere tax shelter promoter. By 1981 his firm, which had grown to an impressive 160 employees, began to diversify. It bought New York Hanseatic, one of a handful of trading companies permitted to buy U.S. government securities directly from the Federal Reserve Bank. It made a $5-million venture capital investment in Fugazy Express. And for $27 million it acquired Southern California Savings & Loan, which had assets of $1.2 billion and a sleek headquarters in Beverly Hills, but was burdened with bad loans and operating losses.

But even as Atkins was trying to establish a genuine investment banking operation, the ground began to crumble beneath him. In 1981 Congress did change the tax code to forbid deductions generated by straddle trades. Instead of closing shop, however, the partners at the Securities Groups discovered they could create write-offs for their limited partners by manufacturing paperwork that would fake tax-deductible interest expenses on the purchase and resale of Treasury bills. Using such a process, they generated almost $750 million of fake losses in 1981 and 1982.

Then, toward the end of 1981, federal agents raided the offices of Sentinel Financial Instruments, a trading firm on Wall Street that, among a host of other illegal activities, had produced some of the paperwork faking trades for the Securities Groups. The name of Joseph Riley, a member of the Securities Groups, was found in the records of Sentinel, and Riley was subpoenaed.

"Riley was upset," Kenneth Kaltman recalled in his testimony at the trial. "He was visibly shaken. He came into my office and said, 'I am really worried.... If this thing falls apart, I am the one taking all of the risk. I am the one that is going to be going to jail....'" Riley added that he should be paid more because of the risk to which he was exposed.

Shortly thereafter, Atkins and some of the other partners met privately to discuss Riley. They considered throwing him to the wolves—that is, firing him and disavowing all knowledge of his illegal trades. But in the end they decided, in a spirit of generosity, to keep him on. They gave him a handsome raise and made him a partner in the firm.

Nonetheless, an atmosphere of suspicion pervaded the firm, much as it had the palaces of the Medicis. Atkins was a "Renaissance man" not only because of his sophisticated education but also because, as he had shown first in his ruthless handling of Markowitz and then in his willingness to sacrifice Riley, he had a Machiavellian capacity for cunning and intrigue. As the situation grew more tense, the partners became mistrustful of each other. One began secretly taping meetings. And they all worried that Atkins, who continued to borrow rampantly from the firm, might be draining it of money. When they questioned him about it, according to Steven Hageman, "he became quite angry . . . and said we should not meddle in his personal business and that it was his right to be able to take whatever money he wanted from the firm."

But by then Atkins was borrowing so heavily that he himself seemed unable to keep track of it. Over lunch in 1982, his partners asked him if he planned to continue to withdraw money from the firm at the rate of $1 million a month. When Atkins replied that he had taken out nothing recently, they had to remind him that he had just borrowed some $800,000 to buy a painting.

Around the same time, the firm's own accountants began to grow suspicious. Arthur Young & Company, which Atkins had hired to audit the firm's books for tax purposes, could find neither telephone numbers nor addresses for one of the companies with which the Securities Groups supposedly traded. In a memo on the matter, the Arthur Young accountant handling the audit wrote that it "smelled shitty— looked shitty on paper." When one of the partners asked Atkins how to respond to the accountant's inquiries, Atkins told him there was no need to be overcooperative, saying, "I don't think we're in business to play nursemaid to auditors."

By that time, too, the Federal Reserve Bank of New York had become alarmed by the staggering size of the firm's portfolio. In all, it claimed to be holding securities worth $24 billion, which rivaled the portfolios of Wall Street's largest firms. But the Securities Groups' was so highly leveraged that there was something slightly unreal about the whole undertaking. Its supposed investment positions were worth more than *200 times* the amount of cash the partners had on hand. It was as if money itself had become an empty abstraction for the members of the firm, with no reference to anything outside the detached world of pure wealth. The

Federal Reserve Bank felt the firm's ratio of capital to investments was "shockingly high" and began to put pressure on the Securities Groups to reduce it.

By 1983 the walls were tumbling in around Atkins. The firm's accountants, having been rebuffed the previous year, resigned when he and his partners failed to clear up discrepancies in the trades they were claiming to have carried out. His savviest investors, among which were the billionaire Tisch brothers, had pulled their money out. The venture capital investment in Fugazy fell apart after a dispute over dividend payments. Atkins, who by then was experiencing many sleepless nights, even had to let his option on the "21" Club lapse.

As the situation deteriorated, the atmosphere at the firm turned somewhat hysterical. The Securities Groups owed William Hack, another tax shelter operator, $1.5 million for paperwork he had generated for it showing fake losses. Hack appeared at the firm one day demanding his money. Atkins, calling him a "bloodsucker," refused to see him. When no one else would talk to him either, Hack lost control. "They owe me!" he screamed at the staff. "They owe me this money! I want to get paid!" One of the newer members of the firm picked Hack up and hurled him against a window ledge, then shoved him out of the office.

Atkins tried to salvage matters by selling the Securities Groups. He approached more than twenty potential buyers, but not one was interested. He then offered to buy out all his investors. Although he could only give them 5 percent of the payment in cash—with the rest in non-negotiable notes—most of the investors leaped at the opportunity. This heaped yet more debt on the firm and sucked out almost all of its remaining cash. As a result, the firm came to a grinding halt. By the end of May 1983, when it had stopped all trading, the Securities Groups had less than $6,000 in cash and more than $400 million in outstanding liabilities.

* * *

When the Securities Groups closed its doors, the hard and powerful people who had invested in the firm turned on its young founder. A number of the limited partners, including John McMullen (the owner of the Houston Astros) and members of the Entenmann's baked goods family, did not sell their stakes in the partnerships back to Atkins at reduced rates. They wanted all their money back. And when Atkins couldn't—or wouldn't—produce it, they sued him, accusing "the boy wonder" of scheming to "defraud investors." They claimed that Atkins was a "horse thief," and that he "withdrew more than $40 million from the partnerships and diverted these funds to his own personal use."

Indeed, while the bank accounts of the Securities Groups were empty, Atkins' personal property—his art, his antiques, his real estate—was believed to be worth more, perhaps considerably more, than $10 million. That property soon became the focus of the suit, and the presiding judge asked Atkins' attorneys for assurances that Atkins would neither sell his $5-million Sutton Place co-op nor remove the $5 million worth of art and antiques it contained without advising the court. Atkins' attorneys told the court that Atkins agreed not to remove any of his "personal property" from the apartment.

By then, however, Atkins had decided to leave New York. Although his reputation was somewhat tarnished, he had amassed a fortune during the five years he had been in the city. It was easily enough to last him for the rest of his life. From 1978 to 1982 his declared net worth had risen from $100,000 to more than $65 million.

Atkins' father, Orin, and his brother, Randy, were living at the time in Florida, and Charlie decided it was the right place for him and his wife as well. In April 1984, the same month that the judge asked for the assurances, a shipment of goods from Atkins' apartment left for Florida. Less than a week later, a rigging crew removed a twelve-by-eight-foot painting from Atkins' apartment, cutting through the iron railing of the apartment's French doors and lowering the work by hoist. Around the same time, Christie's auctioned four George II mahogany wood chairs and a Regency writing table that had been listed as "the Property of a Gentleman"; Atkins' signature appeared on the presale forms. And at the end of the month, Atkins' wife air-freighted half a ton of something—she later said it was her school alumni records—to her hometown of Pine Bluff, Arkansas.

When word of this moving and shipping and selling got out, it appeared to some that young Atkins had not honored his assurances to the court. But he had, he said, he had. "[My attorney] was saying that 'You shouldn't remove any property that was at One Sutton Place that was *yours*,'" Atkins recalled later. "And I said, 'Uh, okay,' without doing a specific inventory of what property I owned at One Sutton Place."

Had Atkins bothered to give that "specific inventory," his lawyers and the court would have found out that nothing in the apartment except a few clothes and personal effects had actually belonged to Atkins. Instead, it all belonged to Atkins' wife, Frances Bellingrath Atkins. A slim and charming blonde known as Marti, Atkins' wife was a model of the modern Southern belle, just as Atkins himself was the model of the well-bred Southern boy. Marti's father ran the Coca-Cola bottling concession in Pine Bluff. She had known Atkins since she'd attended Madeira, a prep school in suburban Virginia outside Washington, D.C., which had ties to Atkins' school. But they hadn't started dating until New York's Southern network brought them together in 1979. They had been married two years later.

Before the wedding, it turned out, the bride and groom had each hired expensive lawyers to negotiate a prenuptial agreement. The lawyers drafted the document, but Charlie and Marti never signed it. They had decided, Atkins explained later, just to have an oral agreement. Charlie would own his interest in the partnerships, and Marti would own their house and its contents. It was so simple, so straightforward. Why bother putting it on paper?

When Robert Dwyer, an attorney for the plaintiffs, learned that valuables from the apartment were being transferred out of state—and beyond the court's jurisdiction—he moved for an attachment on what the defendants were calling Marti's assets. That meant serving Marti notice.

But Marti had disappeared. Dwyer's firm tracked her down by scouring Arkansas papers for the announcement of the birth of Charlie's and Marti's child, which they knew was imminent. The announcement, when it appeared, duly recorded the name of the hospital. "Mr. Dwyer had my wife served," Atkins later said in outrage, "one day after her cesarean birth, in the hospital in Arkansas...*while she was nursing our child.*" According to Dwyer, however, the process server waited until Marti was finished nursing and gave her flowers along with the complaint.

Some two weeks later Dwyer heard that Charlie and Marti were about to buy a huge cotton plantation in the South. There was also a story that the co-op at One Sutton Place was on the market. One of Atkins' attorneys, reporting statements from his client, told the court that the allegations about a South Carolina plantation were "flatly incorrect" and that no sale of the apartment was imminent.

He didn't know that some months earlier, Atkins had bought the 800-acre Mulberry Plantation outside Charleston, South Carolina, for $2.3 million and then sold it to his wife for $3. Nor did the attorneys know that the prominent investment banker Leon Levy had offered to buy Atkins' apartment for $4.5 million, that the board of One Sutton Place had approved the sale, and that Atkins had even signed closing papers on behalf of Marti, who, Atkins kept reminding everyone, owned the apartment. (In the end the sale did not go through.)

Alarmed by this apparently deceptive maneuvering, the attorney Dwyer asked for permission to inspect the art and antiques in Atkins' co-op. It was granted, and on a warm day in May 1984 Dwyer, another attorney, an appraiser, and a photographer took the elevator up to Atkins' co-op on the ninth floor of One Sutton Place. But when Dwyer stepped through the door he halted in astonishment. The apartment had been stripped. Some moving cartons and crumpled packing sheets sat in the center of the room, but otherwise the walls and floor were bare. The paintings, the rare books and rarer prints, the Fabergé matchboxes, the Tabriz rugs and giltwood tables and Louis XVI bureaus had all vanished. It was, for practical purposes, an empty apartment. Charlie Atkins had fled the city. Shortly thereafter, presenting himself as a man of little property, he filed for bankruptcy in Florida.

A constellation of factors seems to have motivated Charlie Atkins. His father, the man who'd once dismissed his own illegalities by saying the applicable rules were "more honored in the breach," was certainly an influence. Then, too, Atkins was among those members of the postwar generation who came of age after 1970, when the Las Vegas Syndrome—the notion that it was all a game and nothing mattered except winning—flourished. That syndrome, which led many to conclude that life was essentially irrational and, as Jimmy Carter said, "unfair," fostered cynicism toward rules and regulations. Rules were for fools. The attitude was thoroughly entrenched on Wall Street, where so many transactions are carried out on the inky, uncertain terrain that lies between what is absolutely correct and what is undeniably illegal. It was hard to know, particularly in those heady days in the early eighties, what was proper and what was not. One of the jurors in Atkins' trial wrote the judge urging a lenient sentence. While he had no doubt Atkins was guilty, the juror explained, the laws he broke "remained largely unenforced."

But another factor is equally important. For certain people, there was *so much* money to be made in the eighties that they just couldn't help themselves.

By late 1985 some twenty other lawsuits had been filed against Atkins and his partnerships, with claims totaling $2.5 billion. It seemed unlikely, however, that the plaintiffs would ever see much of the money. Upward of $10 million, and perhaps far more, was in investments in his wife's name, safe from the reach of the bankruptcy courts. Even if his conviction was upheld and he served a short prison term, he had, in four years on Wall Street, earned enough to live handsomely, doing nothing if he chose, for the rest of his days. And whatever the future held, he would always be able to say that for a few brief shining years, when he was young and the promise of life seemed limitless, he had been a Prince on Wall Street.

3

PRISONERS OF SUCCESS: THE ART WORLD OF THE EIGHTIES

THE NATIONAL MULTIMEDIA CELEBRITY

Mark Kostabi was sitting at a marble-topped table in his living quarters in the back of his New York studio. Kostabi was an artist. He was twenty-seven years old. In the first six months of 1988, he said, he had sold more than $1 million worth of paintings. He had also recently published a book called *Sadness Because the Video Rental Store Was Closed*. It consisted of reproductions of some of his paintings grouped to form loose narrative lines. Kostabi was explaining how it came to be published.

"Though by all definition it's not vanity press, everyone knows that an art book is subsidized to some degree," he said. "I bought two thousand copies of this book before it was published. I also gave the publisher two paintings. Things like that are usually not talked about but it goes on. I don't think artists usually buy two thousand copies of their own books, but they usually give up some paintings."

Kostabi loves to talk about things that are usually not talked about. He loves to provoke even more. He was promoting his new book by running an advertisement that quoted from critics who hated his work. Under the heading "A Real Advertisement," he included, among other culled statements:

"A sad attempt to be fashionable."

"Kostabi's work seems to weaken with each exposure...monotonous, figurative—photographic gimmickry."

"The only viable antidote is to ignore it and leave it to its inevitable resting place in the garbage bin of worthless product."

"Indifferent, clumsily painted."

"Too much, too soon."

All publicity is good, Kostabi is fond of pointing out, even good publicity. Bad publicity, he will then explain, is infinitely preferable to good publicity because it creates controversy, and nothing attracts people's attention like controversy.

As Kostabi went on about all this, Ned, one of his young assistants, hesitantly stuck his head through the door.

"What's up?" Kostabi asked.

Ned explained that Kostabi's agent—not the art dealer who represented him and not a literary agent, but his theatrical talent agent—was on the telephone.

"Do you know what she wants?" Kostabi asked.

Ned didn't know.

"Can you just take a message?" Then, as Ned withdrew his head from the doorway, Kostabi had an afterthought. "If she's telling me I got that movie or the Coke commercial, come back and tell me."

Ned returned shortly.

"You had a callback on the film," he told Kostabi.

"Oh, that's great," Kostabi said. But he did not become overexcited.

On the dust jacket of Kostabi's book was a large photograph of the artist. Kostabi is not a handsome man. He is slender and on the short side. He has a thick jaw with a somewhat Neanderthal jut to it. His eyes bat and flutter when he becomes nervous. In the book jacket photograph, however, he looked almost pretty.

"That's my acting head shot," Kostabi explained. "I have makeup on, and it's one out of a hundred photographs that were taken to make me look as if I were a saleable commodity, to see if I could get national TV commercials."

Like many young artists in the eighties, Kostabi was not particularly interested in the physical act of painting. The whole process of stretching canvases, priming them, mixing paint, then applying the paint to the canvas with a brush—not to mention having to think up something to paint—was simply too tedious. It was also too messy. Paint splattered your clothes. You smelled of turpentine. What fun was that? Sitting down by yourself and painting your own pictures was like paying dues. It was a laborious initial career step, something you had to do before the arrival of the collectors and dealers whose money enabled you to hire teams of assistants, and before the shows and invitations and press coverage that meant you had become an art star.

But for the truly ambitious artist, becoming an art star—a painter who could command $50,000 or more for a canvas, who enjoyed automatic entrée to the most exclusive nightclubs and who had paintings hanging in the Modern and the Guggenheim—was little more than another temporary career step. The real goal was to transform yourself into a National Multimedia Celebrity. Painting was just one way of achieving that. It was not an art form you were wedded to for life. Robert Longo, to give an example, was one of the most successful art stars of the eighties. Before breaking through as a painter he played in a rock band. And no sooner had he succeeded as an artist than he gave the novelist Richard Price a couple of canvases to write a screenplay, which Longo then began shopping around Hollywood with the hopes of directing.

For other artists in the eighties, recognition was a step on the way to creating their own corporate franchise. It provided an opportunity to go into a real business. Since the birth of bohemianism in nineteenth-century Paris, artists had reserved their greatest scorn for the shopkeeper. No one, to their way of thinking, more completely epitomized the narrowness, the prejudice, the hopeless banality of the *petite bourgeoisie* than the shopkeeper: the harassed and stunted fellow chained to the cash register who spent his days counting out change.

But in the 1980s established artists—the very ones whose paintings cost $50,000 and were hanging in the Modern and the Guggenheim—found the idea of selling goods appealing, *more* appealing than the idea of iconoclastic avant-garde freedom. They pursued merchandising licenses, product endorsements, retail outlets. Keith Haring, one of the original and most successful of the so-called graffiti artists, had first attracted attention by the chalk drawings he made on New York City subway station billboards. That was all very much in the venerable anti-establishment tradition of modern art. Haring was promptly discovered and turned into an art star. He had an income from the sale of his paintings in excess of $100,000 a year. And so what did he do? He opened a store, the Pop Shop in lower Manhattan, selling T-shirts, shoelaces, lapel buttons, and other trinkets he and some of his artist friends designed. He became a shopkeeper.

"This is the way everyone wants to work," said Kostabi. "Artists that are in art school now don't want to be the isolated lone visionary laboring in their small studios." By the summer of 1988 Kostabi had twenty assistants working for him in the two large studios he maintained. In addition to turning out paintings, he had designed soda bottle labels and shopping bags for Bloomingdale's. He had created animated television commercials for Japanese newspapers and water filter companies. He had appeared in five television commercials for Levi's 501 jeans. In one he sat in an empty loft uttering statements like "I've been called a money-hungry opportunist" and "Put a dam in your stream of consciousness" while he completed a sketch and then set it afire. He had put together a "reel" of these commercials along with his appearances on television talk shows. His theatrical talent agent was sending the reel to Hollywood casting directors. Now Kostabi had gotten the callback. It was for a role as an eccentric performance artist in a movie starring Jessica Lange. He was on a roll. He had momentum. If he could sustain it, he had a shot at becoming a National Multimedia Celebrity.

The art of the eighties may well turn out to be esthetically worthless, but the art world of the eighties is an anthropological treasure trove. An extraordinary artistic revolution took place during the decade. For more than a hundred years, the public had been led to believe that art was a spiritual mission, a calling, with all of the attendant religious implications. Artists, according to the Romantic tradition that shaped public perception, performed rites of denial, suffering, penance, and purification. For the annointed among them, those deprivations were followed by immortality. While many of the Impressionists had an accommodating attitude toward the marketplace—Degas and Monet, to name just two, produced certain types of paintings simply because they knew they would sell—the twentieth-century artist tended to see himself as a pilgrim. He was an existential hero. He was a source of moral authority in a godless world. His destiny was to rebel against commonplace assumptions, to seek out and articulate the hard truths. While yearning for commercial success, he would never compromise his art for the sake of it. He preferred instead to wallow in working class squalor, though in his work he devoted himself to standards that were intellectually and esthetically elitist.

In the eighties, a new generation of artists reversed this equation. Dropping the posture of the anti-establishment iconoclast, they embraced materialism and consumption and luxury. Abandoning the elitist approval of peers, critics, and curators, they sought "the validation of the marketplace." In the eighties, art became much more of a business. And the artist became much more of a businessman, or, to use the word of choice, an entrepreneur. He hired accountants and bookkeepers and invested in tax shelters. The approach could be called either pragmatic or cynical. It was certainly devoid of illusion. But after all, there was really no such thing as truth in art. There were, as the painter Eric Fischl has said, only opinions. That meant success in art depended not on your ability to articulate the truth but on your ability to command attention for your opinions. And *that* was marketing.

In the seventies, art was dominated by movements like minimalism and conceptualism. Minimalist artists painted mathematical cubes or bands of color that were supposed to express the artificiality of paint or the two-dimensionality of the canvas or the objecthood of the work. But only a handful of critics and museum curators cared about, much less understood, the theories that legitimized this work. The public certainly didn't. And, as the seventies progressed and the theories became increasingly arcane and labyrinthine, artists themselves lost interest. Art, they began telling each other, had become the victim of pretentious "art babble."

At the same time, it had become almost impossible for artists to act like rebels. They had, by the late seventies, succeeded in reducing to rubble almost every esthetic assumption the public had held. In increasingly drastic "conceptual art" statements, artists had buried automobiles in sand, wrapped bridges in plastic, twisted rusting iron into ugly shapes, exposed their sexual organs, offered themselves up for electrocution. They had so harried and confounded the bourgeoisie that, like some animal exhausted by overexposure to Pavlovian stimulus, it had lost the capacity to be shocked.*

For artists, this was a true crisis. As Peter Frank and Michael McKenzie write in *New, Used & Improved*, an account of the art world in the eighties, "Western society no longer exhibits the resistance to new ideas that made an avant-garde possible in the nineteenth and early twentieth centuries. Thus artists cannot position themselves effectively against social norms without quickly being absorbed by those norms. New art forms and movements once took years to sway younger generations even as they shocked older ones. Now new forms and movements have instant influence.... From then on, no matter how radical, new artistic developments enjoyed, or suffered, substantial acceptance as soon as they appeared."

In other words, avant-garde artists had won the war. But like all victorious soldiers, they suddenly found themselves

---

*An example of just how insensitive to shock the public had become was found in the 1988 exhibit of work by the photographer Robert Mapplethorpe at the Whitney Museum of American Art in New York. Middle class New Yorkers of all ages and sexes strolled through the galleries dispassionately contemplating pictures that included, among numerous studies of penises and buttocks, a self-portrait of Mapplethorpe with a long leather whip inserted into his anus. Shortly after Mapplethorpe's death from AIDS, the exhibit moved to Chicago, where it featured even more graphic photographs.

with nothing to do. Frank and McKenzie appeared not to see the irony, much less the humor, in this situation. They seemed dismayed that society, by accepting whatever artists did, now deprived them of their right to rebel. Any position the artist staked out, no matter how outrageous or provocative, was immediately accepted. His work, no matter how subversive, was greeted with enthusiasm. It was frustrating! It was insidious!

The artist who had most successfully negotiated these paradoxes was, of course, Andy Warhol. Opinion is still divided on the esthetic value of Warhol's work. Whatever that turns out to be, unquestionably his greatest contribution was to redefine the role of the artist. Warhol, to put it simply, demystified the profession. Having started his career as a commercial illustrator, he addressed issues like popular culture and mass media while most of his contemporaries were mired in abstruse theory. He hired assistants to mass-produce lithographs and silk-screened images. He and Salvador Dali made it socially acceptable for artists to explore areas previously considered improper because of commercial implications. Warhol's contemporaries had been reluctant to admit association with any enterprise linked to commerce. When Jasper Johns and Robert Rauschenberg collaborated on the design of windows for Tiffany's in the early fifties, they used a pseudonym. Warhol embraced commerce. He created advertisements; he appeared in commercials; he designed record jackets; he published a magazine; he made movies. Most importantly, he made money.

And not only did he make money—many artists have done that—he proclaimed his adoration for it. While painters such as Cézanne and Toulouse-Lautrec had come from affluent families and didn't need to worry about making money, and while others like Renoir openly courted success by celebrating the middle class, it became almost obligatory for twentieth-century artists, even the rich ones, to express utter contempt for money and for those who valued it. Unsuccessful painters—those who couldn't persuade the public to buy their work and therefore couldn't afford to live in material comfort—were merely making a virtue of necessity. Drawing on the examples of a few prominent but atypical artists, such as Gauguin and Van Gogh, they insisted that they preferred to live among the peasants or working classes, which, unlike the insincere middle class, were composed of *real people*, authentic spirits uninhibited by proprieties and so capable of spontaneity.

Warhol, the son of Polish immigrants and a native of Pittsburgh, broke the twentieth-century artist's Romantic association with the working class. He made it legitimate for contemporary artists openly to delight in bourgeois luxury and the accumulation of wealth. Warhol brazenly sought portrait commissions. He painted pictures of dollar signs. At one of his birthday parties in the seventies, friends showered him with thousands of dollar bills. He made statements like "Being good in business is the most fascinating kind of art. Making money is art and working is art and good business is the best art."

This was all supposed to be campy, a joke, an ironic conceptual art statement. But at the same time, Warhol believed it.

While there were notable exceptions, such as David Wojnarowicz, most of the young artists who transformed the art world in the early eighties took Warhol as their inspiration. They were part of the group that novelist Tama Janowitz has referred to as "Andy's Children." They were born in the late fifties and early sixties. During childhood and adolescence they were saturated with American popular culture: cartoons, comic books, situation comedies, fast food, tract housing. Warhol was the only artist whose work explored this sensibility, and they worshiped him. Toward the end of the seventies, they began to appear in New York. They moved into squalid apartments on the Lower East Side and wore versions of Warhol's signature black leather jackets. They talked about video art. They were more fascinated with the manipulation of existing images than with the creation of new ones. They also had little interest in adopting the posture of Anguished Romantic Hero or of Tormented Genius. Both implied angst, anger, darkness, and gloom. That stuff was too heavy. The new artists for the most part were too young to have been stamped by the intellectually fashionable pessimism of the sixties and seventies. Their creed was to have fun.

"I like to have fun," Kenny Scharf said in a 1985 interview with *Art News* magazine. Scharf is one of the most successful young eighties artists. His work mixes cartoon characters, Day-Glo colors, and surreal graffiti backgrounds. "I think everyone wants to have fun," he went on. "I think that having fun is being happy. I know it's not all fun, but maybe fun helps with the bad. I mean you definitely cannot have too much fun. OK, it's like I want to have fun when I'm painting. And I want people to have fun looking at the paintings."

THE RETURN OF
THE COLLECTING CLASS

A young Manhattan couple who were thinking of purchasing a Kostabi were in the artist's studio one day looking at his canvases. The woman saw one she liked. But because it was on an easel and a paper plate with daubs of oil paint rested nearby, she asked if it was finished.

"I don't know," Kostabi said. "What do you think?"

At first the woman thought Kostabi was attempting some

sort of confrontational, conceptual art kind of game. He was putting her on the spot, challenging her assumptions, and so forth. But then she realized that he was actually quite serious. He went on to ask her if she thought it needed more color, more figures, more detail. At first this seemed to the woman to violate some canon of artistic integrity.

Then she thought: well, why not? As artists had for centuries prior to the emergence of the bohemian avant-garde in Paris in the 1830s, which created the perception that the task of the artist was to *épatez* the middle class, Kostabi was willing to accommodate the patron. All businessmen want to please their customers. His solicitous behavior was simply an acknowledgment of the critical role collectors had come to play in the eighties in setting prices, establishing artistic reputations, and even shaping the look of paintings.

By the late seventies, the private collector of contemporary art, bored if not revolted by the pessimistic and incomprehensible work of the times, had all but disappeared. The market for art was shaped by the museums, who for the purposes of exhibition tended to be interested in art that was part of a theoretical school, and by foundations, who tended to give grants to artists who could write articulate theoretical proposals.

But then the artist Julian Schnabel appeared on the scene. He had the sort of megalomaniacal, charismatic personality that excites collectors. His canvases were big and his colors were bold. They dealt with issues like religion. Some had fragments of pottery—plates and whatnot—attached to them. Schnabel's work also included human figures. After years of stripes and cubes and splotches and twisted metal, someone was finally producing paintings with which the public, in however simplistic or misguided a fashion, could make some connection.

The rising young art dealer Mary Boone recognized Schnabel's potential. She arranged a one-man show for the artist in 1979 when he was twenty-seven. His paintings were priced at around $5,000 apiece. The public reaction was astonishing. Private collectors, who had not shown much interest in new art since the pop artists like Rauschenberg and Johns, clamored for Schnabels. Two years later the artist's paintings were selling for $40,000 apiece. "Whatever you think about Schnabel, he brought back the American collectors," Robert Longo told the journalist Lynn Hirschberg. "And we all wanted to get in on that."

The work of Schnabel's contemporaries such as Longo, Eric Fischl, and David Salle was even more representational, and by the early eighties, collectors were returning in droves. One reason was the huge surge in income enjoyed by individuals in the higher income brackets. Accountants, rock stars, lawyers, movie producers, hedge fund barons, arbitrageurs, real estate developers, and investment bankers had more money than they knew what to do with. They built mansions in Bel Air and Brentwood, they renovated vast lofts in lower Manhattan, they knocked down walls to create apartments that occupied entire floors and sometimes several entire floors in sparkling glass towers on the East Side. All of these spaces had enormous walls that required large-scale paintings.

But the art was not merely decorative. It enabled the collector to acquire, instantly and with no exertion, a patina of culture. Rough, gravel-voiced men who grew up in Brooklyn and attended city colleges and became wealthy speculating in commodity pits surrounded themselves with art. Quite often they hadn't even bought it themselves. It was selected by their "interior designer" or "art adviser." The presence of these people at New York auction houses contributed greatly to the galloping pace of the art market throughout the eighties.

During an Impressionist auction at Christie's in the winter of 1986, just such a young man (with a wide tie and too-small glasses) and his strikingly attractive wife (in a full-length raccoon coat) were discussing their growing collection with an equally young art adviser.

"We're unhappy with the Cézanne," the husband told the adviser. "We got it back and hung it up, but it wasn't what we thought it was."

"But that's okay because we're going to *trade up*," the wife said.

"Terrific idea," said the adviser.

"Did we tell you we moved to Seventy-second and Park?" the wife asked.

"High ceilings?" the adviser asked.

"Wonderfully high," the wife told him.

"I always thought your Sutton Place apartment was a little claustrophobic," the adviser remarked.

"Well, it had those tremendous views," the wife said somewhat defensively.

"I didn't mean that," the adviser apologized. "I just meant that eleven-foot ceilings are so fabulous. All that space to hang paintings on. I can't wait."

The arrival of all these new collectors altered the art market in several fundamental respects. Many of these collectors were frankly more interested in art as an investment than as a means of cultural certification. Dealers exploited this. Mary Boone promoted art as an investment. So did Citibank's art advisory service. *Barron's*, the financial publication, even began running an art market index, complete with charts, showing average auction prices in various categories such as Old Masters, Impressionists, Modern.

Although most dealers and collectors protested (too loudly, perhaps) this approach, price patterns did support it. Jackson Pollock's paintings were selling for less than $10,000 at the time of his death in 1956. Twenty years later they were fetching more than $2 million. Jasper Johns' and Robert Rauschenberg's prices had similarly increased.

Only the super rich and the museums could afford the work of those artists now, not to mention Old Masters or Impressionists. But the young professionals pouring into New York—the lawyers, brokers, advertising account executives, photographers, sales representatives—could afford $5,000 to $10,000 for a painting. And they were more than willing to buy, particularly because of the possibility for staggering appreciation. After all, as dealers took every opportunity to point out, Schnabel's prices had increased eightfold in three years. A collector who acquired the work of some young artist before everyone else discovered him could make a killing. Buying a hot new artist was like investing in the right penny stocks. The upside potential, as they are fond of saying on Wall Street, was enormous.

Thus began the great hunt for the *newest* artist. Artists in an earlier generation might wait decades before having their first one-man show. Willem de Kooning did not have a one-man show until he was forty. It was assumed by such painters that you had to discover your subject matter, master your technique. In the eighties, however, no one had time for a long apprenticeship. As a result, artists barely out of their teens were lionized as the next Warhol, the next Jasper Johns, the next Picasso. Jean Michel Basquiat, the graffiti artist who died of a drug overdose at the age of twenty-seven, had his first solo show in New York in 1982, when he was twenty-one. Rodney Allen Greenblat held his first one-man show when he was twenty-three. Kenny Scharf and Keith Haring were established artists by the time they were twenty-five, making well over $100,000 a year. They were just *kids*.

One of the most telling indications of the feverish demand for new art is the fact that between 1970 and 1985 the number of art galleries listed in New York increased from 73 to almost 450. So great was the demand for paintings that many artists had waiting lists of collectors who wanted to acquire their work. Dealers, meanwhile, contributed to the overheated atmosphere by manipulating the market. Certain dealers agreed to represent aspiring artists if they made their paintings more saleable by producing them in a specific size or by using popular colors. To keep prices at a premium, other dealers discouraged established artists from producing more than twenty paintings a year. Certain dealers were said to require a new collector to buy an inferior example of an artist's work as a demonstration of faith before selling the person a good painting. Collectors desperate for art capitulated to such brazen demands. They held onto paintings they had tired of because they were afraid of offending the artist, more of whose work they might want to buy in the future, or whose friendship lent them social cachet. "We'd like to sell it, but he's certain to hear of it and would get very upset," said a young collector stuck with a Kostabi.

This swarm of collectors was at times frightening to artists. The collectors could be not only aggressive but actually predatory. The British advertising tycoon Charles Saatchi, who with his brother Maurice had created one of the world's largest advertising agencies through rampant acquisition, was among the most avid collectors of contemporary painting. He approached art with the same calculation that he used to value corporate stocks, buying the works of painters in volume—as if, people said, he were acquiring stock in some undervalued company before announcing a hostile takeover.

And indeed, this tactic could make an artist's reputation, and the price of his work, fluctuate as wildly as the stock of a company rumored to be a takeover target. In 1984, for example, the art world learned that Saatchi was selling off a large number of paintings he had acquired by the artist Sandro Chia. No one knew why Saatchi was selling the paintings. He was divorcing his wife and may have needed money. Nonetheless, other collectors began to wonder if Saatchi had come to the conclusion that Chia was an overrated artist (there was no truth in art, only opinions) and had therefore decided to dump Chia's paintings while their price was high. The other collectors began to wonder whether they, too, should dump their Chias. In other words, they were reacting exactly like arbitrageurs to the rumor that a corporate raider would not proceed with a hostile takeover. Chia could do nothing but sit it out, for such were the perils of marketplace validation. He had become a prisoner of success.

Like rock stars and movie stars and other prisoners of success, artists in the eighties were consumed with constant anxieties about their position on the charts. Who was hot? Who would be hot next? Who was no longer hot? Robert Longo, who had his first show in 1981 at the age of twenty-eight, was afraid by the age of thirty-three that he was, as he put it, "washed up," shoved aside by rising younger talent. At the age of twenty-four, three years after he burst onto the scene, Jean Michel Basquiat, like Longo, worried that he was "washed up."

Their uncertainty was all the more pronounced because the payoff for success had become so great, and because they had, compared with earlier artists, done so little work to deserve it. Lacking inner conviction, artists in the eighties allowed commercial success and media attention to define them. But having become celebrities, most artists, as is the case with most celebrities, were capable of sustaining intense public interest only for a short period. The crowd, always restless, moved on to some new star. For that reason, artists, like island natives who despise the tourists on whom they depend, began to hate the collectors. They felt *exploited* by the people who acquired their work. One of Mark Kostabi's paintings is called *The Merely Rich Buy Art, the Truly Rich Buy Artists.* Another is called *I Give Them What They Need, They Give Me What I Want.* Yet a third painting, *Pure Product,* portrays, in Kostabi's words, "an artist being strangled to death by the public demanding that he produce."

THE ARTIST AS ENTREPRENEUR

On a sweltering summer day, the air conditioners throbbed away in Kostabi's main loft on West 37th Street at the fringe of New York's garment district. A young woman with a tattoo of a bird on her shoulder was listening to rock music on the radio and applying paint to a large Kostabi canvas. She was one of Kostabi's twenty assistants. Six or eight other assistants were working on canvases that were in various stages of completion. Some of the assistants were standing, some were sitting, some were squatting.

Kostabi stood in the center of the studio surveying the work in progress. He wore a dark blue shirt covered with red stars. In the fashion of the day, the top button was buttoned. His hair in its natural state is brown, but he had taken to dyeing it all sorts of colors—chartreuse, peroxide yellow—and that week it was white. Sometimes he liked to make his hair stand up in spikes. That week it was chopped close on the sides, making the top seem a sort of bleached animal pelt.

Kostabi described how his studio operated. He and a thin pretty woman named Fontaine sketched out concepts for possible paintings. Fontaine was Kostabi's "idea person" as well as his girlfriend. She used to be his "image person"— that is, his hairdresser and clothing adviser. The sketches Kostabi and Fontaine made were usually some variation on a faceless gray android figure called Everyman that appears, engaged in various surreal activities, in most of Kostabi's painting. All those in the studio then voted on which of the sketches to turn into paintings. "All along my work was never mine," Kostabi said. "It was the product of everyone involved. If four out of six people in the studio think it's a good idea, it will get painted."

After a decision was made, one of the assistants copied the selected sketches onto a transparency. The transparency was projected onto a canvas. Colors were selected by Claude, the "color theorist." Assistants then applied the oils. Some of the more experienced ones painted an entire canvas. Claude, who had worked for Kostabi for three years and was one of his fastest painters, could finish a painting in a day; it took other assistants two or three days. The more junior assistants were not trusted with entire canvases. They began with relatively untaxing tasks like filling in gray background space.

Kostabi said he was able to produce about thirty paintings a week with this system. They sold for an average of $12,000, though some fetched $20,000 or more. It cost Kostabi about $100 in labor and materials to produce a painting, and he figured that if for some reason the art market collapsed and the price of his paintings fell as low as $500, he would still come out ahead.

One of Kostabi's claims to fame is that he doesn't paint any of these pictures himself. "I haven't painted at all myself for the past year. I direct. But while I was away these past two weeks there were at least two dozen paintings done. I didn't give a nod of approval on one. Some of them were great. Some of them had to be painted over. One of the idea people came up with the idea, projected it, picked the colors, someone else executed it, all while I was away."

Racks of Kostabi canvases filled the studio. Kostabi, afraid that the presence of all these paintings might suggest that the supply of his work exceeded the demand, explained that he had been "warehousing" paintings for several large shows he planned to have that fall in Europe and Japan. As a matter of fact, he had just recently returned from a two-week trip to see dealers and collectors in Europe and Asia in preparation for the shows. "My studio looks jam-packed right now, but it's usually empty," he said. "It sells all over. Dealers buy my work in bulk and distribute it to other galleries. It sells in California, Chicago, Minneapolis, Japan."

Indeed, Kostabis can be found just about everywhere. The Metropolitan Museum of Art, the Guggenheim Museum, and the Museum of Modern Art all own Kostabis. Corporations own them, too: The Chase Manhattan Bank has one, as does Macdonald's Corporation. Mostly, however, they are in the hands of private collectors. Japanese and Europeans own them. So do movie stars: Sylvester Stallone bought two Kostabis.*

The majority of them are bought by more or less ordinary people. John Fernandez, the owner of a company in Hoboken, New Jersey, that makes signs, has six. His favorite is called *Mergers and Acquisitions*. It shows five android figures standing in a circle. They are painted in brilliant flame colors of orange and red. Three wear blue snap-brim hats. Two are shaking hands. The brokerage firm Smith Barney used the painting on the cover of one of its annual reports. John Fernandez loves it because it's "about business."

Despite the undeniable demand for his work, Kostabi may well be the most roundly denounced painter in the eighties. "A bad boy artist," scolded a critic for the *Chicago Tribune*, "whose work epitomizes the nasty cynicism that pervades today's art world." "Kostabi's works are so bad

---

*One of the paintings, called *Lovers*, depicts two android women embracing on a bed. Kostabi told a reporter that Stallone acquired it because he likes "T and A." When Stallone heard this, he said he was going to get rid of his two Kostabis. Kostabi apologized, explained that he was just joking, and offered to buy them back.

they even subvert the good name of 'bad painting,'"
complained a writer for *Artforum*. "This work celebrates the
notion of artist as entrepreneur," a critic for the *Los Angeles
Times* said in yet another diatribe. "Because its bottom line
is sales, it is the perfect art for the yuppie mentality of the
80s."

But the onslaught of collectors has diminished the role of
critics and museum curators in providing artistic validation.
The commercial success enjoyed by the new generation of
artists enabled them to jettison the intelligentsia, who, as a
rule, had little good to say about them anyway. For validation they turned to the marketplace.

"It makes me look good to have those uptight critics
worrying about me," Kostabi said contentedly. He didn't
even take the opportunity to posture intellectually when it
was offered to him. Asked to explain his technique of
"quoting" from other artists, inserting elements of their
work in his, he said, "A year ago I could have given you a
very rational, intelligent explanation of having a dialogue
with art history, but I don't think about it anymore. It
happens so naturally that I can just as comfortably say it's
just plain theft."

Kostabi is not without his supporters, who include individuals such as Paterson Sims, a former curator at the
Whitney Museum. They argue that Kostabi is making a
"valid statement" about the contemporary art scene. His
entire studio setup is one grand work of performance art
designed to parody the commercialism of the art world. It
embodies the prevailing American esthetic: a veneration for
the product, for the commodity, over the creative process
itself. It also forces people to ask themselves why they buy
art. Is a painting an investment? Is it a status object, with
the artist's name conveying simply the same empty certification that a fashion designer's label brings to clothes or
perfumes or sheets? Or is the collector buying a painting

because he likes it and wants to live with it? And if so, does it matter who actually painted it? "People who buy my work are going to get what they deserve," Kostabi is fond of saying.

But even his supporters have urged Kostabi to be a bit more ironic about his position, to give a wink now and then that will let the critics and other insiders know that he sees himself as a parodist, that he is not really the shameless and greedy publicity-monger he pretends to be. But Kostabi won't play along. "The truth is, I don't want art historical validation for what I'm doing," he said. "I'd rather be invalid and therefore completely new and different and therefore I'll have achieved my goal in conceptual art, and that is to be nothing but different. Anything to get attention, anything to be a little weird. That's what I was taught was good art."

Kostabi's office was just off his main studio. It contained file cabinets and a desk with an electronic typewriter and an impressive multi-line telephone. Against the wall was a case with a collection of conventional art books. On the walls were signs saying:

WHEN YOU'RE BOUGHT YOU'RE HOT

TAKE THE R OUT OF FREE

CASH IN ON PASSION

I AM BOUGHT THEREFORE I AM

USE PEOPLE BEFORE THEY USE YOU

A PICTURE IS WORTH A THOUSAND DOLLARS

THE PERFECT PAINTER NEVER PAINTED

"Those are Kostabi-isms," Kostabi explained. "They are meant for the TV stations to zoom in on." And indeed, because this is all so very outrageous, television stations love to do stories on Kostabi, invariably structured around the question "Mark Kostabi, is he an artist or a con artist?"

But that misses the point entirely. What Kostabi has done is simply revive the studio system, an ancient and venerable artistic tradition that dates back to the Renaissance and prospered until the early nineteenth century. The Renaissance was created by the emergence of a new social class, personified by the merchant princes of Venice and Florence. Their wealth came from commerce, from banking and trade rather than inherited land. They were, in other words, the first nouveaux riches. They built grand villas and palazzos requiring decoration that was large in scale and sometimes secular in subject. This demand, along with the development of oil-based paint and the rediscovery of classical Greek and Roman art, was responsible for a dramatic change in the role of the artist and the type of work he produced. Artists were liberated to a certain degree from the church, where they had spent the Middle Ages, illuminating manuscripts and making pictures that explained the Bible to the illiterate. They became independent operators. Though they maintained strong ties to the church, which commissioned more art than anyone else, they also produced paintings for anyone who could afford them.

It took one man a long time physically to apply the paint needed to cover the gargantuan canvases that hung on the walls of the merchant princes. And if he had commissions for more than one work, then doing it all himself was out of the question. So the great painters of the Renaissance, such as Raphael and da Vinci, hired assistants. This practice was taken to much greater lengths by the Flemish painters of the seventeenth century, such as Rubens, who were also providing large works for a new merchant class. The painters trained these assistants and oversaw their work. Assistants who had proven that they could execute work in the manner of the master were trusted to paint entire pictures, which the artist, who had conceived them and overseen their execution, then signed. Art was considered a business, and the studio system provided a more efficient means of producing, enabling the artist to turn out a greater number of works than would have been possible if he had had to paint them all himself. In the eighties it has openly become a business once again, and no one was more eager to acknowledge that than Kostabi.

As he stood in his office, Kostabi was approached by Shawn, one of his assistants. Blond, muscular, and handsome, Shawn functioned as sort of operations officer to Kostabi's chief executive. "He is my double, my stand-in," Kostabi said. As a gag and a conceptual art statement, Shawn sometimes took Kostabi's place at parties and even occasionally gave interviews for Kostabi. "He is like a good-looking version of Mark Kostabi. I'm this weird creature. I'm good on film for gangsters and things like that. He's more commercially attractive."

Shawn had a problem with one of the paintings then being completed, and he asked Kostabi to look at it. Out in the studio, an assistant stood next to a large canvas. It was devoid of the usual Kostabi androids. Instead, it was a surrealistic conglomeration of lines and colors and "quotations" from other painters. On the right side was a large eye. Shawn was not happy with the eye.

"It doesn't work," he said. "It's too derivative and obvious."

Kostabi studied the painting, his chin cupped in his hand. "You're right," he said. "Let's take it out."

"Take it out?" the assistant asked.

"Take it out," Shawn told him.

Kostabi and Shawn decided to go up the block to Kostabi's second studio to check into the work in progress there. Kostabi explained that demand for his paintings was so great that, to fill it, he had been hiring additional assistants at the rate of one a week for the last couple of months. He paid his assistants between $7 and $10 an hour. Almost all of them were aspiring artists themselves. Many had masters degrees in fine art. Kostabi had hired so many assistants in the last few months that his staff no longer fit into his loft, so he had rented the second loft.

In the elevator down, Shawn, who was very talkative, began to complain about a bad stock tip he had received from corporate raider Saul Steinberg. Like others in the art world these days, Shawn read the *Wall Street Journal* and kept abreast of financial news. He had been aware that Steinberg had filed a form 13-D with the Securities and Exchange Commission stating that he had accumulated more than 5 percent of a company called Lomax & Nettleton. Wall Street analysts were speculating in the papers about whether Steinberg would attempt a hostile takeover of the company. Shawn had been sitting next to Steinberg at a dinner party and had asked him what his plans were. Steinberg just smiled. Shawn interpreted this as a confirming signal, so he bought stock in Lomax & Nettleton. He took an arbitrage position. The stock had run up on all the takeover speculation, and when no takeover actually materialized—Steinberg seemed to have wanted merely to buy some Lomax & Nettleton—it dropped again. Shawn lost money.

"I'm pissed," Shawn said in the elevator. "When he gave me that tiny smile I thought for sure that meant he was going ahead."

In the second loft two young women were working on large canvases spread across the wooden floor. Kostabi explained that with this new studio he was able to separate those of his assistants who didn't get along.

On a shelf near the door was a time clock. The expansion of the staff and the addition of the second studio, together with the fact that many of the assistants preferred to keep odd hours, had made it difficult to know who was working when. So Kostabi had bought a time clock.

"I must be the only artist with a time clock," he mused, as if its incongruity had not occurred to him before. He turned to Shawn with the inevitable conceptual art reaction to this thought. "We should emphasize it and make an altar out of it."

ROLODEX ARTISTS

Mark Kostabi was born in 1960 in Whittier, California—the same town that produced Richard Nixon, he is quick to mention, thereby suggesting but not explaining a similarity between himself and the former president. Both Kostabi's parents came from Estonia. They had emigrated to Canada after World War II, then settled in Whittier. His father worked in a factory that manufactured French horns, trumpets, tubas, and other musical instruments. His mother had a job soliciting donations for nonprofit organizations over the telephone.

Kostabi, whom his parents had named Kalev, started drawing at an early age. He soon demonstrated remarkable technical proficiency. Unlike many contemporary artists, he is capable of turning out the sort of detailed realistic or academic painting, in the vein of Andrew Wyeth, that the art world considers hopelessly banal and that most impresses middle Americans. (In fact, this kind of work remained a secret vice; after he moved to New York he would go to Central Park on weekends to paint pictures he neither showed nor sold.)

As a teenager Kostabi was not popular. He was obsessed with his face, which he considered ugly, and he would engage in ritual bouts of self-humiliation, drawing attention to himself by standing on tables and making loud noises and otherwise misbehaving. But he also drew constantly. He had decided he would try to become a magazine illustrator, perhaps one day work for *The New Yorker.*

While in college at California State University, Fullerton, Kostabi was exposed to conceptual art. It appealed to him, this idea that you could hammer a nail into a post and call it art, or set fire to a book and call it art, or fish some piece of detritus from the dump and hold it up and call it art. He liked it because it was defiant, because it was, he felt, a concept the average person could neither understand nor accept. He could do anything he wanted, literally, and justify it by saying, "This is art."

Kostabi continued drawing, however, and while in college he developed in outline form his trademark cartoonish android. He refined the figure in countless sketches, some of which were shown in glass display cases around the campus. He collected the best of these in a book he published by himself, which he paid for by painting realistic portraits for local suburbanites.

In the back of Kostabi's book, *Sadness Because the Video Rental Store Was Closed,* is a realistic portrait of his father, a balding gray-haired man wearing a blue polo shirt and sitting pensively in the golden light of late afternoon. "I was painting like that," Kostabi said one day. "I would agonize over a painting like that—well, it really wasn't agony... I would spend three days on a work like that to earn two hundred dollars when I was in school. I painted about three of those to earn money to publish the book of line drawings, which is what I really wanted to do."

He sold the books on campus. Then one day he walked into the Molly Barnes Gallery in Los Angeles and showed the owner a copy. Barnes liked the drawings. They were funny and offbeat and hip. They were slick but ironic about their slickness. They had, in other words, a particularly

Hollywood sensibility. Barnes thought they might not look bad on the walls of a studio executive's office, and she agreed to represent him.

The drawings, on eighteen- by twenty-four-inch paper, proved a big hit in Hollywood. Barnes sold the first two for $20 apiece, then quickly raised the price to $100, then to $150, then to $200. Entertainment executives like Norman Lear, Ray Stark, and Daniel Melnick all purchased Kostabi drawings. Kostabi was then asked to design the menu for Ma Maison, a restaurant for movie industry powers. A critic for the *Los Angeles Times* saw his work and wrote a positive review.

All of which meant to him that it was time to move to New York. Though Kostabi had another year to go before graduating from college, he had no real interest in acquiring a degree, because he had already decided he would never work for anyone else. "I refused to have a regular job early on. I absolutely refused. I'd commit suicide before I took a job working for another artist or for anyone. I had that attitude. I knew my work was better than the people out there who were making it."

Consumed, as he puts it, with "pure raw ambition," Kostabi arrived in New York with his book of drawings in the beginning of 1982. The East Village art scene of the eighties was just blossoming. Jean Michel Basquiat, who had six years to live, had been discovered and was being kept by a dealer in the basement of her Soho gallery; she supplied him with canvases and paint and sold his work, people joked, "before the paint had dried." Keith Haring was promoting graffiti art in shows held at downtown nightclubs. The Fun Gallery, one of the first of the East Village galleries that would proliferate within a few years, had opened and was showing work by Kenny Scharf. Robert Longo had held his first solo exhibit at the Gallery Metro, igniting the art world with his large cinematic canvases of well-dressed people clawing at each other or writhing in pain. Richard Hambleton was painting ominous black shadow figures on walls through the city.

Kostabi sublet an apartment on Central Park West, and in the next eight months visited more than sixty galleries. He brought with him his book of drawings. This, after all, was how he had done it at the Molly Barnes Gallery, and he had succeeded effortlessly. But Kostabi was only one of tens of thousands of aspiring young artists haunting New York's galleries, ambushing dealers in restaurants or outside their apartments. One winter's day, for example, an art dealer slipped on ice and fell to the sidewalk in the East Village. While she was still prone, a young artist materialized at her side and opened his box of slides.

Kostabi didn't even have slides. That was because he had no paintings. All he had were his drawings. But though Kostabi was unaware of this, the money that New York dealers stood to make on the sale of drawings was so negligible, and their overhead was so high, that they rarely showed them, and then only when the drawings were by an established artist.

In order just to arrange to see dealers, Kostabi had to resort to subterfuge. Leo Castelli's secretary gave him an appointment when he said he wished to interview the influential dealer for a book he was writing on pop art. Once in Castelli's office, he produced his drawings. Castelli praised them, as he did the work of most young artists, but he told Kostabi, as he did most young artists, that he didn't have space to exhibit his work.

Kostabi also managed to get in to see Ivan Karp of the OK Gallery. Karp was less impressed than Castelli. Kostabi's work struck him as so much obsessive fantasy. He didn't think Kostabi would make it in New York, and he wasn't interested in taking him on as a client. "But," Kostabi recalled, "he said, 'If you're going to try, you should at least be making paintings. It's not worth any gallery's while to show works on paper. Where are the canvases? Where are the paintings?'"

Kostabi was understandably chagrined by Karp's lack of sympathy, but he returned to his apartment determined to take the dealer's advice. If they wanted canvases, he would give them canvases. "I looked at my drawings. People had been telling me they would make good sculptures, so I said, 'What would it look like if it were a sculpture.' Falling back on my knowledge of academic realist painting, I made black and white paintings of my images as if they were sculptures, with strong side lighting."

It took Kostabi a year to complete six paintings. By then he had moved into a small studio in Hell's Kitchen. From the paintings he made slides to show dealers. Interest in his work picked up. People no longer dismissed him as a potential *New Yorker* cartoonist with a sheaf of charming but hopelessly unsaleable line drawings. They saw that he actually could paint, that he understood light and color. But though dealers had begun to treat him with more respect, he still found no one to display his work. The fact of the matter was that he did not have enough paintings to put together a one-man show. The most he could aspire to was a group show. But he didn't know other artists.

In the summer of 1983, after he had been in New York a year and a half, after experiencing dozens and dozens of rejections, Kostabi attended an opening at the Leo Castelli Gallery. Years later he could not remember the name of the artist. But that was no matter. Because when he stepped into the gallery, with its wood floors and white walls and track lighting, what caught his attention was not the artist's paintings but the crowds of people there for the opening. They were in tight black clothes, Italian suits over T-shirts, studded leather jackets, hand-painted sack dresses, sunglasses, bangles, and spiky hair. Holding plastic champagne glasses, they talked and smoked while cameras flashed. The paintings seemed merely the backdrop for this hot seething tangle of bodies and conversation. Kostabi remembered a parody he had once read in an art magazine about artists who spent all their time cultivating social connections rather than painting.

"It clicked. I understood instantly that, as far as making it in the New York art scene—making it fast, that is—it's ninety-nine percent social networking and one percent talent." He plunged into the tangle. "I invaded conversations. I heard some people talking about how much money they made each year. I said, 'How much was that?' The person said, 'Thirty-five-thousand dollars." I said, 'That's pretty good.' I became part of a conversation."

Not everyone responded with enthusiasm to this approach. "Some people made it clear that I was below them. They wouldn't talk to me and they still won't." Nonetheless, as a general strategy it worked. "I was introduced to five people by one person. They introduced me to another five. I went to about ten openings after that. In a matter of a few weeks I had met just about everyone in the art scene who goes to openings. I would go out every night and come home with a stack of business cards that I would feed into my address book, which soon became a Rolodex. The next thing I knew I was in a group show. A week after that I was in three group shows that opened in one night."

From the Renaissance up until the nineteenth century, European artists tended to fall into one of two categories. In countries driven by commerce with a thriving merchant class, such as Holland and England, they were independent entrepreneurs such as Rembrandt and Gainsborough. In less progressive countries, like France and Spain, they were by and large court painters like Goya, Boucher, and Fragonard. Fragonard, in fact, was one of the last of the French court painters. Many of his patrons, including Marie Antoinette, had been beheaded in the revolution. The eclipse of the French aristocracy cut into the demand for huge paintings. The big art studios, such as the one Boucher had operated, grew obsolete. After the revolution, the rise of the middle class, who lived in houses rather than palaces, created a demand for smaller paintings, though of course large canvases, such as Courbet's *The Peasants of Flagey* and Couture's *Romans of the Decadence*, continued to be produced.

The court artist lived on in the person of the society painter. The artistic center, however, had been seized by the bohemians. Inspired by the example of the revolution, which had challenged and toppled the entire social order, the bohemian artists first advanced the notion, later to be refined by the modernists, that the task of the artist was to challenge comfortable public assumptions, to produce an esthetic shock much as the *sans cullottes* had produced a political shock. This reversed the historical relationship between the artist and his audience. Instead of seeking their approval, he now attempted to provoke them. (By challenging his audience, the artist also began to challenge himself in a new way—to ask himself, "What is art?" and thus to set in motion the tightening spiral of self-absorption that marked twentieth-century art and that finally became coiled so tensely it sprang apart in the eighties.)

The bourgeoisie often rejected the new work. As these mutually antagonistic positions were staked out, artists repudiated the idea of entrepreneurial success as their counterparts before the revolution had pursued it. They became accustomed to the fact that they might have to forego public acceptance for a lengthy period.

In fact, those long years in the wilderness came to be seen as a necessary rite of passage in the career of the artist. Some artists had literally to go to the wilderness before they could be taken seriously. Gauguin, for instance, had been a stockbroker until he was thirty-five. He couldn't interest anyone in his paintings until he left France for Tahiti. Although the work he sent back from the South Seas did not create a popular stir, he did develop an ardent following among the younger generation of French artists. Gauguin was horribly bored in Tahiti, and no sooner had he become successful than he rushed back to Paris. The works he began producing there, however, failed to interest many people. So, rather reluctantly, he sailed off again to the wilderness of Tahiti, began again to paint Polynesian nudes, and was again a success. When he then contemplated yet another return to Paris his dealer advised him against it.

With Van Gogh, the notion of the artist's wilderness years took on the character of religious redemption. It was an act of self-abasement and mortification he was required to perform in order to acquire profound creative vision. Van Gogh's suffering, the artistic and personal rejection he experienced, the wandering in the south of France, the intensity of personal expression in his work, the association with laborers and prostitutes, the self-mutilation, the insanity, the early death all came together after he was discovered by the art world to form the irresistible picture of the Tormented Genius. He literally gave his life for art, people came to believe, and it was this suggestion of quasi-religious sacrifice that helped turn the modern artist into the Voice of Moral Authority in a Godless World. The canonization of Van Gogh made deprivation and rejection seem to aspiring artists to be a badge of artistic integrity.

But by the time Kostabi showed up at the opening at Castelli's gallery, the very idea of suffering for art had begun to seem hopelessly retrograde. People in the East Village had begun to speak mockingly of "the Van Gogh Syndrome" or "the Van Gogh Complex," the notion that art was produced by solitary, suffering geniuses who usually were not recognized until after their deaths. "An artist can't really create masterpieces in isolation," Kostabi said, "or very, very rarely. Millions of people think they can, and they're trying, but surely there can't be more than three or four who are actually doing anything significant."

New York, Kostabi felt, was full of untalented artists suffering from the Van Gogh Complex. They used Van Gogh's example to reassure themselves that the rejection they experienced was merely a tribute to their genius. Artists suffering from the Van Gogh Complex resented those who succeeded. And they despised those who courted success. "I didn't learn about the Van Gogh Complex," Kostabi said, "until after I moved to New York and started dealing with artists who lived in Soho and didn't make it in the seventies and who were mad at me for putting my paintings in a window on Broome Street."

After all, why should an artist suffer? What was the value of it? With a little savvy and hustle, he could have a table at Mr. Chow's, Armani suits, an American Express Gold Card with a $15,000 line of credit, a waterfront house in Bridgehampton, and lithe young assistants to fetch and carry. That was the fun part. Why forsake it just to maintain some obsolete artistic posture? Agony was not the necessary spiritual condition of the artist. Van Gogh just hadn't marketed himself properly. Networking—collecting business cards, making connections, acquiring the right dealers, befriending the right artists, participating in the right group shows—was 99 percent of the game. And so it was that the eighties saw the rise of the Rolodex Artist.

HIRED HANDS

By the summer of 1983, when Kostabi sold his first painting, the new downtown art scene was in full swing. The optimistic mood of the Reagan years was gathering momentum. A feel-good spirit had invaded the country. The Reagan Administration had invaded Grenada and overthrown the Marxist regime in power there. Female vocalists with bright voices and upbeat lyrics like Cindy Lauper ("Girls Just Want to Have Fun") and Madonna ("Material Girl") were beginning to dominate popular music. Hollywood was soaring with success parables like *Flashdance* and comedies like *Risky Business*. Wall Street was a year into the great bull market. Restaurants and nightclubs proliferated in New York. Young professionals in yellow ties were moving into the East Village.

Prices for Kostabi's first six paintings ranged from $1,500 to $2,000. It wasn't much for a year's work, but, like Wall Street, like the city, like much of the United States itself, Kostabi, too, began gathering momentum. It had taken him a year to do his first six paintings, but he had now defined both his subject matter and his style, and he began to produce works at a rate of one a day.

Having studied cartoons and magazine illustrations, Kostabi knew the value of a strong caption. It drove the message home. The same was true, he decided, with paintings. At museums, so many people head first for the little box of text beside a painting that explains it. A number of modern artists, concerned that titles were distracting or even fraudulent, had taken to calling their works *Untitled I, Untitled II,* and so on. This forced the viewer, they told each other, to confront the canvas without the comfort of literary crutches.

That didn't bother Kostabi. He began to use caption-like titles to reinforce the "commentaries" that his paintings were supposedly making on contemporary life: *Materialism; Climbing; Yuppies; To See Through Is Not to See Into; If You Can Buy Neatness, You Can Afford Sloppiness; Dress for Success; Post Yuppie Transcendence; The Interpenetration of Aesthetics and Economics; Everyone I Meet Has an Account in My Memory*

Bank; Great Art Must Have Intelligence in Front of It as Well as Behind It.

These epigrams were modeled after those by Andy Warhol. Warhol was, of course, Kostabi's hero and role model. Warhol's commercialism-as-esthetic-statement was a strategy that Kostabi had, in the language of the times, appropriated. Kostabi's painting production line resembled Warhol's factory, just as his multimedia dabbling resembled Warhol's. Kostabi admired Warhol's public style. He read all he could about and by Warhol, and studied the interviews Warhol gave. He thought Warhol's *faux naïf* answers were filled with depth. Kostabi took humor very seriously, and he thought Warhol was very funny.

Most of the other young artists Kostabi was getting to know hoarded their paintings until an established gallery deigned to represent them. But by the end of 1983 Kostabi was producing so many paintings that he was willing to show anywhere: clubs, bars, restaurants, scruffy little galleries sandwiched in between *bodegas* and record shops. Most of these places had insurance, but Kostabi would show with them even if they didn't. He had plenty of paintings, and there were plenty more coming. The risk of having one or two damaged was easily offset by the exposure he gained.

In 1984 Kostabi won the "proliferation prize" from the *East Village Eye* for participating in more shows that year— thirty-seven altogether—than any other artist. He also began to receive critical attention. "Kostabi has risen from the mountain of young ambitious artists who, like rock stars, aspire to dazzling success," Hedy O'Beil wrote in *arts* magazine in 1985. "He reflects the emptied-out, machine-like automatons that one fears will result from the technological age, with its threat of anonymity, its computers, VCRs, and word processors.... A given time calls forth an individual who embodies that time. Surely Mark Kostabi personifies *now* better than anyone else."

In 1986 he was picked up by Ronald Feldman, a prominent Soho dealer who, to begin with, sold Andy Warhol's prints. Feldman's staff had first noticed Kostabi's work in the window of the storefront on Broome Street that Kostabi had rented. (The technique that so offended the artists suffering from the Van Gogh Complex had worked.) The *New York Times* reviewed the first show Feldman arranged for Kostabi. While the critic, Vivien Raynor, complained about the "verbal bluster" of his titles and aphorisms, she quite liked the paintings and said in conclusion that Kostabi was "holding his own with glistening, sometimes morbid, sometimes witty fantasies."

Kostabi by that time was doing well enough to have moved out of Hell's Kitchen to a loft across the street from the Odeon in Tribeca. Formerly a cafeteria, the Odeon had been transformed into an expensive avant-garde restaurant. During the evenings, limousines idled outside. Inside could be found artists like Warhol and Basquiat and Longo and Schnabel. Shortly after his show at Feldman's gallery, Kostabi had lunch at the Odeon with the painter Gregor Stefan. During the lunch, Stefan, an established and successful artist, wondered if Kostabi could use any help on his paintings. At first Kostabi thought Stefan was suggesting that his paintings were artistically inadequate. But that wasn't the case. Stefan explained that since Kostabi's work was so systematically executed, he could easily have assistants blend colors and fill in the large monochromatic areas of the canvas.

Kostabi knew other artists hired assistants not just to mix paint and prime canvases but actually to apply paint to the surface. Lichtenstein didn't fill in every one of those dots himself. Warhol's assistants executed a lot of his work. Robert Longo's assistants applied paint while he stood at a distance, studying the image on the canvas and feeding them instructions, like a film director. Kostabi had even heard of an artist, named, say, Jones, telling his assistants on his way out the door, "Just make some Joneses." While Jones was shopping or at a movie screening or in bed with a girl—whatever it was—the assistants would produce paintings in the Jones manner. So it was done all the time, though everybody stayed quiet about it. Even Warhol, whom one might have expected to be the most candid about this, kept the precise nature of his assistants' involvement in his work shrouded in ambiguity.

Stefan's suggestion struck Kostabi as a wonderful idea. For the past two years he had had an assistant stretching canvas for him and serving as a porter, carrying his work from show to show. Kostabi, to be frank, found that certain passages in his work had become increasingly monotonous. He was getting bored with the mechanical application of paint required for his style. He knew exactly what it was going to look like beforehand. It made perfect sense when Stefan proposed that he hire other people to apply paint. That would free Kostabi to concentrate on the images and the ideas and the design—the creative part.

Stefan, in fact, knew a girl Kostabi might want to hire. He sent her over. The standard artist's assistant, she was young and attractive and worked in the evening at Nell's, a fashionable nightclub at the time. Unfortunately, she wanted $15 an hour, the wage most artists paid their assistants. Kostabi thought that a bit steep. There was another problem, too. "She could not do a Kostabi painting very quickly," Kostabi said. "She didn't have the craftsmanship in oil painting. She was a watercolorist. I said, 'Oh, maybe you could do watercolors for me.' So she did a few Kostabi watercolors, but she was doing them slowly, and not as well as I could have. I had to fire this assistant, even though she was nice and she was great-looking. I thought, 'There's got to be a better way to do this.' So I took out an ad in the *Village Voice*."

> ARTIST'S ASST—Skilled, academic, realist painters wanted to execute lge, wet into wet oil canvases after drawings by Mark Kostabi. Bring slides or origs to interview. Absolutely no expressionists. Bring resume if poss. $7/HR. M–F. 12–6. Please read ad carefully before calling (212) 629-4182 bet 12PM–6PM ONLY.

Kostabi wanted no expressionists because that style "was so far removed from my approach, which was much more calculating and systematic, almost mechanical, robotlike." Even so, he had, he said, more than seventy applicants, many of whom had master's degrees in fine art. Claude was one of the last. He brought with him some remarkable copies he had made of Old Masters paintings, and Kostabi hired him on the spot.

Claude began showing up daily at Kostabi's loft to paint the ideas Kostabi sketched out. As Kostabi learned to trust Claude, he allowed him to make decisions about color. The paintings they produced sold for an average of $8,000, and demand for them grew steadily. In the spring of 1987, shortly after Andy Warhol's death, Kostabi moved into the new loft on West 37th Street and took out another ad for more assistants.

By that time Kostabi had more or less stopped applying paint with his own hands. Only a philistine, he reasoned, would think there was some fundamental difference between the artist using his mind to direct his fingers to paint in a specific fashion and the artist using his mind to direct an assistant to carry out the same task.

Kostabi's paintings looked pretty much the same: endless variations on the Everyman android, many with themes and titles relating to commercialism, capitalism, materialism, and so on. Despite the repetitiousness of this work, Kostabi felt that his esthetic was evolving. As he worked it out, he was no longer making statements within each painting. The paintings, instead, were part of a grander statement about the nature of art. "Everything I do is part of my style: the media manipulation, the images—it's all mixed up in one. My painting factory is a prop in my gigantic work of conceptual art."

THE MYTH OF
ARTISTIC ORIGINALITY

Early in 1988 Kostabi was presiding over the opening of a new exhibit of his paintings at a gallery in Chicago. On such occasions it is important for the painter to play the role of Crazy Artist. Kostabi wore a black shirt with white polka dots. His hair was dyed white, and he had dabbed it with large spots of black paint, creating the reverse image of the pattern on his shirt.

One of the tactics Kostabi adopts when he is playing Crazy Artist is to insult collectors. "Anyone who buys a Kostabi painting is a total fool," Kostabi likes to say. "I think they should be doing something much more intelligent with their money."

Followed by a CBS television crew, Kostabi circulated through the crowd. He fell into conversation with a well-dressed middle-aged couple who were studying one of his works.

"How do you feel knowing that I didn't paint it?" he asked.

The question made the woman, who had short blond hair and was wearing a black mink coat, shriek with nervous laughter.

"I don't care," the man said. He was wearing a jacket and a tie. He did not look at Kostabi as he spoke. Instead, his eyes swiveled around the gallery.

Kostabi attempted to provoke them further. "I didn't even think it up," he said.

The woman shrieked louder. The man's eyes swiveled around the gallery.

Many of the aristocrats and rich merchants who commissioned art in the sixteenth, seventeenth, and eighteenth centuries seem to have had little interest in who actually applied the paint to the canvas. Whether or not the artist had painted it himself, the work came from his shop. He had overseen its execution; it carried his imprimatur. What concerned these patrons most was whether or not the work was pleasing. They would have been baffled by the endless debates and scandals in the twentieth century over which works were actually painted by the great artists themselves, which were collaborations, and which were the work of students or assistants.

The issue of attribution has become so important these days in part because of the vast sums of money art can command. What philosophically justifies those sums—and, in fact, helps prop up the entire art market—is the assumption that a great work of art is an original and therefore irreplaceable product of individual genius. While this may not be just a sentimental fallacy, it certainly has not always been the shibboleth it became in the twentieth century. A very different attitude was held by no less an artist than Rembrandt.

In the popular mind, Rembrandt is the very personification of the introspective genius. Moral authority, psychological penetration, spiritual transcendence, technical virtuosity, stylistic innovation—his paintings had all the features of artistic originality. Along with Bach and Shakespeare, he has long been considered one of the truly godlike artistic geniuses of Western civilization. But he was also a business-man. One of his biographers, Gary Schwartz, has complained that he was untrustworthy and greedy. He was certainly money hungry. He had a large house in Amsterdam, and he filled it with expensive odds and ends: suits of armor, busts, prints. (Many of these objects, however, were used as props in his work.)

In his studio Rembrandt was surrounded by students and assistants, and, according to some scholars (though it is disputed), he felt no compunction about sending out their work under his name. The five art scholars on the Rembrandt Research Project in Holland have spent twenty years exam-ining every work attributed to the artist and deciding wheth-er it is or isn't or might be his own work. And they still are not finished. Some of the most renowned Rembrandts in existence, *The Polish Rider* and *Man with the Golden Helmet*, are now considered by certain scholars to be the work of his pupils. But, as Kostabi and his defenders say (probably echoing the consensus of Rembrandt's patrons), if you like the painting, who cares who did it?

The art critic Svetlana Alpers actually blames Rembrandt for transforming works into commodities. In *Rembrandt's Enterprise: The Studio and the Market*, she described him as an "entrepreneur of the self" who "invented the work of art most characteristic of our culture—a commodity distin-guished among others by not being factory produced, but produced in limited numbers and creating its market, whose special claim to the aura of individuality and to high market value bind it to basic aspects of an entrepreneurial (capital-ist) enterprise."

During the eighties several presumptions about the na-ture of art were attacked. Primary among them, as Frank and McKenzie have pointed out, has been the idea that what gives a work of art its value—indeed, what actually defines it as a work of art—is its originality. Dissatisfaction with the cult of originality came about because of the suspicion that for those who have come of age in the era of television, life has been essentially derivative. Popular notions about everything from love to death are appropriated from TV dramas, news programs, commercials, top-forty music. Experience is mass-produced. It was impossible or irresponsible, according to the thinking of the eighties, for the artist to try to ignore this fact. Originality had become irrelevant. The thing to do was to appropriate material from popular culture, then strike an attitude toward it.

The whole "art of appropriation" may be nothing more than a rationalization for imaginative failure; the artists of this school may simply lack the talent needed to do original work. Whatever the case, artists in the eighties energetically devoted themselves to the appropriation of the work of others. The graffiti art that kicked off the decade was itself an appropriation of—what else?—graffiti. As the appropriation movement gathered momentum, artists made clever little concept statements by painting copies of paintings, taking photographs of photographs, and restaging moments in art history. Writers appropriated titles and paragraphs from great novels. Performance artists appropriated characters from television shows and news. But since appropriations have always been a feature of art—Manet's *Olympus* is an appropriation of Titian's *Venus of Urbino*, Dali added a moustache to the Mona Lisa—none of this was terribly inventive.

Also, none of these supposedly sophisticated appropriations in fact challenged the notion of originality at the core of art. They all presumed that the idea that motivated the artist to rework the earlier artist was somehow original. His creative contribution was to make a new statement, to cast in a new light an existing work. What makes Kostabi so infuriating to so many people is that he has shamelessly, brazenly renounced any claim in his paintings to personal originality.

In 1987 Kostabi ran a second ad in the Help Wanted section of the *Village Voice*.

> ARTIST'S ASST—Inventive artists wanted to provide IDEAS for Mark Kostabi paintings. Submit sketchbooks, notebooks, or miscellaneous artifacts displaying ingenuity. Have resume avail if poss. $7/HR. 12–6 M–F. Call (212) 629-4182 bet 12PM–6PM M–F ONLY

This naturally outraged everyone, as it was in part intended to do. People who saw the ads telephoned Kostabi just to insult him. "Someone called and said, 'What a stupid idea,' and hung up," Kostabi recalled. "Then someone called and said, 'What's the matter, don't you have any ideas of your own?' and then he hung up." But others found the idea clever. "Some people said, 'This is the ultimate job; this is my dream job come true.' Some people thought it was an interesting semiotics project, whatever that means. I got some very sophisticated people and I hired two of them."

And on a certain level it made perfect sense. Some people had good ideas for paintings but lacked the talent to execute them. Others could paint well but had no ideas. Why not bring them together?

Kostabi's New York art dealer, Ronald Feldman, was initially a little leery about a public acknowledgment that any part of Kostabi's work was undertaken by assistants. The members of his staff who first found out about it were shocked and alarmed. Not with the fact that Kostabi had assistants producing ideas and executing work (everyone in the art world knew that went on), but with the fact that Kostabi was admitting it, even emphasizing it.

After all, if Kostabi came out of the closet, he might scare off the collectors. It was the notion of creative originality that provided works of art with value. That was what drove the art market. Kostabi was challenging it. He was saying that a work of art was in effect nothing more than the sum of the paint, canvas, wood, and craftsmanship used to produce it. This could undercut or even destroy the whole immensely lucrative assumption that the artist, through the alchemy of his talent, converted those cheap materials into a very valuable commodity. What would happen if that alchemy lost its mystique? What if, as Kostabi was beginning to do, other artists admitted that there was no alchemy at all, that they were not—to reach back to the original meaning of the word *genius*—vessels inhabited by a divine spirit? The public might then decide that art was one giant fraud perpetrated by a group of smirking cynics. This was dangerous. So Feldman asked Kostabi to play along. He suggested Kostabi put some notation on those paintings he had done himself to distinguish them from those his assistants had executed. This would reassure the collectors who cared that they were getting the real goods. Kostabi refused.

Some of the more conventional collectors whined about it. But others shrugged it off as a logical extension of the mass market culture. And much to Feldman's surprise, not to mention his relief, it didn't dampen the demand for Kostabis one bit. In fact, it turned out to be a great publicity stunt. It was perfectly designed to fit into the classic media formula, even more widespread in the eighties, of exploiting the sensationalism of some outrage while posturing against it, of perpetuating hype while claiming to scrutinize and criticize it, as in the *Business Week* cover story on Donald Trump that asked, "What's Behind the Hype?" and the

Newsweek cover story on the Warhol auction that announced "Art for Money's Sake."

Kostabi likes to say he is providing entertainment through controversy. His concept, which others but not himself refer to as performance art, worked so well that now Feldman gets in on the joke as well. "He recognizes talent in others," Feldman will tell the interviewer who makes the trip down to his Soho gallery. "He has advertised, then hired, an incredibly talented staff. They're much more talented than he is."

But while the idea for the ideas person is a joke on one level, it is not merely a joke. Kostabi takes the hiring of assistants and his economy-of-scale production of art very seriously. "I wanted it to be a real business," he explained. "I didn't want the assistants to be just props. These are real people who have real talent who can execute the work. It's not like I'm some rich kid who decided he wanted to play a fun game with the media and hired all these people to make these paintings that no one wants. People want these paintings. There is a real demand for them."

THE NEW VAN GOGH

"I don't think of myself as commercial," Kostabi said. "It's obvious the work sells. Red sells. It's easy to make something that sells. But I think I'm beyond that. That's not the motive behind every painting. Sometimes I will tell the press: 'What makes a good painting? Whether it sells or not.' 'When is a painting finished? When the collector's check clears.' But those are just very simple-minded, provocative statements."

The controversy around Kostabi was such that by August of 1987 the *Village Voice* had anointed him the "next superstar hype artist." It also, of course, earned him numerous enemies. Many of the other successful artists of the eighties—Schnabel, Longo, Haring, to name a few—disliked Kostabi intensely. Since many artists dislike each other, that may mean little. Still, so much about Kostabi annoyed people. More than his pose and his colored hair (though those were annoying enough to some), it was the bottomless cynicism he seemed to represent, the willingness to exploit.

Diana was the first idea person Kostabi hired. A tall, pretty woman with long brown hair, she had previously worked as a model, which was one of the reasons Kostabi hired her. He told her that giving interviews would be part of her job. She would gamely tell reporters things like "I'm concerned with the art of business, and Mark's concerned with the business of art." But she quit after six months. She felt used. She had given Kostabi *her* ideas. And while he was earning money on them, she could scarcely pay her rent. One day she learned that a painting made from one of her ideas was actually hanging in the Guggenheim. She had received no credit for it. The whole thing was sick, she decided, and so was Kostabi. He was full of hatred. He hated other artists for their talent and integrity. He hated himself for his lack of talent and his dependence on the talent of others. This self-hatred was revealed in his compulsive need to humiliate himself publicly.

One day I asked Kostabi how he saw himself. Did he think of his paintings as comic? Did he see his whole conceptual art extravaganza—the assembly line production of paintings, the outrageous pronouncements, the insulting of collectors—as a comic statement about the current art world?

"The idea is not to have a private joke," Kostabi said. "At this stage I think no one will believe me, but it's actually deep and it has to do with sadness. People usually laugh when they're scared or frightened. They don't know what else to do. It's a very deep thing."

I said that what seemed to upset people most was the way he belittled cherished romantic notions like artistic integrity and spiritual torment.

"Don't you think," Kostabi said, "I'm exhibiting myself somewhat as a tormented soul by saying to the public, 'Only a fool would buy a Kostabi,' and 'You're a total idiot if you buy one of my paintings.' That's kind of weird and tormented. Why would someone want to say something like that?"

He went on to say that such behavior revealed as much spiritual torment as Van Gogh had displayed. In its own way it was the same sort of agonized gesture Van Gogh had made by cutting off his ear. Despair was brought on, however, not by rejection but by success. Like Sandro Chia, Kostabi was a prisoner of success. "It's anti–Van Gogh," he said, "but at the same time I'm becoming a new kind of Van Gogh."

4

NEW YORK'S
PARTY PALACE AND THE
STATUS RITUALS OF
THE NOUVEAUX RICHES

THE NOUVEAUX RICHES TRIUMPHANT

The limousine crush in front of the Metropolitan Museum began to form around eight o'clock on the night of the party for Sid Bass and his bride-to-be, Mercedes Kellogg. One could tell what kind of a crowd it would be by the preponderance of Mercedes 450SLs in the line. The 450SL had emerged by the late eighties as the car of choice for the nouveaux riches. Only a few years ago a stretch limousine had been considered de rigueur, but it had subsequently come to be regarded by the more discerning as a vulgar and dangerous rattletrap. A stretch also seemed so *rented*, particularly if driven by a chauffeur in a black suit and cap. It had become almost imperative to have a Mercedes 450SL or at least a Jaguar XJ6 and to have behind the wheel a casually dressed young man—an aspiring playwright or something—whom one referred to not as "the chauffeur" but as "my driver."

So, the backup of Mercedeses and Jaguars in front of the museum was mildly annoying, but because the entrance to the Met was so grand, the wait was never long, and anyway, the impatience of the guests was tempered by the fact that all would be allowed their own unhurried entrance, their own opportunity to sweep with casual hauteur and perhaps a patronizing smile past the flashing strobes of the society photographers.

As they waited their turn, the guests peered out at the museum's columns, majestic in the silver floodlight, at the fountains tumbling whitely, and at the sail-like banners luffing and snapping in the icy wind. Although tens of thousands of tourists and students tramped through it during the day, the museum really belonged to *them*, the princes and princesses of the city's irresistible and fluid aristocracy. It was their own Palace in the Park.

After all, their names were on the wings and the galleries and on the plaques lining the walls of the main staircase. They sat on the board and the Chairman's Council and the visiting committees. They, not the director Philippe de Montebello, decided on the important acquisitions, and quite often—especially if the influential trustee Jayne Wrightsman, in that deliciously direct way of hers, let them know how essential it was—they would write that extra $30,000 check for some obscure but actually quite beautiful lapis statuette that Philippe had had his eye on but that the acquisitions budget couldn't quite be stretched to include.

It was not, however—and this point could scarcely be overemphasized—*merely* the money they gave. Their paintings and their furniture adorned the galleries. And the galleries even looked like their homes. Shrewd maneuvers by the trustees of Robert Lehman's foundation ensured that the rooms housing the Lehman Collection were an actual replication of the rooms from his father's townhouse. And, were it necessary to point out an even more intimate association, the very clothes off their backs hung in the Costume Institute, which in the right company could be referred to—with a wry smile—as one's walk-in closet. They celebrated their birthdays and their weddings and their triumphs here. The museum was theirs.

For the Bass party, which cost around $500,000, the Charles Englehard Court was ablaze with pink and gold lights. Philip Baloun, the florist of the hour, had installed eight Christmas trees and surrounded them with dozens of pots of white narcissus. After drinks in the adjacent Medieval Hall, Mercedes led the guests, who ranged from Nancy and Henry Kissinger to Jane and Michael Eisner, into the court, where they sat down for a dinner of lobster followed by pheasant bouillon followed by quail followed by poached pears with spun sugar.

When the meal was over, the toasts began. It was a long evening, with a fair amount of drinking, and the Texans who had flown up for Sid and Mercedes' wedding the next day at the Plaza Hotel began accompanying each toast with boot-stomping, hog-calling Texas yells. *Yahoo! Yahoo!* Some New Yorkers joined in. And why not? There was much to celebrate. Sid Bass had taken over Bass Brothers Enterprises from his father in 1969, at the age of twenty-seven, and had built it into a $4-billion conglomerate with holdings in gas, oil, and real estate. In the early eighties, he also began to use it as a vehicle to launch hostile takeovers. Sid Bass and his brothers, who were all based in Fort Worth, had become known as corporate raiders and greenmailers.

Sid's reputation improved, however, when he became involved in the takeover battle for Walt Disney Productions in 1984. Although he never actually tried to acquire the company himself, he did become its largest shareholder. His support of Michael Eisner was one key reason the Disney board named Eisner as its chairman and chief executive. Within two years the price of Disney's stock had appreciated so dramatically under Eisner's guidance that the Basses enjoyed a profit of $850 million on their investment.

After that the Bass brothers went their separate ways. Sid's own interests shifted from finance to culture and society, and he and his wife, Anne, moved their base from Fort Worth to New York. That same year, Sid met Mercedes, then the wife of Ambassador Francis Kellogg, at a ball given by the Duke of Marlborough at his country estate, Blenheim. Mercedes Kellogg was a rail-thin woman of Iranian extraction. She had dark hair, a broad face, and exotic prominent eyebrows. She was extremely interesting and vivacious, and though she and Sid Bass were both in their forties, an infatuation developed that neither could resist. Both left their spouses and moved together into a suite at the Carlyle. Anne Bass was of course chagrined but, by receiving almost $200 million in the divorce settlement, she became one of the richest women in the country.

Now, two years later, Sid and Mercedes were about to be married. After the other toasts, Sid stood up and surveyed the 166 guests at the seventeen tables. "I have a wonderful woman and we're very much in love," he told the room. "I've never done this into a microphone before, but there's only one way to say it. Yahoo!"

Other guests took it up and the walls of the museum rang with their jubilation. *Yahoo! Yahoo! Yahoo!* Oh, what a glorious time it was to be alive and rich in New York!

THE PARTY PALACE

By 1986, people at all levels of society dedicated themselves not only to wealth creation but also to the delineation of social distinctions that testified to their wealth. BMWs and Mercedeses became as popular with inner-city crack dealers as they were with investment bankers. Exclusivity and elitism flourished among the younger as well as the older. Debutante parties once again became fashionable. At the Silver and Gold Ball in New York, fourteen-year-old girls arrived in Oscar de la Renta dresses. "They looked adorable," said one of their chaperones. Only a few years earlier private clubs had faced dwindling membership rolls that had threatened their continued operation, forcing some to close and others, such as the Yale Club and the Dartmouth Club in New York, to merge. But by the mid-eighties these clubs had waiting lists years long.

The money culture was becoming institutionalized, and four events that occurred in 1986 illustrate just how advanced that process was. The first was the opening that March of Polo/Ralph Lauren. The store, which was to be Lauren's flagship retail outlet, was located in the restored Rhinelander mansion, a five-story neo-French Renaissance house on Madison Avenue in New York. Decorated to resemble an English country house, the store had polished mahogany walls, oil paintings, worn oriental carpets, cracked leather wing chairs, and table surfaces cluttered with picture frames, stopwatches, little leather jewelry boxes, and other casual appurtenances of the country gentleman. The fact that this atmosphere of gentility and tradition had been assembled almost overnight offended no one. The store was a sort of elaborate stage set on which the professional classes could act out the seemingly bottomless well of aristocratic aspirations that Lauren, who was raised in the Bronx and whose original name was Ralph Schwartz, had tapped with success.

Aristocratic aspirations also defined the Manhattan night club Nell's. Like Ralph Lauren's store, Nell's was decorated in the *faux*-Edwardian manner, with velvet sofas, embroidered cushions, and club chairs. Its opening in the fall of 1986—the second of the events that revealed the institutionalization of the money culture—raised the exclusivity of the eighties to new heights. Although exclusivity had been a feature of New York nightlife since the late seventies, when Steve Rubell and Ian Schrager opened Studio 54, a populist ethic of sorts had operated, since anyone willing to dress up wildly enough to impress the doorkeeper could count on being admitted. But at Nell's admission was largely limited to those who, in the eyes of the management, had some form of social cachet. In one possibly apocryphal story, a young female doorkeeper turned away the actress Cher— her cachet was simply insufficient.

Nell's in other words, was literally a club, and like all clubs, it was defined by the self-congratulatory smugness of its members. That gloating tone often translated into disdain for those without the good fortune to be admitted into the circle of the elect. And as the passion for exclusivity grew, it became increasingly ominous. In 1988 a new club called MK opened in Manhattan. Its owners, who tried to make it even more exclusive than Nell's, established the club's atmosphere with a pair of huge stuffed Doberman pinschers that greeted those lucky enough to be admitted. Later that year, in what seemed just another extension of this ethic, Rubell and Schrager opened a hotel called the Royalton and were soon battling charges, which they denied, that they had instructed the staff to turn away blacks and orthodox Jews.

The third event indicating the institutionalization of the money culture was the New Four Hundred Ball, which was held in the spring of 1986. In 1876, more than a century before, Mrs. William B. Astor had held a Centennial ball to mark the first hundred years of the nation's existence. Ward McAllister, the social arbiter of the day, had limited the number of people invited to the party to four hundred, supposedly the maximum that could fit into the Astor ballroom. To be among the Four Hundred was to be acknowledged as a member of New York's ruling social elite.

In a similar attempt to establish social distinctions 110 years later, a young Wall Street lawyer named George Carroll Whipple III and a friend of his named Marc de Gontaut Biron organized the New Four Hundred Ball in the Seventh Regiment Armory on Park Avenue. Whipple told journalist Patricia Morrisroe that the party was "an amusing concept." Biron explained, rather more pretentiously, that he was trying to create a "new society."

But while Whipple and Biron seemed to imagine themselves as latter-day Ward McAllisters, the power to confer social authentication in the eighties rested less with individuals—even individuals of much greater consequence than Whipple and Biron—and more with cultural and philanthropic institutions. It was the interaction of these institutions with the nouveaux riches that produced the status rituals peculiar to the eighties. Each was uniquely qualified to satisfy the needs of the other.

Thus the fourth, and most significant, event announcing the triumph of the money culture in 1986 was the official inauguration of the Metropolitan Museum's party policy—a policy designed, it would seem, to offer the nouveaux riches previously unparalleled opportunities for ostentatious displays of wealth.

In earlier years, if someone wanted to hold a party at the museum, a written request had to be made to the board. The event had to be related to art, and a donation to the museum in the range of $5,000 was required. As the eighties progressed, the museum received an ever increasing number of requests to hold parties in its galleries and courts. As a result, its officials decided that, for a fee of $25,000 (later raised to $30,000), anyone who wanted to could hold a party at the museum for just about any purpose. The event need not be related to art. (Subsequently, one of the halls was even rented out to launch a new perfume named after the actress Catherine Deneuve.)

Officially, the museum did not concede it had gone into the catering business. "We don't lend out the hall," explained John Ross, the museum's public relations director. Instead, a company or an individual became a "sponsor," and that expression of commitment to the arts entitled one to hold a party there.

Which is not to say that the museum was uncomfortable or even circumspect about exploiting its mystique. "Many public relations opportunities are available through sponsorship of outstanding special exhibitions at the Metropolitan Museum," it boldly declared in a letter sent to corporations in January of 1986. "Learn how you can provide creative and cost-effective answers to your marketing objectives by identifying your corporate names with Vincent Van Gogh... Canaletto...Remington, Fragonard, Rembrandt or Goya...."

Museum officials also printed a colorful brochure promoting use of the institution's facilities for parties. "Entertain in its magnificent spaces," stated the brochure, which contained pictures of the Great Hall bedecked with flowers and of the Blumenthal Patio, the Engelhard Court of the American Wing, and the Temple of Dendur furnished with big round linen-draped tables, china, glassware, and more explosively colorful floral arrangements. Entertain in its magnificent spaces! Rent a palace! Party! Party! Party!

THE NEW SOCIAL ORDER

The nouveaux riches accepted the museum's invitation, and within two short years, they had converted it into a sort of arena for their own status rituals, a circus for the enactment of social ambition. Parties were held there evening after evening after evening. During the fall of 1988, in the months preceding the Bass-Kellogg affair, Marvin Traub, the head of Bloomingdale's, threw a party at the museum for Robert Campeau, who had recently acquired the department store in a hostile takeover battle for its parent company. John Gutfreund, the head of Salomon Brothers, and his wife Susan, held a cocktail reception. Henry Kravis, who would negotiate the $25 billion leveraged buyout of RJR-Nabisco that same fall, and his wife, the clothes designer Carolyne Roehm, had a sit-down dinner for 140 people. Social columnist Billy Norwich found himself writing so often about the shindigs and hoo-has at the museum that he took to referring to it as Club Met.

In fact, so intense was the desire to hold parties at the museum, to be a part of the circus of ambition, that it often had what the museum staff called "doubleheaders." On those occasions as many as five hundred people might attend a reception in the Temple of Dendur while another five hundred viewed an exhibit. At the appointed time, the members of the museum's "special events" department switched the two groups the way ranch hands move separate herds of cattle around a feed lot. Dinners were even more complicated. Talk about logistical headaches! The architects who designed the museum had not anticipated its future in the catering business and had failed to incorporate kitchens into the various wings. So, every time there was a party, temporary kitchens had to be set up in the halls between galleries. The aromas of poached salmon and roast rabbit wafted down the echoing halls, past the ancient treasures.

Sometimes the parties seemed to take over the entire museum. When Iris and B. Gerald Cantor held an affair there in the fall of 1988, the guests started off at the special Degas exhibit, where actors and actresses dressed to resemble figures from the artist's work strolled through the galleries striking the poses in the paintings. The guests then proceeded to the Temple of Dendur. Tables were laden with saddles of beef. Waiters served Puligny Montrachet while an orchestra played. Quick-sketch artists drew portraits of the guests, and a hired video film crew circulated—light packs and all—around the overcrowded tables. Meanwhile, in the American Wing, a country-western band was holding forth for those in a more raucous mood. For the finale, everyone gathered in the Great Hall, where yet more tables were heaped with dessert confections of spun sugar, and only then, sated and dazed, did the guests depart.

The capitalist economy of the United States has always produced a steady supply of nouveaux riches. By and large, they have been assimilated with little more than a brief twitch of revulsion into the bosom of the establishment. But three times in the past 125 years a confluence of economic conditions has created arrivistes in such great numbers and with such immense wealth that they formed a critical mass and created a whole new social order with its own new rules of acceptable behavior.

This happened after the Civil War, when the westward expansion and the development of national rail lines provided unheard of opportunities for speculation, innovative financing, and corporate restructuring. The result was the Gilded Age, or as Vernon Parrington called it, "the great barbecue." "Everywhere," he wrote of that period in *Main Currents in American Thought*, "was a welling up of primitive pagan desires after long repressions—to grow rich, to grasp power, to be strong and masterful and lay the world at its feet.... A world of triumphant and unabashed vulgarity without its like in our history, it was not aware of its plight, but accounted its manner genteel and boasted of ways that were a parody on sober good sense."

A new social order was created a second time, though to a lesser extent and in a less permanent fashion, after World

War I, when the booming automobile and radio industries and the development of assembly-line production techniques created the machine age and the surge in corporate underwriting that was responsible for the great bull market of the roaring twenties.*

It happened a third time in the eighties, when undervalued stocks and the growing wave of takeovers again provided extraordinary opportunities for speculation and innovative financing, and led to the creation of the current money culture. These watershed eras, particularly the post-Civil War years and the 1980s, came at a time of delirious economic expansion, when corporate restructuring visibly affected the public welfare. That, together with the creation of radical and controversial new ways to raise capital, made it possible to amass large fortunes at a pace so rapid it was shocking, and thrust finance to the front of the national agenda and Wall Street to the center of public attention.

For the rich and the ambitious during the Gilded Age, New York—the national center of finance and speculation— was the only place to live. In his 1908 memoir, *Fifty Years in Wall Street*, the financier and socialite Henry Clews wrote that the nineteenth-century nouveaux riches were drawn from across the country to New York because of the city's "imperial wealth, its Parisian, indeed almost sybaritic luxury and social splendor.... Soon nothing remains for the wives of the Western millionaires but to purchase a brownstone mansion, and swing into the tide of fashion with receptions, balls and kettledrums, elegant equipages with coachmen in bright-buttoned livery, footmen in top-boots, maid-servants and man-servants, including a butler...."

---

*As noted in chapter 1, the nouveau riche financiers of the twenties did not have as profound an impact on their times as did their counterparts in the Gilded Age and the eighties. This was true in part because no fundamental reordering of the nation's corporate structure took place in the twenties, as it did in the Gilded Age and the eighties. The nouveau riche financiers of the sixties, which also enjoyed a strong bull market, had virtually no impact on society and culture.

New York also served as the sacred city for the money culture of the eighties. The Basses of Texas and the Gettys of California and hundreds of other lesser luminaries from the West made the pilgrimage to Manhattan, bought wood-paneled co-operative apartments on Fifth Avenue and Park Avenue, joined charities, retained decorators and art dealers, cultivated social columnists, hired handsome young men to drive them around town in gleaming automobiles with tinted windows, and like their forebears in the Gilded Age, acquired what Clews so aptly called the "adjuncts of fashionable life in a great metropolis."

Another striking parallel between the Gilded Age and the eighties is that the nouveaux riches of both ages had so much money that it became necessary to recalculate completely the sum that qualified individuals as wealthy. "A fortune of a million was worth nothing now," Ward McAllister wrote in 1890, though he might just as well be describing the current era. "One needed a fortune of ten, fifty, one hundred million to be counted rich."

This vast wealth gave the nouveaux riches so much power and so much momentum that it enabled them to create a new social order. They more or less displaced the older establishment, which if it didn't disappear altogether at least had to jump quickly to avoid being trampled in the stampede.

"What do you do with one hundred million dollars?" one of New York's socially connected art connoisseurs asked over lunch in the fall of 1988. "How do you begin to spend it, even part of it?"

The problem is a complicated one, particularly in New York. It is universally accepted that the object of spending by the wealthy has always been, in the words of Thorstein Veblen, conspicuous consumption. Money is spent only ostensibly to acquire goods; the real purpose of spending is to display an ability to spend. "In order to gain and to hold the esteem of men it is not sufficient merely to possess wealth or power," Veblen wrote in 1899 in his classic study, *The Theory of the Leisure Class.* "The wealth or power must be put in evidence, for esteem is awarded only on evidence." Veblen traced this urge back to the primitive hunter-warriors, whose trophies of scalps and captured shields and whose "conspicuous leisure" while slaves labored on their behalf all testified to "successful predatory aggressions or warlike exploits." The modern equivalent of the hunter-warrior provides evidence of the wealth acquired during his predatory exploits by demonstrating an "ability to sustain large pecuniary damage without impairing his superior opulence."

Traditionally, that ability has been demonstrated through the creation of a great house (lavishly furnished) requiring a huge staff (in archaic costumes) and with all sorts of impractical but obviously exorbitant features (such as curving cobblestone driveways). And so it was in New York. Until the construction of Central Park, which began in 1859, New York's older society had lived around Washington Square in Greenwich Village, while parvenus like J. P. Morgan settled twenty blocks north in Murray Hill. But as the park began to take shape, the nouveaux riches bought up the underdeveloped land near it to build houses that gave *real* testament to their money.

The Vanderbilts were among the first. William Henry Vanderbilt's house at Fifth Avenue and 51st Street occupied an entire block. Built in the Greek Renaissance style, it took two years to complete and was furnished with, among other items, Italian tapestries, Japanese lanterns, medieval armor, and a carved walnut wainscoting taken from a French chateau. Meanwhile, his relation, William Kissam Vanderbilt, built his own opulent house across the street. To celebrate its completion, he and his wife planned a costume ball that would, the papers of the day announced, "surpass in splendour, in beauty...in luxurious and lavish expense any scenes before witnessed in the New World."

The ball, held in 1883, proved to be one of those pivotal events that announced the arrival of a new social order. At the time, "old New York" considered the Vanderbilts hopelessly arriviste, even though they had been a force in the city for some thirty years. Mrs. William Astor, the social queen of the day who had held her Four Hundred Ball only seven years earlier, had never once called on Mrs. W. K. Vanderbilt. But she and her circle were so alarmed at not being invited to the Vanderbilt ball that Mrs. Astor "unbent her stateliness," in one account of the event, and paid Mrs. Vanderbilt a visit. And there it was—social surrender, the passing of the scepter, an act of obeisance announcing that the nouveaux riches had achieved critical mass, displacing the older establishment.

By the late 1800s, hordes of other parvenu merchants, speculators, and corporate monopolists—"nature's noblemen," as Henry Clews called them—had followed the Vanderbilts north, and they turned Fifth Avenue from 42nd Street to 79th Street into a dazzling boulevard of palaces. Known as the Billionaires' District and as Two Miles of Millionaires, it consisted of block after block of mansions in Gothic, Italian Renaissance, German Renaissance, Georgian, Oriental, Baroque, and French Chateau styles—all amply demonstrating their owners' ability to "sustain pecuniary damage."

Such opportunities for extravagant displays of wealth remain today in most American cities. Drive through Beverly Hills and you will see any number of mansions being torn down so a new arrival can make his own statement of opulence. In late 1988 the television producers Aaron and Candy Spelling were in the middle of building a gigantic $45-million house in Holmby Hills that was truly on the scale of the seventeenth-century palaces built by the European nobility. It was 315 feet wide (Buckingham Palace, by comparison, is 464 feet wide). Built in the French Regency style, it was four stories tall and had 123 rooms, including an indoor bowling alley, a fifty-seat cinema, a doll museum, a flower-arranging room, a dressing room that occupied an entire wing and contained a catwalk to reach all the shelves, and a windowless "anti-terrorist room" with steel walls and its own oxygen supply into which the Spellings could retreat in the event of an attack. The house was so large that neighbors compared it to a Hyatt hotel.

But the crushing realities of New York real estate denied the city's parvenus similar possibilities for conspicuous consumption. Except for a handful of people like pet food magnate Leonard Stern, who lived in one of the few remaining mansions on Fifth Avenue (a mere townhouse, nothing the Vanderbilts would have considered a mansion), the wealth of New York's newly wealthy was locked away in co-op apartments. These were huge, naturally. (Gayfryd and Saul Steinberg lived in a thirty-four-room triplex filled with paintings by artists from Titian to Renoir to Bacon.) But they were invisible.

True, gilt-edged shelter magazines like *Town & Country*, *HG*, and *Architectural Digest* provided some outlet, but it was frustratingly narrow in scope. True, there were rural estates, but these were too remote to do the job. Hidden away in the dunes of the Hamptons or the hills of Connecticut and the Hudson Valley, they were just not conspicuous enough. A genuine statement of wealth and power needed to be made within the urban milieu. And in New York in the late eighties, the sole remaining venue for conspicuous consumption on a pharaonic scale was the Metropolitan Museum.

LEGITIMIZING WEALTH

The nation's prestigious cultural institutions are legion. They range from the Los Angeles County Museum of Art to the Art Institute of Chicago and the Smithsonian Institution in Washington, D.C. But because New York has been the center of the money culture, its philanthropies and cultural institutions afford the greatest prestige. They include the New York Public Library, the Metropolitan Opera, the American Ballet Theatre, the New York Zoological Society, and the Museum of Modern Art. Towering over all of these august institutions, however, is the Metropolitan Museum of Art. No other club, church, philanthropy, or fraternal order in the United States enjoys quite the same prominence or confers quite the same radiant status.

To be listed in the back of the annual report as a fellow or a member of one of the visiting committees became as important in the eighties as a mention in the Social Register. To be invited—one naturally could not apply—to join the Chairman's Council or the actual board was to have one's name linked with the names Astor, Dillon, Heinz, and Reed. It was to be counted among the one hundred or so most select families in New York, to have arrived finally at the true pinnacle in a city where, no matter how high one climbed, there always seemed to be yet another pitch to ascend, yet another slope curving upward and out of sight.

Several factors accounted for the museum's peculiar social authority. There were, of course, the great works, the aura of accumulated culture, the distinguished tradition of philanthropy to which it had given rise, and so forth. There was also the Met's sheer size—it has a hoard of more than 2 million art objects, only a fraction of which are ever on display. And there was its economic power. The museum was New York's biggest tourist attraction, drawing more visitors than the Statue of Liberty, more fans than any sporting event. Museum officials liked to boast that visitors to the 1986 exhibit "Van Gogh in Saint Rémy and Auvers" spent $223 million while they were in town.

For the rich the museum also had that prized New York commodity—location. If one lived on Fifth Avenue, the Met was so extremely convenient. Jacqueline Onassis lived just across the street from the museum. Douglas Dillon, the former investment banker and Secretary of the Treasury who had been the museum's chairman for years, was in the neighborhood. Arthur "Punch" Sulzberger, the publisher of the *New York Times* who also became chairman of the Met in 1986, had lived within a stone's throw of the building all his life and liked to explain that he didn't personally collect art because, as he told me, "the greatest art collection in the city is right across the street."

Art museums generally are more prestigious than cultural institutions like libraries, because books—most books, anyway—have some practical purpose, which means that as a whole they lack the wastefulness necessary for a pure act of conspicuous consumption. Also, art is more expensive than books, and thus provides a greater opportunity to sustain pecuniary damage. Between 1983 and 1989 the Met took in $10 million from Laurence Tisch, $10 million from Milton Petrie, and $10 million from Henry Kravis, to mention only three of the largest bequests. The ability to absorb such huge amounts of money helps explain why art museums are more prestigious than ballet or opera companies. Furthermore, a gift to produce a ballet or opera disappears as soon as the curtain comes down. A gift to the Met for an acquisition or even a gallery—hardly anyone gives to the operating budget—provides evidence of the donor's power and wealth for a long, long time.

An additional reason for the Metropolitan Museum's surpassing prestige can be found in the special relationship that has always existed between art and newly minted wealth. This can be traced back to the Renaissance, the time in European history at which wealth from commerce (new wealth) began to become as significant as wealth from land holdings (old wealth).

So often fortunes are amassed at the expense of someone else. Thus, a certain taint attaches to them, and those who have accumulated them often seek expiation in one fashion or another. The Roman Catholic Church took advantage of this in the late Middle Ages by selling papal indulgences to raise money to build churches and to decorate them with paintings, statues, tapestries, and relics. The logic of this enterprise seemed to suggest that donating money for art and architecture made it somewhat easier to enter heaven.

In 1515 Pope Leo X, who was the son of Lorenzo de Medici and thus no stranger to finance and power, began to sell papal indulgences to finance the rebuilding of St. Peter's and also to pay off secretly the debts of a young cardinal. (Catholics refer to such transactions as "abuses" of the practice of granting indulgences, or temporary remissions for sins.) In exchange for 50 percent of the money to be collected, the investment banker Jacob Fugger provided the Pope with a sort of "bridge loan." Martin Luther became so outraged by the cynicism of this behavior that he drew up his ninety-five theses and tacked them to the door of the All Saints church in Wittenberg, touching off the Reformation. The *Catholic Encyclopedia* dryly notes that Pope Leo X was "perhaps the last of the Renaissance popes who looked upon the papacy as primarily a temporal monarchy."

Nonetheless, the notion that art purified or at least legitimized wealth persisted. It was responsible for the flourishing of American museums during the Gilded Age. "Probably no age and no city has ever seen such gigantic fortunes accumulated out of nothing as have been piled up within the last five years," Joseph Choate, one of the Metropolitan's trustees, said in a speech marking the opening of the museum's Central Park building in 1880. "Think of it, ye millionaires of many markets—what glory may be yours, if only you listen to our advice, to convert pork into porcelain, grain and produce into priceless pottery, the rude ores of commerce into sculptured marble, and railroad shares and mining stocks—things which perish without the using, and which in the next financial panic shall surely shrivel like parched scrolls—into the glorified canvas of the world's masters, that shall adorn these walls for centuries. The rage of Wall Street is to hunt the philosopher's stone, to convert all baser things into gold, which is but dross; but ours is the higher ambition to convert your useless gold into things of living beauty that shall be a joy to a whole people for a thousand years."

The same impulse expressed itself in the eighties. Henry Kravis sat on the board of, among other charitable organizations, the New York City Ballet, and had donated large sums to, among other deserving institutions, Mt. Sinai Hospital. But after giving his $10 million to the Met for the Kravis Wing, he said, "I've never been so excited about making a gift to any institution."

VICARIOUS CONSUMPTION

In the middle decades of the twentieth century, the board of the Met was controlled by a clique of Wasp aristocrats. Among them were the surviving remnant of New York's nineteenth-century nouveaux riches. They had names like Rockefeller, Whitehouse, Redmond, Bingham, Dilworth, and Brown. They were, in a word, patrician.

That meant they were conservative. This attitude shaped their artistic tastes: Henry Luce, the founder of *Time* magazine who was a trustee, once rejected a now celebrated

Matisse, saying it was the ugliest thing he had ever seen. It also shaped their behavior generally: Wealth, they tried to convince those who lacked it, imposed a serious, even grave responsibility. Thus, to be seen openly enjoying one's money was considered unseemly. The personification of this somber restraint among New York women was Blanchette Rockefeller, daughter-in-law of the money-burdened John D. Rockefeller, Jr. When she was out at night, she invariably wore a severe black or gray dress and a single strand of pearls. At the time, understatement was considered the purest expression of taste, breeding, and virtue.

By the early seventies the patrician Wasps had begun to die off. Their heirs showed little interest in the sort of grand establishment institution the Met represented. They had become instead preoccupied with less orthodox ventures. Abby Rockefeller, most notably, devoted a great deal of time and money to promoting a toilet that would recycle human waste. Consequently, museum officials like Ashton Hawkins, the in-house counsel and de facto social facilitator, and Thomas Hoving, who was then the director, began to cast around for new sources of patronage. During this period Hawkins told a friend over dinner that the old days had come to an end. The museum needed "new blood." "This is what's happening," the friend recalled Hawkins saying. "We've got to get new money."

But this was nothing new. As Joseph Choate's speech indicated, one of the primary functions of the American museum has been to seek out the nouveaux riches and, in exchange for handsome donations, bestow its approval on them and their fortunes. When J. P. Morgan was named president of the Met's board in 1903, he was widely regarded as the very epitome of the grasping nouveau riche financier.

Hoving's most widely remembered contribution to the Met was the development of the blockbuster exhibit. But just as significant—or just as insidious, depending on one's point of view—were two other steps he took. First, in 1972 he hired Diana Vreeland, the former editor-in-chief of *Vogue*, as a consultant to the Costume Institute. The Institute had been started in 1936 by a group of rich women who thought it was a shame to throw away their expensive gowns after wearing them only once or twice, so they began a museum of fashion to which they donated their clothes. Under Vreeland, the Institute's annual dinner, known as the "Party of the Year," was transformed from a rag-trade benefit to one of the glamorous social events of the fall season. By bringing in women such as Jacqueline Onassis and Pat Buckley, and then by connecting them with fashion barons like Halston, Oscar de la Renta, and Bill Blass, who were emerging from the swirling flotsam of the late-sixties party scene to become social figures in their own right, Vreeland helped induce the cross-pollination of the fashion crowd and the moneyed establishment that was to give society in the eighties its intoxicating blend of power and glitter.

This cross-pollination was greatly aided by the second step Hoving took: building the cavernous Sackler Wing, which houses the Temple of Dendur. After it opened in 1978, parties began to be held there. It was a wonderful space for parties, people felt, so wonderful, in fact, it seemed almost as if it had been designed for entertaining. Some, such as the art critic Hilton Kramer, insisted that it was. The Temple of Dendur, he argued, had negligible esthetic and historic value. It had been a gift from the Egyptian government in appreciation for American help in saving several monuments, notably Abu Simbel, that would otherwise have been flooded by Lake Nasser after the construction of the Aswân Dam. Several museums competed for the temple; it went to the Met after Hoving offered to build the Sackler Wing to contain it. The artificial pond next to the temple that symbolized the River Nile was, to Kramer, an "incredible joke."

But what a *great* place to party!

And indeed, as wealth was amassed in the eighties, the party became an important vehicle for ostentatious display. It began with corporate entertaining. Flush Wall Street firms created departments devoted to planning and holding parties. Gone were the cucumber sandwiches and generic scotch popular during Blanchette Rockefeller's era of understatement. They were replaced by salmon and Perrier Jouet. Much of this was known for tax purposes as business entertaining. It was not Marvin Traub himself but Bloomingdales that held the dinner for Robert Campeau in the fall of 1988. It was not John and Susan Gutfreund but Salomon Brothers that gave the cocktail party. But that simply indicated that the old distinction between business and private entertaining had blurred. As the nouveaux riches achieved critical mass, they showed less interest in cultivating friendships with pedigreed society figures who had no ties to commerce. Clients, competitors, and colleagues *were* their friends. It was to them that they wished to demonstrate their status.

But during the eighties, private entertaining flourished on a whole new scale as well. Henry Kravis was making around $100,000 a year in 1976 when he left Bear Stearns to start Kohlberg Kravis Roberts. By 1988, even before his firm's $25-billion leveraged buyout of RJR-Nabisco, he was worth at least $330 million. For such people, with so many friends and so many social debts to repay, the private dinner party—twenty or thirty guests sitting down in the dining room of one's Park Avenue duplex—simply did not suffice. It could not do justice to the size of one's fortune.

As Veblen pointed out, once an individual's wealth reaches a certain level, it becomes impossible for him to consume conspicuously enough on his own to demonstrate the extent of that wealth. Thereafter, he must resort to vicarious consumption. Others must consume on his behalf. "Costly entertainments, such as...the ball, are peculiarly adapted to serve this end. [The guest] consumes vicariously for his host at the same time that he is a witness to the consumption of that excess of good things which his host is unable to dispose of singlehanded."

It comes as no surprise, then, that as the eighties accelerated, the Met began receiving more requests to hold purely private parties there. The museum, which like all non-profit organizations is eternally short of funds, was happy to comply. And thus in 1986 it instituted the $30,000-party policy.

When the policy was first being formulated, no one really knew where it would lead. In a largely flattering profile of Philippe de Montebello in the *New York Times Magazine* that appeared at the time, art critic James Mellow fleetingly referred to the matter and asked, "What next? Weddings in the Temple of Dendur?" Mellow clearly intended his question as rhetorical hyperbole, a joshing hypothetical example of the excesses that might occur if these parties ever got out of hand. The museum's officials, Mellow seemed to suggest, were too sensible ever to allow that to happen.

Who knows, maybe it was the Mellow article that planted the idea in the minds of Laura Steinberg, the daughter of Saul Steinberg, and Jonathan Tisch, the son of Laurence Tisch, or in the minds of their parents. Whatever the case, two and a half years after the piece appeared Steinberg and Tisch celebrated their marriage right there in the museum in one of the most ostentatious parties of the decade. The Tisch-Steinberg affair, which cost $3 million, featured 50,000 French roses, gold-dipped magnolia leaves, a dance floor hand-painted just for the night, and a ten-foot-high wedding cake that cost $17,000. It was conspicuous consumption at its most exuberant, a bellowing declaration of wealth from individuals unfettered by the guilt that so often inhibits the anxious wretches who have inherited their money.

Museum officials hastened to point out that the affair was not an actual wedding, it was a reception; that it was not in the Temple of Dendur, it was in the restaurant; and that while it may have been a trifle expensive, it was nonetheless in the best of taste. Punch Sulzberger attended the wedding. He and Saul Steinberg had long since patched up the misunderstanding that had led Steinberg to threaten a hostile takeover of the *New York Times* at the beginning of the decade. Sulzberger thought the wedding was fantastic.

But New York society was nonetheless aflame with gossip over the staggering ostentation. To Hilton Kramer the wedding represented "the nadir of the museum." And some museum officials rolled their eyes at the unseemliness, the outright scandal of it all. Hell, members of the staff said, people were always trying to rent the Cloisters, the museum's medieval branch on a wooded hill overlooking the Hudson River, for weddings. If the museum was going to have wedding parties, it might as well go all out. The staff began to joke that the museum should just install in the Cloisters a chapel of the sort found in Las Vegas. Dozens of couples a day could be whisked in and out for brief ceremonies.

The problem for the Steinbergs was that they had violated what Veblen called the "instinct for workmanship." In *The Theory of the Leisure Class* Veblen used that phrase to describe the predisposition among humans to be disgusted by inefficiency, lack of productivity, and waste. This instinct, he said, comes into conflict with conspicuous consumption and creates "an abiding sense of the odiousness and aesthetic impossibility of what is obviously futile." As a result, paradoxically, it becomes necessary at times to find a pretense of useful purpose for conspicuous consumption, the real purpose of which, of course, is to waste money. The lavish charitable benefit emerged precisely as a means to avoid offending this instinct for workmanship. It gave the pretext of raising money for the needy to what was actually an exercise in conspicuous consumption. This had long been understood by everyone and joked about in private, but it was considered bad form to point it out publicly, and worse to moralize about it, which accounted for the small uproar created in 1986 when investment banker Felix Rohatyn and his wife, Elizabeth, both of whom seemed to be reacting in an unconscious way to the institutionalization of the money culture, piously complained to reporters about the motives of those attending charity balls.

Even the nouveaux riches of the Gilded Age recognized the need to give conspicuous consumption some small pretense of usefulness, as Matthew Josephson pointed out in *The Robber Barons.* "Against the outcries of moral bluenoses in times of hardship, the modern Sybarites declared that their carnivals were designed to create employment, and that the proceeds were to be devoted to charities." Thus the end of the nineteenth century witnessed the rise of the "poverty social." The poverty social was a costume party, but instead of coming as Arab sheiks or eighteenth-century French courtesans, the guests dressed up like *poor people.* At one such party, according to Josephson, they appeared wearing tattered rags, sat on soapboxes, were served scraps of food on wooden plates, used newspapers as napkins, and drank beer from rusty cans. What fun it must have been to pretend to be poor! The party, however, was not cheap. It cost $14,000. But it was all for charity.

And so it was one hundred years later, when a new wave of nouveaux riches once again sought pretexts for conspicuous consumption. Gayfryd Steinberg threw herself into PEN, the writers' organization devoted to promoting freedom of expression around the world. She and her husband hosted fund-raising parties for the organization. Arbitrageurs and greenmailers mixed with writers like Gay Talese, Norman Mailer, and Jerzy Kosinski. Everyone wore black-tie. They drank champagne and chatted in a grand salon whose walls were covered in red silk and hung with Old Masters. The women exclaimed over the pretty little Renoir in the powder room.

Socialites everywhere spoke of "my charities." They hired society publicists to arrange for them to receive invitations to the right charity balls. The publicists also promoted the parties their clients gave with gossip columnists, who at times were even provided with limousines rented by the charities. Husbands complained—in a good-natured way— about having to attend three or four charity balls a week, about "dancing for death," and "dancing for a different disease every night."

The point, of course, was to provide pretexts for conspicuous consumption, to avoid inciting the "odiousness and aesthetic impossibility of what is obviously futile." Even the young men who arranged the New Four Hundred Ball recognized that necessity. Marc Biron, a native of France who said he was a count, explained that while the ball was not a charitable function the first year it was held, he and his friend George Whipple III wanted to transform it into one. "We could do something like charity of the year," he told Patricia Morrisroe. "But it should be an amusing charity, like for the homeless."

When the nouveaux riches, carried away with the fun they were having spending their money, forgot to abide by the stipulations of the prevailing hypocrisy, the outrage was inevitable and prompt—as the Steinbergs learned. Interestingly enough, however, each successive violation of the instinct for workmanship seemed to weaken its moral authority. The Steinberg wedding, while the subject of exhaustive malicious gossip, did not put an end to lavish private parties at the Metropolitan Museum. If anything, it seemed to make it easier for the next private party to be held there. By the following fall, the nouveaux riches were holding parties that had no charitable purpose with such regularity at the museum that they seemed to have secured the right to turn it into their private house of revelry in the evenings.

THE PERFECT PARTY

That October, Henry Kravis and Carolyne Roehm gave a party at the Met that was considered one of the most sumptuous affairs of the season. Gossip columnist Aileen "Suzy" Mehle, who was asked to attend and chronicle these affairs, described it as "the perfect party." The invitation was on paper as stiff as Sheetrock, and when one arrived at the appointed hour Carolyne and Henry were greeting their guests just inside the wrought iron gates of the Medieval Court. Carolyne looked simply stunning, with her huge dark eyes, retroussé nose, and the glistening cabochon emeralds that adorned her white throat. The extraordinary thing about Henry and Carolyne was that despite their frantic paces they managed to keep up on everyone. They knew all one's accomplishments and they praised them all in those few seconds at the gate before the glittering swirl drew one in and they receded.

While it was customary to groan about having to attend them, they were actually exhilarating, these evenings at the Met. Most of the men were powerful. Those who were not powerful were art dealers and interior designers who had, through sophistication and wit, insinuated themselves into the circle of the powerful. The women were beautiful, but if not beautiful then handsome, and if not handsome then grand. Certainly they were all vivacious. Their conversation sparkled. They wore gowns and jewels worth hundreds of thousands of dollars. It was all, quite frankly, electrifying— more euphoric and intoxicating than any chemical stimulant.

What added to the electricity was that everyone knew only too well just how precarious was the wealth on display. One had only to think of what had happened to Ivan Boesky, to Harry and Leona Helmsley, to Bess Meyerson, who had been, until overtaken by scandal, an ex officio member of the Met board and a regular attendant at parties such as this. Even divorce could bring one down. Look what had happened to Anne Bass who, for all her $200-million divorce settlement, was not the woman she had been when married to Sid.

Scandal aside, a sense of uncertainty still hung over these fortunes. Would they endure? Were they destined to cast a shadow into the next century, as fortunes amassed during the Gilded Age had? Or would they evaporate in some upcoming market debacle, as happened with many of the speculative fortunes made during the twenties? That uncertainty gave the behavior of the nouveaux riches of the eighties a superstitious cast. Their world resembled Rome in the days before Christianity introduced the idea of compassion for the unfortunate. In pagan Rome it was believed that good luck and bad luck were contagious. People attached themselves to the successful for as long as they were successful, and they shunned those whose luck had turned. Pity simply did not exist. It was a vicious world, the world of pagan Rome, and so was the world of high society and nouveau riche ambition. But that viciousness—that pagan sense of the world as a place of pervasive danger and cruelty—only added to the intoxication.

After champagne and cocktails, the lights were lowered and everyone took seats around a small stage to listen to the gifted young violinist Midori. Henry and Carolyne sat in the front row on the far right, and one suddenly noticed that a single spotlight seemed to have been positioned to shine directly on Carolyne. Whether intentional or not, there she was, illuminated, her hands clasped together at her chest, a look of poised rapture on her face.

Dinner in the Blumenthal Patio followed—and Carolyne's seating plan was brilliant. There was no head table, and because every table had top people, no one felt slighted. The meal was marred only by the rabbit, or *lapin*, as the menu called it. Many found it exquisite, but it also produced a lot of titters, and in a surprising display of provincialism, a few people separated the meat from the rest of the casserole and pushed it to one side of their plates. Where *do* they come from?

Fortunately, when dinner was over Henry resisted the temptation to say a few words. Fortunately, too, no other tycoon decided to hold court. How many affairs had one been to where the most aggressive tycoon present stood up as soon as he finished eating and just planted himself in the center of the room, remaining there for the rest of the night talking deals while the rest of the men approached him like supplicants?

Instead, the guests repaired to the new Tisch Gallery to see the Degas exhibit. It was marvelous to contemplate the works without being jostled by crowds and forced to endure their inane chatter. Then, as the guests left, each was given a beautifully wrapped hardcover copy of the catalog, which cost $45 apiece. Delightful and lavish gifts were a Carolyne trademark, and a welcome relief, too, from the bag of trifles—lipstick, cologne samples—usually thrust at departing guests by the coat-check boy.

But as the driver maneuvered the car down Fifth Avenue, the main image that one carried away from the party was of the beautiful Carolyne illuminated by that spotlight: her clasped hands; the jewels; her white throat; the rapturous gaze. So, though it may well have been an accident, that spotlight was altogether appropriate. For Carolyne was a princess in the new social order, and the Metropolitan Museum was her palace.

5

"LOSERS ARE BORING": THE MANIA FOR CONTROL IN HOLLYWOOD

"CONTROL THE ENVIRONMENT"

The offices of the producers Don Simpson and Jerry Bruckheimer were in the Cecil B. DeMille Building, just inside the gate of the Paramount Pictures studio in Hollywood. They were generous quarters, with a reception area decorated in the powerful but hip design scheme favored by executives in the fashion and entertainment business. There were couches made of black leather and a glass-topped table with copies of *Rolling Stone* and the *Hollywood Reporter*. The soundtracks from all but one of Simpson and Bruckheimer's movies had gone platinum, that is, sold more than 1 million copies—*Flashdance* sold 17 million copies and became the biggest-selling movie soundtrack in history—and the gray fabric–paneled walls of the reception area were adorned with platinum records.

Simpson and Bruckheimer themselves shared a large room that was down a hall and through a bullpen of assistants. The two producers could each have had their own office, of course—to keep Disney or 20th Century–Fox from luring them away, Paramount would probably have

given each his own building if he wanted—but since they
conferred constantly, it made more sense to be together in
one room. They even shared the same desk. It was a vast
piece of furniture in the shape of a T. Each partner sat in
one of the two angles.

Although it was late afternoon on an early spring day
in 1988, with the shadows lengthening across the small
pastel bungalows around Melrose Avenue, Simpson and
Bruckheimer had only recently arrived at the office.
They were between pictures. *Beverly Hills Cop II*, their
most recent movie, had opened the previous summer
and was no longer playing. Paramount expected them to
deliver another movie for release in Christmas of 1989.
Though they had twenty projects in development, they
had yet to decide which one to make. The 1988 writers'
strike, which would last 150 days and ultimately end in a
victory for the studios that would generate comments
about "corporate hardliners" and "1980s-style capitalism," was only a month old. Writers were laboring over
scripts at home and furtively showing them to producers
in what had become known as a "Mulholland Drive
midnight drop-off." But officially it was impossible to
proceed on anything. So Simpson and Bruckheimer were
taking it easy.

"Isn't this the life?" Simpson would tell people, in a way
that emphasized that such inactivity was quite novel. "We
are doing absolutely nothing and loving it." Indeed, after
their midafternoon arrival at the office they would spend a
few hours returning calls. At six or so, they went into
screenings, then afterward they would have dinner at Mortons
or Spago or some such exclusive retreat for movie industry
powers. Simpson and Bruckheimer, who were part of the
group of hippies, Yippies, leftist radicals, and anti-establishment poseurs that had moved into Hollywood in the seventies, used to disdain such centers of establishment power in

favor of more egalitarian spots like El Coyote, just down the
road from Paramount. But those days were long past.

Simpson was sitting with his feet on his desk, sifting
through his mail. He had a lined, fleshy face and alert hazel
eyes that watched you while he talked. He had a rock-star
haircut—short bangs, long in the back—and a four-day
beard. He wore an expensive white shirt, faded Levis, black
cowboy boots, and a western belt with a hammered silver
buckle. He used to have something of a gut and, to
disguise it, would dress in loose floppy clothing, but recently
he had checked into an exclusive health spa, Canyon Ranch,
where he lost fifty pounds, then hired a personal trainer
who put him on a special exercise program. It was working.
The expensive white shirt was tucked into his jeans.

Simpson finished one letter and started another. It had
arrived with a manuscript attached. He frowned and pushed
a button on his desk. His assistant Beth appeared.

"I can't read this," Simpson told her. "The people who
are opening the mail are supposed to know. I'm not supposed to receive unsolicited scripts."

The letter was from a man with whom Simpson had gone
to high school. The man had written a screenplay, and he
hoped to interest his former classmate in it. The idea almost
certainly was not registered with the Writers Guild. If
Simpson read a letter with a story proposal, much less if he
read an actual script, and then sometime in the future made
a movie that in even the most remote fashion resembled the
idea, he could be sued. And given the fact that, according
to one school, there are only some six plots in all literature,
the chances that some resemblance might exist were not
insignificant. But even if the movie did not resemble the
idea in the slightest, Simpson could still be sued by someone claiming it did and hoping to wring an out-of-court
settlement from a rich producer with deep pockets and no

time to spare for frivolous litigation. Just about every successful movie made in Hollywood spawned lawsuits by people claiming credit for the screenplay's idea. To avoid adding to the pretexts for litigation, Simpson forbade himself to read unsolicited manuscripts.

He told Beth to handle it. "But he's an old friend, so do it nicely," he said. "And I'll write a note to add to it."

All this time Jerry Bruckheimer was sitting next to Simpson in the other angle of the magnificent power desk, talking on the telephone. Unlike Simpson, Bruckheimer was quiet, almost shy, and thin. He, too, had a beard, but it was a serious beard, not like Simpson's fashionably roguish growth. Generally, Bruckheimer was put together in a more conventional manner than Simpson. He wore a tailored gray suit and a charcoal gray shirt that was open at the collar. He had on a pair of black loafers made of some exotic skin. His feet, too, were up on the desk.

"Ten o'clock tomorrow morning," he said. With his hand over the mouthpiece, he explained that he was talking to representatives from Kodak, who had asked Simpson and Bruckheimer to appear in a commercial.

"You're going to be in a commercial?" I asked Simpson.

"We *are* the commercial," he said rather grandly, then smiled.

The advertisement was part of a series that Kodak had run featuring filmmakers such as Martin Scorsese who, like Simpson and Bruckheimer, used Kodak film stock to shoot their movies. Before Simpson and Bruckheimer agreed to appear in the commercial, they had insisted on total control. They would decide what clothes to wear, where to pose, and what angle the photographer would shoot from. They wanted to approve the final photograph that was used and the copy and the manner in which the art director laid out the ad.

"Control the environment," Simpson said. "That's what it's all about."

THE QUEST FOR CONTROL

Control has been one of the overriding psychological preoccupations of the eighties. For many, control was actually seen as the object of a sort of existential quest. This provided a striking contrast to much of the sixties and seventies, when Americans—following the lead of the young—were driven by the spirit of emancipation. As in the twenties, they sought release from conventional and inhibiting forms of behavior. Self-expression became a fetish. Americans took up painting, dancing, poetry, the guitar, photography, and macramé, all as part of the grand effort to liberate their spirits and express their inner feelings. And while some educators and therapists genuinely believed that *everyone* was creative, talent was not really the issue. Personal fulfillment was. Without some sort of creative outlet for self-expression, according to prevailing thought, an individual could not be truly fulfilled, indeed, could not be truly alive.

But one more result of the upheavals and failures of the seventies was to reverse this drift. Americans found themselves unable to contain inflation or thwart terrorists. Carter's fatalistic view of an age of limits indicated his inability to exert influence over the course of events. "Citizens observe that success and economic security no longer depend on the usual virtues of hard work and saving, but on inflationary currents over which they have *no control*," Paul Blumberg wrote in *Inequality in an Age of Decline* (my italics).

In fact, everywhere Americans looked things seemed to be out of control. The fetish of self-expression had been carried to extremes, resulting in moral chaos, religious cults and mass suicide, drug overdoses, and declining test scores in schools that had dropped traditional curricula for "alternative" approaches. In 1980 Jerry Falwell, who rose to prominence largely by exploiting the panic this perception created, toured the country with an audio-visual presentation that showed pictures of Charles Manson, Times Square adult film theaters, nuclear bomb explosions, young men caressing one another, and dead fetuses in bloody hospital pans.

As indicated by the title of Falwell's presentation, *America, You're Too Young to Die*, a feeling had arisen that the nation's very survival was at stake. Consequently, the liberating impulse, the desire for release and self-expression, began to yield to the desire to conserve and control. People began to see the act of imposing their will, of mastering a situation, as intrinsically gratifying. Physical strength and masculine aggression, repudiated in the sixties as the dumb brutishness of athletes and soldiers, again became socially acceptable, while the sixties ideal of the sensitive frail male fell from favor. Falwell, once again, articulated the new values by attacking the image of Christ as a gentle pacifist, insisting that He was a "he-man," not a "sissy." The term *control freak* began to enjoy a vogue. And after the assassination attempt on Reagan, Alexander Haig made his marvelously self-revealing assertion: "I am in control here."

The quest for control could be seen even in the sexual arena. One of the main avenues for self-expression in the sixties and seventies had been sexual expression. But first herpes and then, much more ominously, AIDS put a chill on sexual activity. People began to practice abstinence, which is, of course, a form of self-control. The degree to which the postwar generation turned away from sexual self-expression in the eighties was found in the emergence among young professionals of the condition known as SIDS or Sexually Inhibited Desire Syndrome. Whether it was due to fear of intimacy, boredom, or simple exhaustion, young people—to the amazement of the sixties generation—were losing interest in sex.

But it was all in keeping with the shift away from the impulse to release and toward the impulse to conserve. The creation of wealth, the glamour of investment banking, and the fascination with the deal were all expressions of the urge to be in control. "Money," Jerry Rubin supposedly said, "is the poetry of the eighties." It was also a metaphor for triumph. Investments from certificates of deposit and gold to mutual funds and real estate provided even the most ordinary citizens with their own personal victories. "It makes me feel smart and gives me more control over my life," a young woman named Carrie Cook told a *Newsweek* reporter in 1984 when asked about the fact that her Boston co-op was appreciating so rapidly she had made more money in one year as a property owner than she had at her job.

Even the characteristic excesses of the eighties—insider trading, stock manipulation, fraud—expressed the desire to control. When the alleged misdeeds of people like Michael Milken and Leona Helmsley were made public, the public was baffled. Why would Milken, who was worth more than $1 billion, manipulate stock prices to enable his firm to increase its fee in a deal by $1 million, as he was alleged to have done? Why would Leona Helmsley, who with her husband, Harry, was worth close to $1 billion, sue the widow of her late son over his $149,000 estate or try to evade $4 million in income taxes?

The answers have nothing to do with money and everything to do with the central paradox of power. The accumulation of power does not provide security. Instead it feeds anxieties—"The wealthy have few friends," as Mary Lea Johnson said—and thus inflames the desire to accumulate more power, to exercise ever greater control over other individuals and events. As Reinhold Niebuhr wrote: "The will-to-power is thus an expression of insecurity even when it has achieved ends which, from the perspective of an ordinary mortal, would seem to guarantee complete security."

Hollywood has always been a revealing laboratory for the study of control. In fact, the whole history of the film business can be described as an ongoing struggle between writers, actors, directors, producers, studio executives, agents, lawyers, financiers, and even legislators for control over what movies will be made, who will make them, how they will be made, how they will end, and whether or not they will contain sex or profanity or a political or moral or social message.

In the thirties and forties, studio heads wielded absolute control over the entire film-making process. Men like Irving Thalberg, Darryl Zanuck, and David Selznick did not just cut deals or put together "packages" of stars and directors and screenwriters. They created stories and assigned them to groups of writers. They approved and at times reworked the scripts. While there were some notable exceptions, such as Howard Hawks, directors generally worked for a single studio, where they were frequently regarded as little more than artisans hired to execute the grand designs of the studio heads. In fact, once the picture was shot, the director usually did not enter the editing room. He had often already begun directing another movie. Before he died, Raoul Walsh, who directed *High Sierra* and *White Heat*, used to describe how he would finish shooting a script at the end of one day and by nine the following morning he would have been assigned a new script and told to start shooting in two weeks. The studio head himself would at times retire to the screening room to review the daily rushes from films then in production, as well as the cut footage the editors were assembling. If he didn't like what he saw, he ordered retakes. Occasionally, after previewing a film, he would insist that an entire new ending be shot. He exercised total control.

In the forties, however, the studio system began to collapse. The Justice Department, concerned about monopoly practices, forced the studios to divest themselves of their theaters. Without those chains, and the demand for product they created, the studios began to reduce the number of movies they produced. They no longer needed the huge stables of writers, directors, and actors who had been kept busy creating large numbers of relatively cheap films. Studios instead began increasingly to negotiate with independent producers to undertake specific projects. Stars and directors also began more often to sign contracts for individual pictures.*

In the sixties, American directors began to be inspired by the control over the script, casting, and production exercised by independent European filmmakers such as Truffaut, Godard, Bergman, Fellini, and Antonioni. They began to imitate the Europeans, and during that decade the success of films by independent American directors like Dennis Hopper (*Easy Rider*) further eroded the position of the studios, which compounded their problems by producing spectacular flops such as *Cleopatra, Tora! Tora! Tora!*, and *Dr. Doolittle*.

Beginning in this period, conglomerates began to take over the studios. By 1982, Warner Bros., United Artists, MGM, 20th Century–Fox, Paramount, Columbia—every major studio except Universal, which was in the hands of Lew Wasserman, and Walt Disney Productions, which was controlled by the Disney family—had been acquired by an investor from outside the film community. The conglomera-

---

*During the Reagan era, with the Justice Department antitrust division in a quiescent state, studios began again to acquire interests in theaters.

teurs, uncomfortable with "creative people," began hiring agents and lawyers—dealmakers, in other words—to run the studios. The new executives had little or no experience actually making films themselves, and they began ceding ever greater autonomy to the directors.

The directors made some remarkable pictures, such as *McCabe and Mrs. Miller, The Godfather, Taxi Driver, Chinatown, Annie Hall, Apocalypse Now,* and *The Deer Hunter,* to name a few. In keeping with the mood of the times, these films by and large were pessimistic. They explored themes of loss, despair, anger, moral degeneration. They focused on the characters of criminals, outlaws, renegades, mavericks, malcontents—the alienated and the disaffected. The directors themselves continued to be very outspoken in their unremitting contempt for the individuals who ran the studios and whom they referred to as pencil pushers or bean counters or money men. Francis Ford Coppola, for one, told people he had only made *The Godfather* in order to earn the money to free himself from the control of the studios.

But one of the great ironies of modern American film history is that in a few short years the directors squandered the freedom they had so recently wrested from the studios by their reckless and irresponsible attitude toward finances. Their behavior, in fact, was a direct outgrowth of the same compulsive self-expression that afflicted the culture at large. As with so many people and social forces in the seventies, they went out of control. The result was a series of self-indulgent, self-important, and horribly expensive flops. Altman's career foundered after *Nashville.* Upon finishing *Apocalypse Now,* Coppola turned out costly disasters like *One from the Heart* and *The Cotton Club.* But the movie that really signaled the end of the brief reign of the directors was, of course, *Heaven's Gate.* Released in 1980, Michael Cimino's extraordinary debacle, which cost $44 million to make and ruined the careers of just about everyone involved with it, was the classic example of the chaos that ensues when creative forces go unchecked. It signaled the end of the era of the director.

Another movie released the same year, *American Gigolo*, foretold the era that lay ahead. Critics denounced it as vigorously as they had *Heaven's Gate*. But unlike *Heaven's Gate*, *American Gigolo* was a success. Opening in February 1980, it was in many respects the perfect movie to kick off the eighties. Neither the director, Paul Schrader, nor the producer, Jerry Bruckheimer, nor the Paramount executive in charge of the picture, Don Simpson, nor the star, Richard Gere, intended it to be prophetic, of course, but the movie did foreshadow many of the attitudes that defined the decade. In Schrader's view, *American Gigolo*, about a high-priced male hooker in southern California, was the portrait of a character who could not accept love. To many critics, however, it seemed preoccupied with surface slickness and pervaded with the horror of sex.

But the true contribution of *American Gigolo* lay not in the film itself but in the fact that it was the first collaboration between Simpson and Bruckheimer. From there the two men would go on to produce a group of films that—for better or worse—helped set the style for Hollywood in the eighties.

Agents had also been moving into the power vacuum left by the studios. Men like Sam Cohn at International Creative Management and Michael Ovitz at Creative Artists Agency became known for packaging their clients: putting together writers, directors, and actors whom they represented into a single deal and presenting it as a fait accompli to the studio. Predictably, critics began to blame the packagers for everything that was wrong with Hollywood, since these packagers were determined to maximize income for their clients (and thus for themselves) rather than to produce movies of enduring quality. But this was precisely the charge made by critics of the old studio moguls. And what Ovitz and Cohn had in fact done was create their own studio systems (with their own stables of talent) without incurring either the risks that came with financing pictures or the overhead that came with operating an actual studio.

For all the power ascribed to them, however, agents were not involved in actually *making* movies. People like Simpson and Bruckheimer were. They were the most prominent examples of a group of individuals who took control of the film-making process away from the directors and placed it back in the hands of the producers. Simpson and Bruckheimer came to run their operation the way Selznick and Thalberg and the other studio heads had run their studios. They exercised total control. It was a development that had consequences not only within the Hollywood power structure but for the American public at large, since it radically affected the types of movies that were to be made.

"LOSERS ARE BORING"

Simpson and Bruckheimer are not creative visionaries. But they are, in a sense, filmmakers, and they like to say they make the kind of movies they themselves would want to see. But they are also under contract at Paramount, a division of a publicly held corporation, with high overhead and an insatiable appetite for revenue. The studio hired them to make films that would make money.

By the spring of 1988 Simpson and Bruckheimer had made five films together. One of them, *Thief of Hearts*, fizzled with domestic ticket sales of less than $10.5 million. The other four, however, did spectacularly well. The first film they produced jointly was *Flashdance*. None of Paramount's executives believed in it. They agreed to finance it, if it could be done cheaply, to fill a slot in the release schedule and move product into the theaters. Critics panned

Flashdance when it appeared—"a ninety-minute MTV rock video" was the general consensus—and there was no reason to expect it to survive for more than a few days before theater owners pulled it. But to the amazement of Simpson and Bruckheimer, the picture struck a chord and went on to sell $207 million worth of tickets worldwide.

Beverly Hills Cop, which Simpson and Bruckheimer brought out in December 1984, became the most successful comedy ever made. It grossed $364 million worldwide and in the process transformed Eddie Murphy into the most successful black film star Hollywood had ever seen. *Top Gun*, based on the Navy's elite combat flight school in Miramar, California, had the astonishing fortune to be released some two months after U.S. Navy aircraft sank two Libyan patrol boats in the Gulf of Sidra. *Top Gun* inevitably became the biggest box office draw of the year, grossing $345 million worldwide. Simpson and Bruckheimer followed that success with *Beverly Hills Cop II*, which was the most popular movie of 1987 with a worldwide gross of $270 million. Since forming their partnership in 1981, Simpson and Bruckheimer had made $1.7 billion for Paramount from tickets, video cassettes, and records. They had provided rather comfortably for themselves as well, having earned—according to studio gossip— more than $10 million apiece on *Top Gun* alone.

Critics have tended to dislike Simpson and Bruckheimer's movies. The characters are thin, they have complained, the plots are predictable or preposterous, the soundtracks are flooded with rock-and-roll. Nonetheless, in a ranking of the decade's most influential movies—the most successful and thus the most imitated, though not necessarily the best— Sheila Benson, a film critic for the *Los Angeles Times*, listed both *Flashdance* ("Cinderella meets MTV") and *Beverly Hills Cop* ("culture clash, cops and comics"). Steven Spielberg was the only other person to have two films on the list.

One indication of the influence of Simpson and Bruckheimer's movies can be found in the fads they have launched. *American Gigolo*, which Bruckheimer produced under Simpson's supervision when Simpson was still head of production at Paramount, inaugurated the male craze for Italian designer suits. *Flashdance* made leg warmers and torn sweatshirts fashionable. When *Top Gun* was showing in theaters, the Navy reported increases in inquiries concerning enrollment in flight school.

But other movies have been even more successful than Simpson and Bruckheimer's. Other movies have started more and bigger fads. *Raiders of the Lost Ark* touched off such a clamor for safari clothes that an entire clothing chain, the Banana Republic, prospered in its wake. Simpson and Bruckheimer stood out, then, for two reasons. They evolved a style of making films that typified Hollywood in the eighties. And they produced the movies that, for better or worse, captured the spirit of the times. "The boys," as people referred to them around Paramount, accomplished this by focusing on two themes, which they called "the Emotion of Triumph" and "the Romance of Professionalism."

Both elements were found in *Flashdance*. Together with the film's music, by Giorgio Moroder, they account for its incredible appeal. Released in 1983, just as the country was pulling itself out of the worst recession since the thirties, *Flashdance* fed the public appetite for fantasies of triumph. Americans had wallowed in pessimism long enough. In *The Culture of Narcissism*, a book drenched in that pessimism, Christopher Lasch pointed out that the spate of disaster movies during the seventies suggested that simple survival was an overriding fantasy. The popular theme song of *The Poseidon Adventure*, "The Morning After," began with the line: "There's got to be a morning after." By the early eighties the public had developed a psychic need for fantasies of obstacles overcome and dreams realized. *Flashdance* provided all that. So what if the plot was ridiculous and the characters lame? It conveyed, in one highly charged package, a myth of success. It made the audience feel good.

"The two of us, we're drawn to stories that are positive in nature and involve people who are productive," Simpson said that early spring afternoon while Bruckheimer continued to talk on the phone with the Kodak representatives. "We love professionals. We're both really, really romantic about professionals."

"It's the inner strength of the character and the conviction to better themselves, to attain their own personal goals, that really interests me," Bruckheimer said after hanging up.

"By and large life is separated," Simpson said. "There are people who are successful and who win. They have moments of pain but they are winners. Then there are losers. Jerry and I side with the winners. We aren't interested in losers. They're boring—to us."

And not just to Simpson and Bruckheimer. To just about everyone in the eighties, losers were boring. It was perhaps the key ingredient in the bull market mentality. Emerging from the threatening, pessimistic wallow of the seventies, Americans devoted themselves wholeheartedly to the pursuit of optimism. They didn't want to be reminded of misery. They wanted to feel good. And so Simpson and Bruckheimer's movies do not wax pessimistic. In them, as in the society at large during the Reagan years, there was no place for losers and their monotonous, whining grievances. There was no place for failure except as a temporary setback, a prelude to triumph.

EROTICIZED SURFACES

Simpson and Bruckheimer liked to describe their movies as "fast-paced" or "full-tilt" or "high energy" or "high octane." "The movies Don and I make say, 'Look at me for an hour and a half,' " Bruckheimer explained. "We're going to take you on a ride. We're going to take you up and down, and when you walk out you're going to feel a little bit better."

Indeed, each of their successful films—*Thief of Hearts* was an anomaly, since a studio, rather than the two producers, developed the project—has employed the same formulaic elements, much in the manner of the studio pictures of the thirties and forties. Although Simpson and Bruckheimer don't think of themselves as having a formula, in each of their movies an attractive central character sets out to attain a goal. Other characters don't believe the main character deserves to achieve the goal, which establishes him or her as a sympathetic underdog in the eyes of the audience. Driving rock music provides the quest with emotion and spirit. Special effects—car crashes, aerial flight sequences, surreally filmed dance numbers—divert the audience along the way. After initial reverses, the character achieves his or her goal in a rousing climax.

Simpson and Bruckheimer fashioned their movies very deliberately. Perhaps more than any other producers in Hollywood, they knew what they wanted.

"There are producers who are packagers," Bruckheimer said. "They'll be friendly with an actor who wants to do something about Chicano beanfields or something. They'll go to a studio and say, 'I have so-and-so who wants to do such-and-such. I control this star. Make me the producer, I'll deliver.' "

That was not the Simpson and Bruckheimer way. "For better or worse, Jerry and I have been the authors of our movies," Simpson explained. "We don't go out and pursue the material in the streets. We in essence invent our movies right here. The ideas have come from our heads."

That may have been something of an exaggeration—

Flashdance, which ultimately went through three sets of writers, was originally conceived by Tom Hedley—but it was not entirely untrue. For example, the situation for *Top Gun* came from an article in *California* magazine about the Navy's flight school at Miramar that Bruckheimer happened to see on a coffee table. "I looked at that story, and it said this is Star Wars but it's real and it's on earth and it's happening every day in our deserts. These guys are playing with thirty-million-dollar machines like in a video arcade, except it's for real." *Beverly Hills Cop* grew out of an evening Simpson spent with Los Angeles police officers on gang detail—or so Simpson has claimed. But let us hold off on that for the time being.

The two producers liked to describe themselves as "Mr. Inside and Mr. Outside," as "two halves of the same brain" and as "verbal and visual" twins. The verbal domain was Simpson's. He handled relations with Paramount and did the cajoling and pitching. He also focused on the script, editing the efforts of screenwriters to ensure that elements such as the "narrative arc," to use one of the phrases Simpson throws around, met their satisfaction. Bruckheimer, who had a background in advertising and still photography, was what is know as a "line producer." He hired the cinematographer, casting director, makeup artists, and all the other members of the film crew. He also oversaw the look and sound of the films, the elements that gave them the packaged slickness known in the movie business as "top spin."

Either Simpson or Bruckheimer was always on the set during filming. Often both were present. They were there not just to keep an eye on costs but also to control the—to use their word—"design" of the movie. They made their thoughts known on matters as diverse as lighting and character motivation. It was no coincidence that Simpson and Bruckheimer relied on relatively inexperienced directors—

Thief of Hearts was actually Douglas Day Stewart's directorial debut. Inexperienced directors were less likely to fight so hard for control. Two of the directors Simpson and Bruckheimer hired, Adrian Lyne of *Flashdance* and Tony Scott of *Top Gun*, previously directed commercials. Commercial directors had a less grandiose vision of themselves. Accustomed to accommodating clients, they tended to be somewhat more practical, more open to suggestion.

The directors who worked for Simpson and Bruckheimer were made to understand who was in control. "What happens with all the directors we have worked with is they start to make the movie their own, they start to shift it to their emotional perspective, which they *should* do," Simpson said. "Thus begins the tug of war between the directors and ourselves—in a very positive way. If it's Tony Scott, who is a madman, he'll start to shift it off to some dark existential axis that's very interesting but strange. Jerry and I will pull it back into what we consider a positive emotional axis. We had great fights with Tony." And with Adrian Lyne, too. "Don and I used to argue almost to the point of blows," Lyne once told the *Los Angeles Times*. Once filming was complete, Simpson and Bruckheimer followed the director into the editing room and argued with him there about how to assemble the movie from the available footage.

Simpson and Bruckheimer's most characteristic movies tended to have a glossy texture. They used backlighting, stylized shadows, closeups, quick cuts, and silky camera pans. This visual style was adopted from advertising. When Bruckheimer worked for the New York advertising agency BBDO, he helped design some of the now legendary Pepsi Generation commercials. Instead of directly promoting the product's virtues—its taste or thirst-quenching powers—these commercials associated Pepsi with a lifestyle. They did so without telling a story. Instead, they established a mood by cutting quickly between a series of elaborately staged, richly photographed, and emotionally charged vignettes of people having fun in different, exciting ways. These lifestyle ads became immensely popular in the eighties. They provided a quick emotional jolt and spared the advertiser the trouble of developing, and the audience the trouble of understanding, any ideas. They packaged a feeling. Chrysler, GM, Levi's jeans, and ATT all copied them. So did Ronald Reagan's advisers. Interestingly enough, it was Phil Dusenberry, the legendary creative director of Bruckheimer's alma mater, BBDO, who produced the "It's morning in America" film for the Reagan re-election campaign, which was shown at the 1984 Republican convention and which shamelessly employed the packaged emotionalism of the lifestyle ads for political purposes. It has been argued that the entire Reagan presidency was essentially a series of elaborately staged, emotionally charged vignettes designed to sell certain topics to the public.

Simpson and Bruckheimer's movies did not sell products— they resisted the temptation, succumbed to by many other producers, to feature products in movies in exchange for a fee—but they did establish moods by taking advantage of some of the techniques developed by the lifestyle commercials. One of the most effective ways commercials established mood was through the exaggeration of detail. The sound of coffee pouring and two voices talking announced morning and suggested intimacy. A closeup of a woman applying lipstick suggested sexual anticipation. Simpson and Bruckheimer's movies used this technique in order to heighten and intensify situations—to eroticize the ordinary.

In the opening sequence of *Top Gun*, a squadron of F-14s prepares for a dawn takeoff from the aircraft carrier *Nimitz*. Hues of rose and pearl bathe everything in a dreamlike light. The planes glide at close range through the camera frame, which lingers on fuselages, wings, wheels, and engines. Suddenly the engines ignite, throbbing rock music fills the theater, the planes are catapulted from the carrier deck, and the movie soars ahead.

Flashdance gets under way in similar fashion. After some preliminary establishing shots, the movie features an extended sequence of close-ups of the actress Jennifer Beals as she dances in silhouette on the stage of a bar. Throbbing rock fills the theater, and the movie soars ahead.

American Gigolo, with which both Bruckheimer and Simpson were involved, helped establish this technique in feature films in the eighties (though it had, of course, been used previously in movies like *Easy Rider* and *Taxi Driver*). The movie worshipped objects, bodies, and machines; it created a world of flawless, eroticized surfaces. "Nothing, neither bosom nor buttock, is photographed more lovingly than the [Mercedes] 450 SL—those taillights, winking provocatively in the velvet night, such as to drive men mad," Charles Champlin wrote of *American Gigolo* in the *Los Angeles Times*.

THE RISE OF
THE HIGH CONCEPT MOVIE

To understand how Simpson and Bruckheimer came to make this particular brand of movie, it is necessary to return to the early seventies, to that period when agents and lawyers were moving into the top jobs in Hollywood and ceding control of the making of movies to directors and stars. One studio that resisted this trend was Paramount Pictures. Charles Bluhdorn, the cantankerous head of Gulf & Western, had acquired the studio in 1966. In 1974, he hired Barry Diller, who was then overseeing ABC's "Movie of the Week," to be Paramount's chairman. Two years later, Diller brought in Michael Eisner as president. Eisner also had a television background. In fact, before coming to Paramount,

Eisner had never worked anywhere but television. The man had never made a feature film in his life.

Eisner's television experience proved to be an advantage. Television networks were run in a similar fashion to the way the movie studios had been run in the twenties and thirties under the moguls. Like the moguls, television programming executives tended to consider directors and to some extent even actors as interchangeable. Their main concern was with story ideas powerful enough to sustain a series. When Eisner arrived at Paramount, he adopted an approach that, while counter to the one then prevailing in Hollywood, resembled the emphasis on story in the television industry. Instead of having his executives take agents and producers to lunch to find out what scripts were coming on the market, he insisted that they originate their own ideas. He felt that if the idea, the *concept*, were strong enough, the movie would succeed.

"I don't care who's in the movie," Eisner used to tell his staff. "I don't care who directs it. I don't care about anything except the idea."

To generate those ideas, Eisner began holding creative meetings. In their intensity and duration, these meetings at times resembled the marathon encounter sessions then popular in California. (According to Paramount legend, the first of these meetings, called shortly after Eisner arrived at the studio, lasted eight hours.) When the staff had gathered, Eisner would say to each person in turn, "Tell me a story." These stories were supposed to be original. Of course, everyone lifted ideas from magazines and wherever else they could find them, but they denied attribution.

Simpson, who was a production executive at Paramount at the time, had a tremendous amount of fun at these meetings. He loved to talk and he loved to make things up. "What I learned after working with Eisner—which I loved, by the way—was that controlling the idea was the answer

to making things work in Hollywood," Simpson said in the
spring of 1988. He was leaning forward, feet on the floor,
gesturing with his hands. "Not *that*"—he pointed to the
telephone—"which I hated anyway. It was *this*." He held up
a script.

But it wasn't even so much the script. A script could be
produced later. It was the idea. Or more accurately, the
concept. And it was better if you could sum up the concept
in a sentence or even a phrase. It was better, in other words,
if it was a "high concept."

High concept has entered the lexicon of the eighties, and
film critics now use it whenever they want to dismiss a
movie as superficial, derivative, insincere, or just plain
stupid. High concept movies were not the inspiration of a
brilliant screenwriter or visionary director. Executives or
producers thrashed them out in meetings like the ones
Eisner held. But they filled a need and so they flourished.

In 1974—the year Bluhdorn hired Diller—it cost $3.5 mil-
lion to shoot, release, and promote the average movie. By
1984, that figure had risen to $19 million. That was a
frightening amount of money. Studio heads had to answer
to the boards of parent corporations, who in turn had to
answer to stockholders, who had become increasingly bel-
ligerent about satisfactory returns on their investment. In
such an atmosphere no one wanted to risk money blindly.
The high concept emerged as a marketing device to enlist
the support of investors and theater owners. It was a sales
tool, a way of explaining a movie that did not yet exist by
relating it to a successful movie or category of movies. Still,
the high concept developed a bad name, and people in
Hollywood began taking pains to dissociate themselves
from the phrase. Some of them, like Simpson, at times even
pretended they hadn't the faintest notion of what a high
concept movie was.

"I've never done a high concept movie and I don't know

if I've ever seen a high concept movie, except maybe *Porky's*," he said indignantly one afternoon.

Why did he take such pains to avoid the term?

"Because, high concept is a definition of bad."

Simpson could muster much support for his opinion that high concept movies were bad, but few would agree that he and Bruckheimer have never made one. Although Simpson and Bruckheimer themselves do not use the phrase *high concept*, their productions are considered *the* classic examples of the high concept picture. What was *Flashdance*? Almost from its inception it was referred to as a *Rocky* for women. What was *Beverly Hills Cop*? A fish out of water. *Top Gun*? *An Officer and a Gentleman* in a jet.

But not only have Simpson and Bruckheimer's movies epitomized the high concept, the term itself was popularized by *American Gigolo*, the film they collaborated on while Simpson was still at Paramount. According to one story, the movie was sold with what would thereafter be known as the definitive, the unsurpassable, high concept pitch. An agent simply held up a large glossy photograph of John Travolta and said to a studio executive, "American gigolo."

The message that Eisner drove home to his young associates at Paramount in the seventies was that if you controlled the concept you could control the movie. If the movie was driven by a concept, the studio could sell it on the basis of the concept. If the movie wasn't a star vehicle, the studio then wasn't in the thrall of a star and his or her entourage. It could negotiate with the star from a position of strength. If the concept was good enough, the movie didn't necessarily even need a star. Paramount under Eisner had a string of phenomenal hits with no stars. *Saturday Night Fever* was one. *Flashdance* was another. In fact, by the time *Flashdance* was in preproduction, casting at Paramount had become, on some movies, almost a casual afterthought.

"That movie was fun to do," Eisner recalled one morning

in his office on the Burbank lot of the Walt Disney Company, where he was now chairman. "Over the years, I had had the chairman of Gulf and Western, Charlie Bluhdorn, say to me, 'You guys don't know what a pretty girl looks like.' The girl in *Saturday Night Fever* wasn't a knockout. 'Every movie you make has these dogs in it,' he would say. 'You have no taste. What are you guys, all gay?' I would say, 'Charlie, we're doing okay.'"

When it came time to cast *Flashdance*, Eisner thought he would placate Bluhdorn. "I had never done this to a movie, but I went down the hall and into every office of every male I thought would be interested. I put everybody in a room and I said, 'Okay, this has nothing to do with acting. This has nothing to do with singing. This has nothing to do with dancing. We're going to have a vote here.' I won't use the colloquial words that I used as to the kind of—

" 'Which of these young women would you rather know carnally?'

"That was the concept of it, yes. All these women came up on the screen and we picked two, both of whom ended up in the movie."

Paul Schrader, the director of *American Gigolo*, once complained that people in Hollywood never remembered what happened. All they remembered, he said, was the stories they told about what happened. But in Hollywood, what really happened was not important. All that mattered was which story got repeated and accepted. Once a movie was released, the battle for control over making it ended and the battle to take credit or place blame for it began. If a successful movie was a star vehicle featuring Clint Eastwood or Sylvester Stallone, the credit went to the star. If it was an imaginative and well-staged film like *E.T.: The Extra Terrestrial* or *The Last Emperor*, the credit went to the director. In a high concept movie, much of the credit went to the person who thought up the concept.

Beverly Hills Cop was just such a movie. Its ultimate success was due to Eddie Murphy. Murphy, however, was not a star at the time he was cast. The movie was not conceived as a vehicle for Murphy and, in fact, Sylvester Stallone was originally supposed to play the lead. *Beverly Hills Cop* emerged from one of the story meetings Eisner held, and ever since it was released Eisner and Simpson have been engaged in a loud but amicable dispute over which of them should get credit for originating the idea.

"*Beverly Hills Cop* grew out of the fact that I was particularly interested in the Beverly Hills police force," Eisner said. "I had become *obsessed* with the Beverly Hills police force the first couple of months that I was at Paramount. I'd never had a nice car in my life. But you can't get into a restaurant here without a nice car. You can't get into a studio without one. They think if you have a nice car you somehow qualify. So as part of my deal with Paramount I finally got a nice car and I was driving down Santa Monica Boulevard with the radio on, probably going seventy miles per hour. I got stopped. I was put up against the car by the meanest people I've ever seen. They put me in the back of the police car. They had computers in there that were incredible. It was like an IBM center. So the next day I came into the office and I said to Don, 'We've got to find a way to depict the Beverly Hills police force. There is something about a force that has the most advanced technology ever but nobody to use it against. There is something about a police force that cannot live in the place it protects. The only way to depict the Beverly Hills police force as it is is to bring somebody from the outside into it.' We wrote eight scripts and nobody got it. We tried it four or five different ways. The script would come in and I'd say, 'This isn't the Beverly Hills police force. What's interesting is they can't afford to live there.' "

"*Beverly Hills Cop* is a movie I invented whole cloth in one of Michael's creative meetings," Simpson claimed. "I re-member the experience vividly. It was a function of me having an experience in the street in Beverly Hills, feeling like an outsider. It also involved a director, Floyd Mutrix." Mutrix, Simpson went on to say, was working on a script about gangs. He had arranged through the Los Angeles Police Department to meet three former gang members who had become government witnesses. Mutrix invited Simpson to have dinner with him and the three gang members and their police escorts at a restaurant on La Cienega Boulevard.

"You had three cops from the L.A. gang beat, all about six-two, two-forty," Simpson recalled. "They wore T-shirts, Levi's, with a gun in the back of their belt, a gun in their ankle, and maybe a coat on. We ended up in the bathroom. There was barely room for all of us. I was by far the smallest guy. There were two huge cops with their guns loaded and two gang guys doing blow over in the corner. It was so fascinating, this world of cops and robbers in the same room, all of them by the way now theoretically on the same side and telling tales of murder and mayhem on the streets.

"What flashed in my mind the next morning, not that night because I was sufficiently inebriated, was: What would happen if one of these cops was transferred from East L.A., where he grew up, to Beverly Hills? I wanted to see a bull—and that's what this one in particular named Buddo was—in that china shop. This guy was half Hispanic, with tattoos. From the gang detail. A real rough-hewn dude. He goes to the pristine, crystal-palace environment of Beverly Hills and he kicks fucking ass.

"That was my idea, which, by the way, was registered with the Writers Guild. I brought it to the meeting with Eisner. He said, 'Great idea.' "

A writer was hired, but the screenplay didn't work. Another writer was brought in. Drafts were produced.

Years passed. The pages flew from the calendar. By 1983 Simpson and Bruckheimer had formed their partnership. They had one surprising success, *Flashdance*, behind them and one flop, *Thief of Hearts*, and they were looking for their next project. Simpson said that he brought up the Beverly Hills cop idea with Eisner again.

"Eisner got excited for the following reason: He had had an experience at his new house in Beverly Hills—we even have memos to this effect. Michael tells stories, we keep records. Michael's wife had seen somebody on their roof. Can you imagine, a burglar on Michael Eisner's roof? They pushed the panic button. The police show up in thirty seconds and they surround the house. Michael's like Howdy Doody in Wonderland, going, 'Wooooo woooo.' He thinks it's great. He comes to work the next day and he tells us about the high tech stuff they had, the guns. And he said, 'Isn't it interesting that all these cops work in Beverly Hills but they can't live here.'

"I said, 'Michael that's interesting but it has nothing to do with my idea.' He said, 'Oh, you'll make it work.' He then wrote us a three-page memo—which we still have—which has nothing to do with anything, but which is where he thinks he had something to do with the movie."

"He wanted to do *Raiders of the Lost Ark* in Beverly Hills," Bruckheimer added.*

THE APPETITE

Don Simpson is one of the great Hollywood characters of the eighties. He grew up in Anchorage, Alaska. His father,

*The descent of the Beverly Hills police force on the house of a rich resident does not take place in *Beverly Hills Cop*. It does take place (twice in fact) in *Down and Out in Beverly Hills*, a movie Eisner brought out at Disney, after leaving Paramount. When this was pointed out to Simpson, he said, "Michael finally got his movie made."

a Southern Baptist, earned a living as a bush pilot and caribou hunting guide. Simpson's wild streak had become fully evident by the time he was a teenager. He liked to pull stunts that drew attention to himself, such as driving his Volkswagen down the hall of his high school. He also ran up a record of four felony convictions by the time he was sixteen. But Simpson was smart, too. He graduated Phi Beta Kappa from the University of Oregon. After working for a while in the marketing department of Warner Bros., he wrote the script for *Cannonball 500* and, after that movie came out, landed a job as a production assistant at Paramount. He caught the attention of Michael Eisner, who promoted him rapidly. By the age of thirty-two, he had become head of production.

Simpson was always controversial. People like Eisner enjoyed him for what they saw as his energy and imagination and forceful personality. He was hated by others, many of them individuals he had had to reject in one fashion or another when he was a studio executive, for what they saw as his irresponsible embellishments, insatiable ego, and loud, grasping manner.

The most extraordinary thing about Simpson was that he was an inexhaustible, virtually unstoppable talker. The man loved speech. The ability to talk articulately, talk spontaneously, and if necessary to talk endlessly was his greatest gift. The *Los Angeles Times* once referred to him as "the Fastest Gums in the West." Simpson rather enjoyed this reputation. "I'll talk forever," he told me at one point. Not only did Simpson talk, he could make the most unbelievable remarks, and his inability to keep quiet had occasionally landed him in trouble. "Paramount has only two assets: Eddie Murphy and Simpson and Bruckheimer," he once told a reporter. It was not the sort of remark to please Frank Mancuso, who replaced Diller in 1984 as the chairman of Paramount Pictures. But Simpson would just as easily incriminate himself.

"People say I will fuck anything that walks, and it's true. I will," he once told a second reporter.

Often people didn't quite know what to make of these remarks, just as they didn't quite know what to make of Simpson himself. Despite the braggadocio, the tales of womanizing and club-crawling, Simpson, a bachelor, spent a lot of his time at home by himself, reading. "When you peel it all away, Don is a closet intellectual," Eisner said. "You got to get away from all the jumping up on tables and saying, 'I am the greatest'—that Muhammed Ali kind of thing. When he worked for me, he was a regular person. He wore a suit and tie when it was called for. The reason Don is successful is he understands. Don is well read. Don knows good from bad. Of the people I've worked with, as far as executives are concerned, he is one of the two or three best."

And anyway, most times Simpson didn't really mean what he was saying. Not in the conventional sense. There was usually a subtext. Sometimes he was just having fun. For example, when discussing his own life, he felt free, as most every writer has, to take the opportunity to practice his craft and punch up the script, editing here, elaborating there, all to make a better story. A good story will, for example, establish a character's motivation early on, and Simpson obeyed this rule. In recounting when and how he decided to pursue the Hollywood dream, he claimed in the seventies that as a child, he saw *The Greatest Show on Earth* and became so upset when Jimmy Stewart, the clown, turned out to be a murderer that he refused to go to school for two days. "I told my mother to tell the theater owner to change the ending," he said at the time. "And from that point on, I knew I wanted to involve myself with that magical form."

But the references to clowns and circuses and Jimmy Stewart and a young child's disenchantment must later have struck Simpson as a trifle square. He subsequently rewrote the script, as it were, and came up with a more hip variation of the myth. The critical moment still occurred at age ten, only in this version the decision to seek out that "magical form" came after seeing a double bill of *Rebel Without a Cause* and *Blackboard Jungle* in the Empress Theater in downtown Anchorage. "Ever since then I wanted to be in the movies," he said in 1988.

Simpson called these shifting details "embellishments." Ultimately, the specifics, the details, weren't important. This was Hollywood, where the story line mattered more than the facts, where publicists manufactured fake biographies, where Reagan had developed his attitude toward facts as easily manipulated irrelevancies. Simpson was totally candid about the role of invention in his life. "Somebody once said, 'You seem to have an aptitude for storytelling,' " Simpson recalled one evening, his feet back up on his desk. "I think they meant 'lying.' I call it 'storytelling.' I love hearing stories and telling stories. I always have."

Simpson's overwhelming personal style was also to some extent calculated. It demonstrated that he had the drive, the fire, the ferocity required to get a movie made in Hollywood. It was so bewilderingly difficult to get a movie made in Hollywood that people can be in the business for years before any project they've been involved with actually reaches theaters. The screenwriters for *Top Gun* had never before had a movie produced, though they had written seven well-received scripts. Because of the exorbitant costs of making movies, as Mark Litwak pointed out in his book *Reel Power*, the individuals who run the studios and thus control the financing of pictures will seize on any excuse to avoid producing a film that doesn't have a major star or is not a sequel with a built-in audience. A project can die because of executive turnover or because a star insists on rewriting the script or because a director goes over budget or because any one of a hundred thousand other things happens.

To overcome such seemingly endless obstacles—to get a

movie made—you had to have what Simpson and Bruckheimer called "the passion for the project." This did not
simply mean that you found the script worthwhile and
believed it would profit the studio and possibly enrich the
human race. To have "the passion for the project" meant
that you would do *anything* to get that movie made. You
would manipulate actors, bully writers, grovel before agents.
You would lie, cheat, steal—whatever was necessary to get
the movie made. To be capable of this and, more important,
to demonstrate to all concerned that you were capable of it,
simultaneously required a raging ego and a shamelessness
that suggested Hollywood had long ago burned away the
last vestiges of dignity, pride, or any other inhibition that
might prevent you from doing whatever it took to get the
movie made.

Paramount in particular encouraged this kind of mentality. Under Eisner and Diller the studio worked on a system
of advocacy. The movies that got made were the ones that
had the strongest advocates among the staff—those who
talked the loudest, argued the longest, fought the hardest
for their pictures. Boundless faith in oneself was an occupa-
tional requirement. Braggadocio simply showed you had
the appetite. "I love that Don takes credit for everything,"
Eisner once said when asked about his protege, "because it
just shows what a great appetite he has."

Simpson and Bruckheimer, in fact, have structured their
movies around characters with that same appetite. And in
the eighties those have been the sorts of characters with
whom audiences identified. Simpson and Bruckheimer identified with them, too. "We are attracted to characters who
were forging ahead because we felt we were living out their
moments on the screen in our lives in minor key ways,"
Simpson said. "If you're smart, and you know what you
can do, and you kick ass doing it, you're going to move
ahead."

THE NEW MALE SEX SYMBOL

Jerry Bruckheimer was born in Detroit. His father was a salesman in a clothing store. His father's clients included the occasional mobster in need of a jacket specially cut to accommodate his gun. Unlike Simpson, Bruckheimer was a nice quiet boy. He displayed an early interest in photography, and an aptitude for it as well, winning a prize for his work from Kodak (which, of course, would later feature him in an ad). After graduating from the University of Arizona, where he studied math and psychology, Bruckheimer found a job in the mailroom of a small Detroit advertising agency. Soon, however, he became an art director/producer and then moved to New York, where he worked for BBDO.

Bruckheimer broke into the movie industry through Dick Richards, a young television commercial director he knew who made Bruckheimer an associate producer on his film *Culpepper Cattle Company*. Bruckheimer did well and became a full producer on Richards' next film, *Farewell, My Lovely*. Neither of these were expensive films by the standards of the time. Bruckheimer and Simpson had met and become good friends and roommates by that time. For his third film, Bruckheimer was brought to Paramount by Simpson, who was then the studio's head of production, to produce *American Gigolo*. The movie was to star John Travolta, then among the biggest stars in Hollywood, and to cost around $12 million. It was a big step forward for Bruckheimer.

The screenplay had been written by Paul Schrader, who would also direct. Before production began, Bruckheimer, Schrader, and Travolta flew to Italy to look at the clothes of a young new designer named Giorgio Armani. Bruckheimer and Schrader were tired of jeans. They had decided it was time to put men back in suits, and they had called John

Fairchild, the publisher of *Women's Wear Daily*, who had recommended Armani.

Armani's clothes looked terrific and they agreed to feature them in the film. Bruckheimer was ecstatic. Here he was with a hot young director and a hotter young star preparing to shoot a picture that was as close to a guaranteed success as you could find. On their return from Italy the three stopped in Paris, and as if to underscore just how wonderful the entire experience was, they all were swept up in a mob of euphoric French girls when Travolta was recognized at Orly Airport. Bruckheimer had dreamed about this kind of thing when he was growing up in Detroit.

But shortly after they returned to Los Angeles Bruckheimer and Schrader were called into Michael Eisner's office at Paramount. Eisner explained that Travolta had dropped out of the picture. Travolta's girlfriend had died of cancer not long before, and someone in his family was sick, and he decided that he was not emotionally prepared to do another movie at the moment. Paramount would need to replace Travolta with a star of similar wattage, Eisner said, because the studio had already received sizeable cash advances from theaters in expectation of a Travolta picture. The only actor that Eisner felt could take Travolta's place in terms of box-office draw was Christopher Reeve, who had become what is known as a bankable star with *Superman*.

All the euphoria Bruckheimer had experienced on that flight back from Paris vanished. He knew that getting Reeve would be difficult, probably impossible. The Reeve ploy seemed to be Eisner's way of killing the project without acknowledging it. Because studio executives are forced to say no so frequently, and because each time they do so they risk making an enemy, they try to avoid direct rejection. In support of this theory, Schrader and Bruckheimer later heard that the studio had asked the auditor on the picture what the "abandon costs" would be. Paramount had invested less than $1 million in the movie and would probably be willing to write that amount off rather than throw good money after bad.

Bruckheimer and Schrader needed to settle on a course of action. That night they decided they wanted Richard Gere to play the lead. He had the surly, sexy quality the role demanded. It would be easier to get Gere than Reeve, who was too wholesome to play a gigolo anyway. And Gere would be a lot cheaper than either Travolta or Reeve. That would undoubtedly appeal to Eisner. Gere at the time was a relatively unknown actor. He had played a psychopath in *Looking for Mr. Goodbar* and had a role in *Days of Heaven*, which was yet to be released. Paramount's executives were not enthusiastic about Gere, but they agreed to finance the picture if Schrader and Bruckheimer could cut its budget from $12 million to $5 million. That seemed impossible, and it appeared that once again Eisner was saying no without acknowledging it. "That was his way of saying, 'You can't make the movie,' of saying, 'Richard Gere is not right,' but it was a very political and a very smart way of saying it," Bruckheimer explained.

Bruckheimer and Schrader did make the necessary cuts, however, and Paramount reluctantly produced the financing. In retrospect, the decision to replace Travolta with Gere had special implications for the eighties. And the fact that Gere and Travolta crossed paths, in a sense, in *American Gigolo* carried its own special ironies. Not only was Travolta on his way down (though that was not clear at the time) and Gere on his way up, but the basic makeup of the American Male Sex Symbol was undergoing a transformation from the type of character embodied by Travolta to the type that Gere represented.

The alienation of the late sixties found expression cinematically in the rise of the anti-hero, a character type initially sketched out in the fifties by James Dean and

Marlon Brando. The male anti-hero came to the fore in the sixties in the romantic outlaws of the sort portrayed by Warren Beatty in *Bonnie and Clyde* and Robert Redford and Paul Newman in *Butch Cassidy and the Sundance Kid*. But these actors lacked the hostility to capture the violent emotions then welling up in the country, and they gave way to the angry and at times even psychotic anti-hero characters played by actors like Al Pacino, Robert DeNiro, and Jack Nicholson who established themselves in movies such as *Mean Streets*, *Taxi Driver*, *Serpico*, *The Godfather*, *Chinatown*, and *One Flew Over the Cuckoo's Nest*, among others. The characters these actors played arrived at existential positions of disillusionment and cynicism in movies that explored a corrupt society.

John Travolta, the leading male sex symbol of the late seventies, was a soulful ethnic in the tradition of Pacino and DeNiro. In *Saturday Night Fever*, *Grease*, and *Urban Cowboy*, his three big hits, he played moody, troubled working class youths. Less hostile than the characters for which Pacino and DeNiro became known, Travolta's characters were yearning if inarticulate young men beset with questions about their identities and goals. They captured the ambivalence, the uncertainties of the period.

But the anti-heroes of the seventies gave way to a new character type, and a new male sex symbol, in the eighties. Michael Douglas, Harrison Ford, Mel Gibson, and Tom Cruise became known by playing characters who were not, by and large, alienated. They were not motivated by hostility or angst but by the desire to succeed. They did not question themselves or society. They knew what they wanted. (Even Richard Gere, for all his angry style, was more an outsider who wanted to belong in society rather than an outsider who had rejected society.) Instead of being overwhelmed by corruption and pessimism they eradicated it. They were not outlaws but lawmen or adventurers. They

were not tortured souls. They were glamour boys. They
rescued women and killed bad guys. They had fun. They
were also unabashedly packaged as sex objects. Movies like
American Gigolo, *Risky Business*, and *Top Gun* all emphasized
the male rather than the female body, featuring extended
scenes of young men either nude or clad in underwear
or towels.

Sylvester Stallone, in his *Rocky* sequels and his *Rambo*
series, was, of course, the extreme cartoonish version of the
eighties male sex symbol. Like Travolta, Stallone had first
come to be known as a soulful ethnic proletarian with his
movies *The Lords of Flatbush* and *Rocky*. After a few expensive flops, Stallone made the transition into the eighties by
devoting himself solely to repetitions of the theme of triumph
he struck in *Rocky*, which recapitulated the struggling-
underdog formula pictures such as *Golden Boy* and *Body and
Soul* produced during the heyday of the studios. And it was
Stallone, interestingly enough, who tried to transform Travolta
into an eighties sex symbol. He beefed up Travolta's mus-
cles and had the hair stripped from Travolta's body in
preparation for his role as a dancer in the 1983 film *Staying
Alive*, which Stallone directed. The movie, supposedly a
sequel to *Saturday Night Fever*, was a critical disaster, though
it eventually made money. After another critical disaster,
the 1985 movie *Perfect*, John Travolta disappeared for four
years.

Tom Cruise most thoroughly embodied the eighties male
sex symbol. He had his first starring role in the comedy
Risky Business, which was released in 1983. By then the
values of the decade were taking clear shape. Cruise plays
a high school senior who damages his parents' car, then, to
make the money to repair it, uses the techniques he has
learned in a class on entrepreneurship and opens a
whorehouse. The business is immensely profitable. On top
of that, Cruise's entrepreneurial success so impresses an

interviewer from Princeton, where he has applied, that the university accepts him.

The psychic distance young Americans traveled between the sixties and the eighties is perfectly captured in the contrast between *Risky Business* and *The Graduate*. In that 1967 coming-of-age film, the character played by Dustin Hoffman rejects all the values his counterpart in *Risky Business* so unquestioningly pursues. In *The Graduate*, money and sex are temptations that involve moral compromises. In *Risky Business* they are the characters' only goals. *Risky Business* elaborates the eighties theme of prostitution-as-business first introduced in *American Gigolo* and, at the same time, provides an astonishingly symmetric inversion of the sixties theme of business-as-prostitution that is an undercurrent in *The Graduate*.

Tom Cruise was not the first of the new male sex symbols, however. It was Richard Gere who initially established the form. But it was not Gere's role in *American Gigolo* that conferred this status on him. Gere came to be seen as the embodiment of glamour and adventure, as a figure representing the romance of professionalism and the emotion of triumph, a figure *Newsweek* would put on its cover under the headline "The Male Idols: Hollywood's New Sex Symbols," with *An Officer and a Gentleman*. It was *An Officer and a Gentleman*, which apparently drew on the Hollywood formula pictures of the thirties and forties such as *Crash Dive* with Tyrone Power, that crystallized the eighties male sex symbol into a figure of virility, determination, and valor. And it was a movie that Don Simpson brought out while at Paramount.*

---

*Gere's career peaked with *An Officer and a Gentleman*. It would falter and never fully recover from *Breathless*, the movie that provided *Newsweek* with the opportunity to put him on the cover. Among the many factors that contributed to the failure of *Breathless*, an expensive remake of Jean-Luc Godard's *nouvelle vague* film, was its sixties plot and theme. Gere played a cop-killer on the run—an anti-social anti-hero—at a time when the country was increasingly unsympathetic to outlaws.

THE MILITARY-MOVIE-MAKING ALLIANCE

Simpson was the head of production at Paramount when he first learned of the existence of the script for *An Officer and a Gentleman*. Before he had even read the script he became excited by a description he was given of the plot, which concerned a young man's attempts to shake off the crippling influence of his degenerate father and make something of himself by graduating from the Navy's officer candidate school. Simpson was also excited by the title. "I loved it," he told me. "I was absolutely drawn to the images that the title evoked, and to the story line that was presented to me—the character with a tattoo coming into a privileged environment on a motorcycle with a father who was a fucking sleazebag. The kid wanted more than anything to be that which he was told he had no right being. To me that's magical and a metaphor for my life. I said, 'Shoot, who doesn't relate to that.'"

The Navy didn't. The war movies Hollywood had produced during the late seventies were for the most part stridently anti-military. *Coming Home* (about a crippled Vietnam veteran), *The Deer Hunter* (about an American soldier in Vietnam who commits suicide), and *Apocalypse Now* (about a renegade American officer) were all released between 1978 and 1980. They portrayed American soldiers as either sadistic and deranged or tortured or as pathetic victims of a misguided policy. The military was upset by the tone of these pictures, and the mistrust of Hollywood it had developed since the sixties deepened.

Douglas Day Stewart's original script for *An Officer and a Gentleman* called for shooting the movie on an actual naval base. But after reviewing the script, the Navy categorically rejected the project. The script's depiction of naval personnel was unflattering and inaccurate, it said, and would hurt the Navy's image. Its sailors, the Navy said, did not curse or whoremonger. "I said, 'Oh really, since when?' " Simpson recalled.

The producers were forced to rent a deserted Army medical facility in a port town in the Pacific Northwest. Scenes in the screenplay involving planes and ships had to be cut. But the Navy's reservations were completely unfounded. *An Officer and a Gentleman*, released in 1982, was an unabashed glorification of military virtues. It celebrated willpower and discipline. It restored the uniform to glamour. The movie also sold $202 million worth of tickets worldwide, and became one of the most successful pictures of the year. It even touched off a surge of interest in enlistment in the Navy, which became somewhat embarrassed by its public repudiation of the movie.

An Officer and a Gentleman was a turning point in many respects for Don Simpson as well. In addition to being a film he identified with personally, it was the most successful film he had been associated with since becoming Paramount's head of production. "It was the film I was the most passionate about in my career up to that date," he said. Although he claimed to be unaware of it, he seemed to use *An Officer and a Gentleman* as the prototype for subsequent films, appropriating not only the sharp focus on goals and desire for accomplishment that motivates the characters, but also their enthusiasm for their work. In fact, many of the plot elements of *An Officer and a Gentleman* reappear in the movies Simpson and Bruckheimer made later. The sympathetic underdog status of the main character is the central feature of *Flashdance*, *Beverly Hills Cop*, and *Top Gun*; the washout and suicide of the main character's best friend would be echoed in *Flashdance* (the main character's best friend despairs when she loses an ice skating competition), in *Top Gun* (the main character's sidekick dies in a flying accident), and less obviously in *Beverly Hills Cop* (the main character's childhood friend is murdered). Even the troubled relationship that the main character in *An Officer and a Gentleman* has with his father, which is responsible for his attitude problems and also drives him forward, reappears in a paler version in *Top Gun.*

As a practical experience, overseeing production of *An Officer and a Gentleman* convinced Simpson he could make this kind of movie himself. He had been more deeply involved with the film than is customary for a head of production. He had supervised script revisions, casting, and set design, and was frequently on the set during shooting. "I did a number of things I wasn't supposed to do as an executive in order to ride herd on the movie," he explained. "This was where I started to get in trouble with management. Eisner would yell and scream at me, saying, 'I don't want you producing movies, I want you running production.' I hated running production. It was being an executive, being a businessman, which is the most boring thing in the world to me. When you're an executive you make decisions, not movies; you make deals, not movies. I was not interested in learning how to package, nor was I interested in learning how to get the best of somebody in a deal. I wanted to make movies."

After *An Officer and a Gentleman* was released, Simpson, at the urging of Bruckheimer, stepped down from his studio job to co-produce *Flashdance* with his friend. Their second movie, *Thief of Hearts*, did little to advance their reputations, but with the release of *Beverly Hills Cop* "the boys" became very, very hot.

After deciding to make *Top Gun* and to set most of the action at the Navy's flight school at Miramar, one of their first steps was to visit the Pentagon to secure the Navy's approval.

170 ♦ CIRCUS OF AMBITION

Simpson and Bruckheimer wore suits and ties for the occasion, but they were still bearded and scruffy in a fashionable way, and they felt distinctly out of place. After walking down endless corridors, they were ushered into a room filled with naval officers in crisp white suits.

An Officer and a Gentleman, together with *The Right Stuff*, had softened the military's suspicion of Hollywood. Interestingly enough, the officer who had rejected *An Officer and a Gentleman* was not present at the meeting—a fact that those who were present subtly brought to Simpson and Bruckheimer's attention. But still, the senior officer in the room told Simpson and Bruckheimer that he wished to know exactly what their movie would be about and how it would reflect on the Navy. And Simpson and Bruckheimer hadn't yet gotten that far with the plot. They had no script or treatment at that point. All they had was the concept.

Simpson, who loved to make up stories, to pitch on his feet, started to invent. He said he and Bruckheimer wanted to make a movie about a character who was the embodiment of the commitment to excellence, who was the embodiment of the Navy today. He and Bruckheimer had recently met some young naval officers, he said, and they were impressed by their intelligence and by their balls. The officers in the room got a chuckle out of that. Simpson began spinning a tale of a young pilot who loved flying and who wanted to get into the Top Gun school at Miramar. But because he was something of a hot dog, his superiors lacked faith in him and he couldn't gain admission. To get into the school, and to succeed once he was there, he had to change his independent maverick style and become a team leader. He had to identify new goals. Simpson went on to say that he and Bruckheimer wanted to do a movie about warriors of the heart. It would have duty, danger, comradeship, heroism, self-sacrifice in the pursuit of noble goals.

Needless to say, the Navy loved it. After the pitch, the

senior officer introduced Simpson and Bruckheimer to a retired admiral. They had drinks, and the retired admiral began telling war stories from Vietnam. He had been based on a carrier, in command of the fighter pilots who escorted bombers on their missions over Vietnam. One of the pilots on each mission, he explained, was called a strike team leader. He had the most dangerous job because he drew most of the flak from the enemy's anti-aircraft guns. After six missions a strike team leader was always rotated out of the position because statistically his chances of surviving diminished at an alarming rate. A critical mission was announced, however, and the admiral chose to keep one particular strike team leader in his slot for a seventh flight.

"The admiral loved this kid; he was the best of the fighters," Simpson recalled. "He thinks he's going to be rotated out and he looks at the board and there's his name on mission number seven. And he says to this admiral, 'Sir, why me?' and the admiral said, 'Son, you're the best I've got,' and the pilot said, *'Yes, sir!'* " Here Simpson saluted briskly. "I tell you, it brings tears to my eyes even now."

Stories like this crystallized for Simpson all the myth-making elements of the Romance of Professionalism. And this story in particular, he explained, had a special twist, one of those twists that spins the plot out of the audience's hands just as they think they've got it firmly in their grasp. The strike team leader survived the seventh mission, but shortly thereafter he submitted his resignation after he almost crashed during one of the most perilous exercises in the book—a night carrier landing. The pilot explained to the admiral that since that seventh mission his wife had had a child, and though he had never seen the child, his sense of responsibility toward the baby had awakened him to his own mortality and undermined his confidence as a pilot. To Simpson, it was a fantastic plot reversal, an apparent step backward that, by revealing hitherto unsuspected emotion-

al depth, turns out to be a step forward. It opened up
tremendous opportunities for establishing character, and
Simpson and Bruckheimer subsequently incorporated it into
the opening scene of *Top Gun.*

When the movie opened in Washington in 1985, a benefit
screening for retired naval aviators was held, followed by a
huge party that took place in an aircraft hangar. Admirals,
pilots, movie stars, producers, and journalists were all there.
The hangar was festooned with *Top Gun* posters and all sorts
of movie memorabilia. Just outside stood a sleek, silvery
F-14. The party was one big mutual love fest. With the
release of *Top Gun*, the reconciliation of Hollywood and the
Pentagon whose interests had overlapped so completely
during the heyday of the studios, was complete. The bearded producers in Armani tuxedos mingling over champagne
with naval officers in starched dress-whites proved that the
entertainment industry and the military establishment were
closer, more united, than they had been at any time since
the early sixties. By restoring the long-lost sex appeal of the
fighter pilot, by re-establishing the old mythic link between
martial prowess and sexual virility, Hollywood sold hundreds of millions of dollars worth of tickets while pumping
up public esteem for the military generally. Each bathed the
other in glamour. Heroic behavior had once again become
acceptable material for actors. That was only appropriate,
for, as every soldier knew, heroism was a form of acting.
Tom Cruise himself referred to the similarities when he
said, "A Top Gun instructor once told me there are only
four occupations worthy of a man: actor, rock star, jet
fighter pilot, or President of the United States."

6

JOHN GUTFREUND AND THE CULT OF RUTHLESSNESS

THE QUINTESSENTIAL TRADER

John Gutfreund and Malcolm Forbes had been friends for years, so when John married Susan Penn in 1981, Susan and Malcolm naturally became friends. John and Susan went ballooning with Malcolm in the south of France. They were among the envied group that spent the Fourth of July watching the fireworks from his yacht in New York Harbor. And when Malcolm was putting together his guest list for the little lunch he planned to throw for Danielle Mitterrand, wife of the French president, he, of course, thought of including Susan.

Now, Susan is a woman they all love to snicker at—all of those snobs and gossipmongers who lunch at New York society restuarants like Le Cirque and Montimer's. But they miss the point about the woman. Her excesses (the four varieties of caviar) and her frivolities (who can forget the spun-sugar apples?) and even her affectations (*"Bon soir, madame,"* she said when she was introduced to Nancy Reagan) are all just endearing expressions of her sense of adventure, her animal spirits, her—as Susan herself might put it—*joie de vivre.*

Because whatever Susan Gutfreund's flaws may be, she is never dull. And to her credit, they remind each other at Mortimer's, she tries to charm and often succeeds. Gianni Agnelli, for example, is absolutely infatuated with her. So Malcolm penciled her in for the Mitterrand lunch.

And Susan did not disappoint. There they all were— Estée Lauder and the Dillons and the Zilkhas and John Fairchild and Susan Newhouse and even, for some strange reason, Donald Trump—sitting at the table in Malcolm's private office in the bowels of the *Forbes* magazine building on lower Fifth Avenue. This was a couple of weeks after Black Monday, and Malcolm's guests were all feeling a little shaky. But no one had more reason to be distressed than Susan Gutfreund.

After all, Salomon Brothers, the investment bank John Gutfreund ran, had suffered heavy trading losses during the crash. Internally, it was still divided by the fact that Gutfreund had sold 12 percent of Salomon's stock to Warren Buffet at a handsome discount to prevent Ronald Perelman from seizing control of the company. So outraged were many of the executives that, even as the guests were being served their cream of pumpkin soup, rumors coursed through Wall Street that a dissident faction at the investment bank was going to force John Gutfreund out as chairman and chief executive officer of Salomon, Inc.

Still, everyone at Malcolm's lunch aspired to gaiety. Susan in particular was in terrific form. An attractive woman with dark blond hair and a wide red mouth, she regaled the table with tales of the difficulties inherent in keeping the staffs of two houses running smoothly (she and John divide their time, as they say, between New York and Paris). At one point, as if in search of just the right insouciant epigram with which to sum up these amusing tribulations, Susan exclaimed, "It's so expensive to be rich!"

Susan Gutfreund didn't come up with this line herself. It was, as a matter of fact, embroidered on a cushion right there in Malcolm's office. Nonetheless, as Susan observed— and this is what made her invaluable—it was true! It *is* so expensive to be rich—for the Gutfreunds, anyway. By one estimate, they spent more than $20 million decorating their Fifth Avenue duplex (though that's not much, considering that a single ordinary Impressionist painting can cost a quarter of that sum). In 1987, while the French decorator Henri Samuel was doing their mansion in Paris, Susan and her young son, John Peter, and John Peter's nanny stayed for months on end in a lavish suite at the Ritz that cost more than $2,000 a day. "My wife has spent all of my money," John Gutfreund confided to a friend in the fall of 1987, "but it is worth it."

Gutfreund was joking, of course, at least about Susan running through his entire fortune. It was true that he was unfazed by her spending frenzies. He not only tolerated them, he relished them. "She's enriched my life," he told a reporter in 1984. She had, in other words, made him appreciate the finer things, like ormulu and Roederer Cristal. One friend of the couple remarked that Gutfreund seemed to think of himself as the frog and of his wife as the princess who had, with her kiss, transformed him.

John Gutfreund was short and pudgy, with thick lips that gave him a vaguely sensual look, and delicate rimmed glasses that added a thoughtful air. Overall, his appearance was rather bland. But people in the securities industry described John Gutfreund as a "brutal trader" whose rule at Salomon was "a reign of terror." They referred to him as a "Wall Street tycoon" or "an investment banking prince" or "the king of Salomon." Those who knew him socially, however, said that at the time of his marriage to Susan,

Gutfreund didn't see himself as much more than a bond-trading grind. From the perspective of his friends, he *was* transformed, just like the frog in the fairy tale, by the beautiful and impetuous woman who became his second wife.

Certainly, Gutfreund's marriage to Susan coincided with his emergence as one of the most powerful and visible men on Wall Street. The couple's social progress, the ascent of the Gutfreund star, occurred alongside Salomon's rise as the country's preeminent investment bank. The installation of his wife in their Fifth Avenue apartment—arguably one of the most sumptuous homes in the entire city—proceeded apace with his plans to move Salomon into what would have been a true cathedral to finance, the mammoth skyscraper that the developer Mortimer Zuckerman was to build at Columbus Circle in partnership with the firm.

Then, too, as the wheel turned, Susan Gutfreund's social setbacks resembled in a most uncanny way John Gutfreund's troubles at Salomon, which began in 1987. If in a sense Susan Gutfreund unleashed her husband's ego, if she enabled him to appreciate more in life than the yield on convertible debentures, she may also be said to have instilled in him a dangerous sense of grandeur, and to have diverted a crucial fraction of his attention from the running of his firm.

John Gutfreund was the very embodiment of Wall Street power in the eighties. It was a period in which vast amounts of money were made without producing anything tangible, and Gutfreund became rich by presiding over a firm that grew in large part by underwriting the massive federal deficit. But the wealth Gutfreund accumulated—he earned $3.2 million in 1986—was a mere trifle compared to the hundreds of millions of dollars amassed by his acquaintances Saul Steinberg and Henry Kravis. Gutfreund's reputation derived instead from the power he wielded as the imperial ruler of the investment bank that was, for much of the eighties, the country's largest and most profitable. In a cover story in 1985, *Business Week* called the firm "The King of Wall Street."

In addition to wealth and power, the eighties have celebrated ruthlessness. And no one has been as ruthless—and as proud of his ruthlessness—as John Gutfreund. At a dinner party the month after the stock market crashed in 1987 he was boasting of how tough he had shown himself to be in firing close to eight hundred Salomon employees. The capacity for political intrigue is a sort of corollary to ruthlessness, and it, too, was elevated to a virtue in the eighties. In this as well, Gutfreund surpassed his peers. Throughout the eighties, his Machiavellian maneuvering made Salomon resemble nothing so much as a Florentine palace during the rule of the Medicis. During his drive for power he betrayed the father figure who made him chairman, plotted against the man with whom he shared power and who had made him rich, and banished the brilliant protege he had hinted might one day replace him.

The era also celebrated excess. Many of the merchant princes of the age left older wives for young women, but none of them was as shamelessly frivolous as Susan Gutfreund. She set new standards for ostentatious consumption at the parties she threw at River House, the prestigious co-operative apartment building overlooking the East River, where the Gutfreunds lived in the early eighties.

At times in the eighties, the ruthlessness, the political intrigue, the ostentatious excess seemed to merge into an attitude of sneering and contempt. It was revealed on Wall Street with the insider trading cases against people like Ivan Boesky, who held securities laws in utter contempt. It was revealed in government with the municipal corruption scandals in New York, the conflict of interest case involving Edwin Meese, and the perjury case of Michael Deaver, to name only two of the most visible examples in the Reagan

Administration. It was, in a less important but just as instructive fashion, revealed in the standards of behavior of the new social order. John Gutfreund personified this as well. One such characteristic display occurred at a party the month before the crash. Turning to his dinner companion, a woman from an old New York family of diminished fortune, he said, so the story goes, "Well, you've got the name, but you don't have the money."

But John Gutfreund was misunderstood, his wife felt. Despite her refining touches, Gutfreund remained a trader. Traders are gruff. They have to be. Have you ever been to the trading floor at Salomon Brothers? It's a barnyard, for God's sake, filled with literally hundreds of bellowing, shrieking, cursing traders. The only way to be heard above that awful racket is to yell. The only way to get someone's attention is to insult him. You can't take it personally. "He's a *trader*," Susan Gutfreund once said to a magazine editor Gutfreund had insulted, as if that excused everything.

Iron lungs and a thick hide are certainly prerequisites for trading. It also requires muscle and daring, quick reflexes rather than contemplative intellect. Traders profit by moving faster than anyone else, not by thinking more profoundly. That explains why traders, all trying to get out in front of each other, often stampede herdlike through the market. If it's up, they buy; if it's down, they sell. "You can't fight the tape," traders say. "The trend is your friend," they say, "and the trend is the last order on the tape."

John Gutfreund was perhaps the quintessential trader. Everything about him seemed an expression of the trading mentality. But then Gutfreund was very much a creature of Salomon Brothers, the only place he had ever worked. And Salomon was the quintessential trading company.

On weekday mornings, Gutfreund got up around six A.M. He was chauffeured down to the financial district and arrived by seven at the Salomon offices at One New York Plaza, directly across from the South Ferry at the southern-most tip of Manhattan. He ate breakfast in the elegant partners' dining room and by seven-thirty was at his desk, where a box of Temple Hall Jamaican cigars and fresh copies of the *Washington Post*, the *New York Times*, the *Wall Street Journal*, the *International Herald Tribune*, and the *Financial Times* awaited him.

This desk was not in Gutfreund's office. He did have an office—decorated by Susan, with black matte walls and Art Deco fixtures—but he used it for more ceremonial occasions. Gutfreund's real desk, a large fan-shaped affair, was at the front of Salomon's mammoth—indeed, unique—trading floor. One hundred feet long and two stories high, it had double-height windows overlooking New York Harbor, a wrap-around visitors balcony, and a massive electronic quote board that displayed the current trading price of approximately two hundred stocks. It was a soaring, even awesome space with the vaulting scale of a cruciform church nave and was referred to at Salomon simply but reverently as The Room.

The location of Gutfreund's desk made him all-seeing and instantly accessible. It put him deep in the information flow—the ruckus of ringing telephones and hollering traders—in a business where privacy was considered dangerous because getting information earlier than anyone else, even seconds earlier, could mean the difference between a profit and a loss on a trade. Gutfreund presided over a true financial empire. Salomon was not the most prestigious investment bank; that honor went to Morgan Stanley or Goldman Sachs. Nor was it the most well known; Merrill Lynch, with 11,000 employees and its huge retail network, was. Salomon rarely traded stocks on a retail level—that is, for private investors. It worked almost entirely for large institutions.

But while it was not the most prestigous nor the best known, Salomon was the most powerful investment bank on Wall Street. Before the crash, it had a capital base of $3.6 billion, which was at the time the largest of any American securities firm. It used that vast capital pool to shoulder aside other firms and buy up massive amounts of stocks and bonds that it resold as quickly as possible for very narrow profit margins. Some $20 billion worth of securities changed hands every day in The Room, more than were traded on the floor of the New York Stock Exchange.

Salomon had a corporate finance and a mergers and acquisitions department, but the heart of the company had always been its trading operation. At other major firms, traders were viewed as a lower order, sometimes as little more than brute savages. But at Salomon the traders ruled. That in turn accounted for the firm's ferocious corporate culture. "You've got to be in shape," Gutfreund told a group of trainees in the early eighties. "And I don't mean jogging and all that crap. You've got to be ready to bite the ass off a bear every morning."

When John H. Gutfreund was born in 1929, the family name was pronounced "Goot-froind." His father, Manuel, who was known as "Buddy," owned a fleet of trucks that delivered meat to restaurants and clubs around New York. Buddy had started his career in the butchery business but got out when he came to believe that it was controlled by organized crime. The family—Gutfreund had a sister—lived in a comfortable but ordinary home in Scarsdale, a suburban town north of New York. Gutfreund attended Lawrenceville prep school in New Jersey, where he became interested in theater and literature. One of his favorite books at that time was Ayn Rand's *The Fountainhead*. Rejected by Harvard, he enrolled at Oberlin and graduated in 1951 with a bachelor's degree in English, having also earned a letter in soccer.

After Oberlin he joined the Army and served for two years as a member of the military police in Korea.

In 1953 Gutfreund was discharged from the Army an returned to New York. He had been thinking of a career teaching literature, but he needed a job in the meantime. The Gutfreund family belonged to the Century Country Club in Purchase, New York, which at the time was a social center for the German Jewish establishment. Among its members were the Salomon family of the then very minor Wall Street bond house Salomon Brothers & Hutzler. William Salomon, a partner at the firm, frequently played golf with Buddy Gutfreund. An interview at Salomon Brothers & Hutzler was arranged for John Gutfreund, who was then twenty-four, and he joined the firm as a $45-a-week trainee in the statistical department.

This was nothing to become excited about. Wall Street in the fifties was not a popular place to work. For most graduates of Oberlin, teaching literature was much more interesting. Wall Street, for most of the people who worked there, simply provided them with a job.

After a couple of months, Gutfreund became a clerk in the municipal bond department. He proved adept at the business and soon was made a trader. Abandoning the idea of teaching, he rose swiftly up the ranks and became a partner in the firm at the age of thirty-four. He displayed drive and ambition in this climb, but he also developed the affable salesman's manner that he would in later life turn on and off at will. "John had a good sense of humor," said Robert Towbin, an investment banker who had known Gutfreund since the fifties. "He could kid around. He didn't take things that seriously. You could go to the Salomon trading floor and ask him what the hell was going on and he would laugh and say, 'I don't know.'"

In the late fifties, Gutfreund married Joyce Low, the daughter of Teddy Low, a prominent partner at the firm of

Bear, Stearns & Company. Joyce Gutfreund was a plain woman of conservative principles. The Gutfreunds moved into a nicely decorated apartment at 61st Street and Lexington Avenue. Gutfreund put in long hours at the office, working late most nights, while Joyce devoted herself to the three sons that were born to them. On weekends the family would go out to Westchester, and the children would help clean their grandfather's delivery trucks. It was a sober, responsible existence.

Through the sixties and seventies, Salomon Brothers (the "& Hutzler" was dropped in 1970) was run by Billy Salomon. He was the son of Percy Salomon, one of the three brothers who helped found the firm in 1910. Under Billy Salomon, it evolved from a relatively small house that specialized in making markets in government bonds to a major force in all trading activities. It also became known for a singular aggressiveness. Though many on Wall Street initially found this quite shocking, the deregulation of the securities business in the seventies made it ever more rewarding. No one at Salomon was more aggressive than John Gutfreund.

"In the mid-seventies a client of mine in the Midwest told me Salomon was calling on him," recalled Robert Towbin, who at the time was part of the small firm of Unterberg & Towbin. "I called John, who was a friend. I said, 'It's an old client. It's my account. It's not a big deal for you, so I'd appreciate it if you'd lay off.' He said, 'Nobody has any accounts anymore.' I was shocked. But he was right, the world had changed. The days of the old boy network were gone. You had to fight in the jungle. He was an old friend, but he taught me that this was business."

William Simon, who ran Salomon's municipal bond department at the time, was the one member of the firm as driven and aggressive as Salomon. But Simon left Salomon to become Richard Nixon's Energy Czar, and in his absence Gutfreund was recognized as the inevitable successor to

Billy Salomon. To many people at the firm, Gutfreund seemed larger than life. He had the capacity for intense concentration. He could grasp problems and make judgments immediately. He could provide fresh perspective. When Billy Salomon stepped down in 1978, it was to the surprise of no one that he appointed Gutfreund chairman.

Gutfreund's professional success had its cost, however. Just at the time he was beginning to be talked about as the successor to Billy Salomon, his wife, Joyce, left him. "We weren't having fun anymore," a friend recalled Joyce saying at the time. Gutfreund moved into a bachelor apartment at 900 Park Avenue. He led a lonely existence, and though he became chairman of Salomon Brothers, he did not seem happy. When an old friend ran into him at a party in Paris in 1978, he said, "Do you remember me? I'm John Gutfreund." He seemed forlorn to the friend.

One of Gutfreund's Wall Street colleagues was a man named Huey Lowenstein, an investment banker at Donaldson, Lufkin & Jenrette. In the fall of 1980, Lowenstein's wife, Sandy, told her husband that a friend of hers named Susan Penn had once bumped into Gutfreund, had become intrigued, and was interested in being introduced to him. Lowenstein arranged for the four of them to have dinner.

RUTHLESS WOMEN

The men making money in New York in the eighties attracted a special breed of woman. These women tended to be in their thirties and had origins that were obscure or exotic but rarely patrician. They were attractive, but many of them, like Sid Bass' second wife, Mercedes Kellogg, were known less for their beauty than for their personalities, their liveliness and daring. They had lived fast and wild in their earlier years, and they usually had one marriage or more already behind them, often to some dubious but rakish character.

Gayfryd Johnson, for example, had grown up in Vancouver, where her mother worked as a clerk for the telephone company. When she was twenty she married a South African, then divorced him and married a New Orleans oil tycoon. He committed suicide after being convicted of tax evasion. But by then Gayfryd had left him and met financier Saul Steinberg at a dinner party arranged by art dealer Richard Feigen. Gayfryd and Saul were married a year later.

Patricia Rose provided a fascinating illustration of this phenomenon. Her father was English, her mother half Iraqi. She grew up in Baghdad, where she learned to belly-dance. As a teenager she moved to London and was discovered by Russell Gay, the publisher of the British skin magazine *Knave*, while belly-dancing in a club. A tall, statuesque woman, Patricia posed nude for *Knave* and wrote a lubricious sexual advice column. Patricia and Russell were married and divorced, and in 1981 Patricia married John Kluge. They reportedly met after he was introduced to her at a party. Kluge, who ran the Metromedia Corporation, was more than thirty years older than Patricia and a head shorter, but by 1987 he was worth an estimated $3.5 billion.

There were many of these women in New York in the eighties. Their racy pasts encouraged the crowd at Mortimer's and Le Cirque to joke about what was imagined to be their highly developed sexual technique. A frequently repeated remark about one such woman was that "she could suck the chrome off a trailer hitch."

Most of these women had no regrets about their pasts. Patricia Kluge once told a reporter that her *Knave* years were "very amusing." But those days were behind most of them by the time they reached New York. They had already had their kicks, and when they arrived in the city they were focused on one goal with an unswerving intensity that was, in its own way, ruthless.

The lives of those who managed either to marry fortunes or to make fortunes in the eighties underwent a magic transformation. So much money was being made so quickly, and people's situations were altered so radically and in such a short period of time, that everything had an unreal quality. It all seemed like a dream, and as a result the behavior of many people seemed dreamy and unreal. Of no one was this more true than Susan Gutfreund, who seemed to think that her actual identity was just as plastic and malleable as her circumstances, and that she could mold it any way she saw fit. She felt free to reinvent herself, to create the past she *ought* to have had. It was the ease with which she and others did this that contributed to the make-believe, fantastic quality of much of the eighties. "New York is wonderful," she once said to a reporter. "It's like living in a fairy tale."

Susan, for example, liked to tell people she had been born in a fifteenth-century house in England with a thatched roof. In fact, she was born in 1946 in Chicago. Her father was Louis Kaposta, a man of Hungarian descent who served for thirty years in the Air Force. Her mother, named America, was of Spanish descent. She had five brothers. Because of Louis Kaposta's occupation, the family moved frequently around the United States and Europe. Susan attended three different high schools during her senior year. She studied at Louisiana State University, then transferred to the Sorbonne when her father was assigned to Paris. While there she was hired as a stewardess by Pan American.

In the late sixties, while working on a Pan Am flight, she met John Roby Penn, the heir to a Texas real estate fortune. They were married in 1970 and set up house in Fort Worth, Penn's hometown, though they also spent much of their time in Fort Lauderdale and sailing in the Caribbean.

The marriage lasted only five years (Penn went on to marry and divorce several other women). Susan Penn (she kept her husband's name) remained in Fort Worth. "Everyone was surprised she stayed around attending all the parties," said Cissy Stewart, a former society reporter for the *Fort Worth Telegram*. "But she was out to catch a rich husband." No prospects materialized, however, and she headed north.

John Gutfreund and Susan Penn were quite taken with each other that first evening the Lowensteins brought them together. They became an item very quickly, and very quickly after that Susan moved into Gutfreund's Park Avenue apartment. One acquaintance attended a Christmas party the Gutfreunds gave at 900 Park back then. Christmas trees would always have a peculiar resonance in the Gutfreund legend, and that year the couple had a big silver tree in the living room. Under the tree the guest saw piles of empty blue Tiffany boxes. Nothing but empty blue Tiffany boxes.

THE CULT OF RUTHLESSNESS

By the early eighties the cult of ruthlessness was spreading throughout the country. With the cavalier destruction of the Bonwit Teller bas reliefs, Donald Trump provided the most visible early manifestation of this trend. But as the money fever swept through New York's real estate market, other developers committed far more astonishing acts. A year later, Paul and Seymour Milstein, real estate developers who had bought the legendary Biltmore Hotel, announced plans to strip it to its skeleton. This prompted New York's Landmarks Preservation Commission to begin studying the possibility of designating as landmarks parts of the hotel's interior, including the celebrated Palm Court and its famous gilded clock.

According to Kent Barwick, the director of the Municipal Arts Society, representatives of the Milsteins asked him which parts of the interior might be designated landmarks. Barwick, thinking the Milsteins wanted to *avoid* damaging those areas while proceeding with their renovation of the exterior, naively supplied the information. Shortly thereafter, on a Friday night in August, the Milsteins suddenly closed the Biltmore, relocated guests, and brought in dozens of workers who began tearing out its interior with jackhammers and crowbars. By the time the Municipal Arts Society found out about the activity and procured a restraining order from the courts, the interior had been destroyed, sparing the Milsteins the cost of preserving it. A few years later, they donated a fraction of the fortune they had made to charity.

The Milsteins' behavior seemed to be exceeded in early 1985 by yet another developer, Harry Macklowe. In January 1985 a contractor working for Macklowe began destroying two small resident hotels on West 44th Street, without securing permits or even turning off the water and gas lines, in order to beat a moratorium on the demolition of such buildings that was about to go into effect. "What can I say?" Macklowe asked in explanation. "It was sloppy." In the end, no one really held it against him. He gave $2 million for housing for the homeless, and three years later was putting up a forty-three-story hotel on the site.

The behavior of developers such as Trump, the Milsteins, and Macklowe provided only the most dramatic illustrations of the cult of ruthlessness. But it permeated corporate America. Like the fascination with investment banking and the veneration of wealth, it stemmed from the industrial decline and management stagnation of the seventies. American executives told each other that their companies had to become "lean and mean" (to use the popular cliché) in order to ward off foreign competition. Jack Welch, the head of General Electric, was one of the most outspoken on the subject. He once explained to a group of *Business Week* editors that he not only closed unproductive plants, he closed plants while they were still productive because he knew they would eventually become unproductive. Welch came to be known as "Neutron Jack" because of his propensity for eliminating vast numbers of employees. Companies he acquired, it was said, looked as if they had been hit by a neutron bomb: The buildings were still standing but the people were all gone.

The cult of ruthlessness also evolved because of the more active role Wall Street began to play in corporate life. The rise of the raiders and arbitrageurs who set takeovers in motion brought about a transfer of power within corporate America. The management class that had come of age in the fifties had for decades run companies with relatively negligible interference from shareholders. But in the eighties shareholders asserted themselves and began to exercise more active control over the companies they owned. Executives who could not produce ever greater returns for investors faced the possibility of a hostile takeover and their own ouster. Managers and executives suddenly found themselves being removed by shareholders as casually as they were used to laying off wage laborers.

These activist shareholders were, for the most part, the institutional investors at pension funds and money management firms, the brokerages and investment banks. They, of course, ran their own operations in a ferocious and pitiless manner. It was a necessity. On Wall Street, small errors, little oversights, minor omissions translated immediately into dollar losses as the market churned ahead. Faced with such pressure, executives on Wall Street drove their employees relentlessly. The weak, the imcompetent, were constantly being weeded out. One day in the mid-eighties, I was in the office of a senior partner at a mid-sized firm. In the midst of explaining his department's business, the partner pressed his intercom and asked his assistant to bring in a presentation. A moment later, a young woman appeared at the door.

"Where's the presentation?" the partner asked.

"Can I talk to you for a minute?" The woman appeared tentative.

"What is it?"

"Well...." The woman hesitated. She wanted a private discussion.

"What *is* it?"

"The presentation's being worked on."

"Just bring it here."

"But we're working on it."

"I said get me the presentation."

"But it's not all in place."

"I said get me the presentation."

As the woman closed the door behind her, the partner turned to me and said, "There's a little girl on her way out."

As the influence of such Wall Street executives spread during the eighties, managers at all manner of companies across the country adopted the hard, unforgiving example they set. And as the cult of ruthlessness grew, ever more brutal behavior came to be seen as acceptable, even virtuous. That cult found its embodiment in John Gutfreund. No one on Wall Street was considered more ruthless than Gutfreund, in whom the trait served as a constant guiding principle of behavior.

Around the time Gutfreund met Susan, his personality began to change, according to old household staff members. Wall Street noticed, too. If nothing else, his ruthlessness reached entirely new depths. When Billy Salomon named Gutfreund to succeed him in 1978, Salomon Brothers was a privately held partnership. Billy Salomon had built the firm into a major force on Wall Street. The task had been his life's work. When he appointed Gutfreund chairman, he thought he was turning it over to a man he could trust.

Four years later, however, without even informing Billy Salomon, much less asking his advice, Gutfreund sold the firm for $554 million to Phibro, the giant commodities trading company.

Gutfreund explained that the firm needed capital to remain competitive and that he did not inform Billy Salomon because his mentor would have opposed and possibly derailed the sale. Though that may well be true, Billy Salomon felt humiliated by his treatment at the hands of his protege. This humiliation was heightened by the fact that he did not even receive a premium for his shares during the sale. Though Salomon had worked at the firm for forty years, though he was the one who had turned it into an institution worth half a billion dollars, he received less than $1 million from the sale. He was so enraged he thought of suing.

Gutfreund, on the other hand, received cash and securities for his shares worth around $32 million. And if Billy Salomon felt cheated, according to professionals on Wall Street, he had no one to blame but himself. It was Billy's fault, observers of the firm told each other. He had put a group of tough, hard-nosed, greedy people in charge. And, quite simply, they were not going to do anything more for him, or for anyone, than they had to do.

Having cut off his mentor, Gutfreund turned against David Tendler, the head of Phibro. Under the terms of the merger, Tendler, an overweight commodities broker, was to be chief executive of Phibro-Salomon, but Gutfreund was to run Salomon Brothers as an independent division. Tendler had believed Phibro would dominate Salomon, but the recession of the early eighties smothered the commodities market while the stock rally that began in 1982 sent profits soaring in trading and investment banking.

Time and time again in the eighties, Wall Street firms were wracked with upheaval when one division's executives decided that the power they wielded was not commensurate with the revenues they were producing. And so it was with Phibro-Salomon. Because his division's earnings were growing, Gutfreund persuaded Phibro-Salomon's board that he ought to be named "co–chief executive." Threatened, Tendler secretly began planning to buy back the commodities operation. The deal collapsed when word of it leaked out, and Gutfreund seized on this act of disloyalty to demand that Tendler be demoted and that he, Gutfreund, be allowed to run Phibro-Salomon singlehandedly.

When the board agreed, Gutfreund set about destroying virtually every trace of the commodities company he had conquered. He sold off a variety of its operations, cut its personnel by two-thirds, and then in 1985, in the final act of obliteration, purged all public memory of Phibro by changing the company's name to Salomon, Inc. It was the corporate equivalent of executing the inhabitants and then razing the town.

ROLE MODELS FOR
THE NOUVEAUX RICHES

One day in November 1986, John Fairchild, the publisher of *W* and *Women's Wear Daily*, was having lunch at Le Cirque. Fairchild was arguably the single most influential person in the entire New York fashion industry. His pronouncements carried such impact that he did more than merely chronicle the ebb and flow of fashion. By highlighting specific designers and specific aspects of their collections in his publications, he came close to actually determining fashion. He exerted a similar influence on high society. His publications scrutinized the social parade as thoroughly as they did the fashion business, promoting and demeaning as they saw fit the men and women who participated in its often ridiculous rituals. Fairchild's publications were read by everyone from Nancy Reagan to Averell Harriman. They had such power to confer social certification that it was said certain people decided to attend certain parties only after ascertaining that a *W* photographer would be on hand.

As Fairchild sat in Le Cirque that November afternoon, it dawned on him that all these people arranged in twos and threes and fours at the tables and banquettes, all these people nibbling and sipping and waving, kissing and table-hopping and flickering their eyes around that peach-colored haven of privilege and glitter—all these people, Fairchild suddenly realized, comprised a new social constellation.

A little more than a month later, *W* ran a cover story entitled "Nouvelle Society." Those included as members of Nouvelle Society couldn't decide if they should be flattered or infuriated. So accurate and timely was the phrase that it eventually entered the vocabulary of the chic and became a reference point for the eighties. The tongue-in-cheek article listed all sorts of characteristics of Nouvelle Society, such as "Believes that when you want something, Money is no Object"; "Rides in Mercedes with phones and drivers"; "Shops at Sotheby's for the ancestral portraits which are now the rage"; "Lusts for big rocks, big furs, big deals"; "Believes in marriage—NS thinks nothing of doing it two or three times"; "Doesn't believe a woman has to be shorter than her man." Heading this list, however, serving as its defining note, was this attribute: "Regards Susan and John Gutfreund as its Role Models. The Gutfreunds represent the best of Old Nouvelle Society."

One characteristic Fairchild might have included was Velocity of Arrival. The members of Nouvelle Society had by and large made vast fortunes at an astonishing rate. As the eighties accelerated, arrivistes appeared in such large numbers and at such a rapid pace that social ascension took on a manic, overwrought quality. The upper-class social circuit came to resemble the entertainment industry. Previously unknown couples could blaze to the top of the charts one season and fade the next. Nothing revealed how hysterically accelerated social ascension had become than the fact that although John and Susan Gutfreund had been married less than five years by the time the *W* article came out, it referred to them as "Old Nouvelle Society." It was as if they were yesterday's stars: distinguished, respected, fondly remembered but somehow past their peak, no longer hot.

Susan Gutfreund had worked hard to become a Nouvelle Society role model. Those five years had been busy ones. She and Gutfreund had married in 1982, around the same time Gutfreund had sold Salomon Brothers to Phibro. For a while they lived in the Olympic Tower, but the building's lack of cachet (it was popular among foreigners like Arab arms dealer Adnan Khashoggi) made it utterly unsuitable as a permanent residence. So in 1982 the Gutfreunds paid $1.1 million for the duplex on the twenty-fourth and twenty-fifth floors of River House—the very apartment that the building's co-op board had refused to sell to Gloria Vanderbilt.

River House was one of the most grand residential buildings in New York. Its other residents included Henry and Nancy Kissinger and Arthur Levitt, the chairman of the American Stock Exchange. Overlooking the East River, it was built in 1931 in the Art Deco manner. Its landscaped grounds were surrounded by a high wall and an iron gate. Its two plinths stood on a wide base. At the twenty-third floor it narrowed into a single tower that rose for another four stories. The Gutfreund duplex formed the lower half of the tower.

Susan Gutfreund hired the modern architects Richard Weinstein and Wayne Berg, who gutted the four-bedroom apartment. By turning more than half—*half*—of the second floor into a vast bathroom and dressing room, with seemingly endless closets, they converted the duplex into a one-bedroom apartment. It was stark and contemporary, with glass bricks and a large spiraling staircase. To the surprise of the architects, Susan Gutfreund then hired society decorators Chessy Raymer and Mica Ertegun, who filled the apartment with eighteenth-century French furniture. The entire effect was dramatic enough to warrant a feature in *House & Garden*. But one hires society decorators not simply for their taste and skill, formidable though those assuredly are. One also hires society decorators for the entrée to society they provide. Chessy Rayner, the wife of Condé Nast editor William Rayner, and Mica Ertegun, the wife of Atlantic Records co-founder Ahmet Ertegun, introduced Susan to their friends.

Susan had by then adopted a frightfully grand style of living. She had a small refrigerator in her bathroom just to chill perfume. She was, according to an acquaintance, one of the first women to start using a limousine for even the most idle, the most casual, the most informal trips, such as the one to her exercise lessons. And she began to throw luncheons and dinners that set new standards for extravagance. Her reputation as a society hostess was sealed when she and her husband snared the honor of giving the sixtieth birthday party for Henry Kissinger. Everyone from Stavros Niarchos to the then Mrs. Johnny Carson attended, but what created the real stir were the green apples of spun sugar that the chef prepared for dessert, using a technique he had learned from the glassblowers of Murano.

But just as the Gutfreunds' social ascendancy was gaining momentum, with Susan doing all the right things, they were turned into creatures of ridicule by the most trivial contretemps. Between the Gutfreunds' duplex and the roof of River House was the penthouse apartment owned by Robert Postel, a former city councilman, and his wife, Joan, an opera singer. The Gutfreunds, who at any given time had up to six servants in their apartment (which was now only a one-bedroom), felt crowded. It occurred to them that if they were to buy the Postels' penthouse and combine it with theirs, the resulting quadraplex would be truly magnificent. According to one couple at River House, the Gutfreunds did offer to buy the Postels out. In any event, those aspirations may have contributed to the ill will that quickly developed between the two couples when they began to squabble over the use of the landing they shared. The Postels claimed that the Gutfreunds, among many transgressions, liked to pretend *theirs* was the penthouse apartment. The two apartments shared a landing, and when the Gutfreunds gave dinner parties, the Postels said, they would turn off the light above the entrance to the Postels' apartment and place large bouquets of orchids in front of it to disguise its existence. This incensed Joan Postel. She was, she claimed, allergic to the flowers, which inflamed her vocal chords and made singing difficult.

The hostility reached full boil during the Christmas of 1982, when Susan ordered an enormous twenty-two-foot-high Douglas fir (four times as tall as her husband) to stand in their two-story-high salon. The tree was so big it could not fit into the River House elevator. So Susan received permission from the co-op board to winch the thing up with a hoist to be attached to the roof.

She did not, however, secure the approval of her upstairs neighbors, whose terrace occupied most of the roof. When Joan Postel found out that laborers were passing through her rooms to hoist the tree from the roof, she became enraged and actually got into a scuffle with the workmen, who, she maintained, had invaded her apartment. Because of their behavior, she was subsequently to argue, she had suffered "severe and extraordinary emotional and psychological distress and damages."

The following Christmas, learning that the Gutfreunds again intended to hoist a massive Douglas fir into their apartment, the Postels filed suit seeking a temporary restraining order. They also demanded $35.5 million in damages on the grounds that the Gutfreunds and their helpers had, among other things, harassed their son and entered their apartment without permission, once surprising Robert Postel in his underwear. The court issued a temporary restraining order, and consequently the Gutfreunds were forced to hoist the tree in from their own balcony. This imposition, they complained, "necessitated the removal of almost all of our living room furniture as well as a window and door to get the tree inside, and resulted in approximately seven moving men being in our apartment for most of the day."

CORPORATE HUBRIS

Though the suit came to naught, the whole affair was made much fun of in gossip columns and other places. But the Gutfreunds could probably withstand the tittering their dispute with the Postels provoked because Salomon was doing so famously. Its bond and equities trading departments had flourished in the bull market, and by the end of 1985 it had amassed a securities portfolio worth $38 billion—quadruple that of its nearest competitor. That December *Business Week* wrote its effusive cover story describing Salomon as "The King of the Street."

The firm had also pioneered all sorts of new speculative products, and the individuals who created them became multimillionaires in a very short time. The best example was Lewis Ranieri, who started out as a clerk on the night shift in Salomon's mailroom and less than twenty years later was a vice-chairman of the firm. What Ranieri had done was create, almost singlehandedly and in less than five years, the $350-billion-a-year market in mortgage-backed securities. By 1984 his department was generating 40 percent of Salomon's revenues, and Ranieri was one of three people on a "short list" Gutfreund had compiled of possible successors.

Success stories like that of Ranieri, who was earning $3 million a year, made Salomon the most exciting firm for the young MBAs who were by then flooding Wall Street. Salomon, they told each other, was doing everything and going everywhere. It had the best people in the industry, the people who displayed the most energy and the most imagination. Salomon was quite simply the place to be. Salomon was where the action was.

The ruthlessness among investment bankers in the eighties, and the rewards they received for their ruthlessness, bred an arrogance or hubris that had an almost Sophoclean dimension. Nowhere was this more intense and palpable than at Salomon. Proclaiming the "globalization of finance," the firm opened offices in Zurich and Frankfurt and Sydney. It expanded its London office, where the staff was to number six hundred by the end of 1986. To accommodate this staff, Salomon acquired a huge space in Victoria Plaza, right above Victoria Station and just a few blocks from Buckingham Palace, and spent a reported £25 million building a trading floor even more majestic than the one in New York.

But plans were afoot for the New York offices as well. Salomon was expanding so rapidly, adding almost 1,000 people a year, that people were squeezed in on top of each other. Only partners had offices to themselves. Extra desks, hundreds of new computer terminals, and miles of cable had been added to The Room. To alleviate the overcrowding, Salomon joined forces with developer Mortimer Zuckerman. Together they would build a new world headquarters for Salomon at Columbus Circle on the southwest corner of Central Park.

Consisting of two soaring towers, one of which would rise to 68 stories, it was a truly pharaonic project. It would also be exorbitantly expensive, requiring Salomon to pay more than 50 percent above the market rate to lease space in the building. But the firm was making so much money—it had a net income of $557 million in 1985, the year City Hall approved the project—that no one there cared about the expense. Salomon's name would be linked with one of the most imposing and visible structures ever raised in New York. It would construct a trading room three stories high, which, together with the building's assertive twin towers, would be a fitting projection of Salomon's power. Susan Gutfreund was so taken with architect Moshe Safdie's drawings that she rushed out and had the building engraved on a set of Swedish crystal vases.

The firm was ruthless in its dealings with those who opposed the mammoth project, which would cast huge shadows over Central Park. Salomon's officials completely refused to negotiate with civic organizations. During the debate over whether the building could be scaled down to create fewer environmental problems, Salomon president Thomas Strauss declared that he wanted it made "perfectly clear" that if the building were shortened or redesigned for "whatever reason," Salomon would abandon the project.

To many on Wall Street, Gutfreund's sudden preoccupation with grandiose architectural schemes was a harbinger of disaster. For thirty years the man had devoted himself exclusively to trading bonds. Now he had become taken up with the creation of a huge monument that would embody his and Salomon's power culture. In retrospect, it seemed he was no longer focusing on business. He had, they said on Wall Street, taken his eye off the ball.

THE OBVIOUSLY FUTILE

People will always gossip about the beautiful young wives that rich men marry, particularly if the women have extravagant tastes. That is due in part to envy and in part to the irresistible targets the beautiful young wives provide when they violate Veblen's "instinct for workmanship," which, as discussed in Chapter 4, causes people to be disgusted by anything blatantly wasteful, impractical, or useless.

To avoid or at least to minimize criticism, it was therefore essential that the wife of a new tycoon find some ostensibly productive way of occupying her time. The preferable solution was to align herself with a charitable organization. Since no one, of course, received compensation for charity work, it served as an instance of what Veblen called "conspicuous leisure." "Under a mandatory code of decency," he wrote in *The Theory of the Leisure Class*, "the time and effort of the members of...a [well-to-do] household are required to be ostensibly all spent in a performance of conspicuous leisure, in the way of calls, drives, clubs, sewing-circles, sports, charity organizations, and other like social functions. Those persons whose time and energy are employed in these matters privately avow that all these observances, as well as the incidental attention to dress and other conspicuous consumption, are very irksome but altogether unavoidable."

Then too, Veblen noted, by keeping the wife busy, it gave the husband the excuse to hire large numbers of servants to run the house, since "the chief use of servants is the evidence they afford of the master's ability to pay."

But some of the wives of the new tycoons also engaged in what Veblen might have called "conspicuous labor." Carolyne Roehm, the wife of the LBO king Henry Kravis, ran her own fashion company, not because she needed the money, naturally, but because she wanted, as she once said, "to become the master of my life and be able to do it all." Similarly, Ivana Trump managed some of the properties owned by her husband, Donald. She, too, claimed that much of what she did was irksome but altogether unavoidable. "I want to be with my husband and children," Ivana Trump once said to journalist Jesse Kornbluth, pretending to complain about the fact that because she operated one of her husband's casinos, she had to spend so much time in Atlantic City. And that was on top of her endless social obligations, she lamented. "We used to go out two nights a week. Now it's every night. Either Donald gets an award or a friend does. And they come to ours so we go to theirs— that's how it's done. But it's hard."

The "work" of women like Ivana Trump and Carolyne Roehm could be seen as a mockery of real labor, of the monotonous, repetitive work performed by the masses to earn a living—just as the "poverty socials" of the nineteenth century could be seen as a mockery of the genuinely impoverished. As evidence for the argument that such conspicuous labor was really pretend, grownup play, Ivana Trump did not even receive a salary. Or rather, her husband paid her a dollar a year and announced that, as compensation, he would buy her all the dresses she wanted. But, of course, the purpose of Ivana Trump's "job" was not to earn money. The purpose was to avoid violating the instinct for workmanship.

A secondary and overlapping purpose was to remain frantically busy. Members of the postwar generation, of which many of the new society women were a part, had been led to believe, in keeping with the teachings of Benjamin Spock, that they were special and unique, loved and desired, in demand. As adults they continued to require the same assurances. Conspicuous labor demonstrated how needed one was. The bulky, appointment-laden Filofax, which women like socialite Blaine Trump—Donald's brother's wife—carried everywhere, acquired its function as a status symbol in the eighties because its calendar pages conspicuously demonstrated how busy, how *in demand* its owner was.

Susan Gutfreund, oddly enough, did not abide by the canons of conspicuous leisure or conspicuous labor. She was apparently aware of them (at least subliminally), since she talked at one point of starting her own import company. But nothing seemed to come of it. While she was on one of the visiting committees at the Metropolitan Museum, that was an honorary position without the responsibilities that came with being a trustee. She went to lots of parties—but not to be seen! "I don't want publicity," she once told a magazine editor. "You can tell that because whenever you see photographs of me in *W*, I'm not looking at the camera. *My* face is in profile."

She spent much of her time accumulating possessions. In 1984 the Gutfreunds, bidding farewell to the Postels and their allergies and hysterias, moved out of River House and into the six-bedroom duplex on Fifth Avenue that they had acquired for $6.5 million. So extensive was the renovation—Susan, of course, had the apartment gutted—that an elevator was built against the back wall of the building just to ferry detritus and laborers and material up and down. She had originally hired Chessy Rayner and Mica Ertegun to decorate, but before long she dropped them in favor of the French decorator Henri Samuel.

Samuel created an opulent eighteenth-century French atmosphere. The capacious double-height entrance hall had stone-paneled walls, one of Monet's water-lily paintings, and a massive central staircase. The library had leather-paneled walls, and there was a plant-filled room with eighteenth-century painted panels and trellises. Working with Henri was a thrill, but it was also downright exhausting.

It left little time for anything else. When one prominent member of the social circuit asked her to work on a major charity event, Susan Gutfreund replied that she too busy decorating her apartment.

Susan also studied French culture under the tutelage of Jayne Wrightsman. When Wrightsman met her husband, the late oil tycoon Charles Wrightsman, who was an ardent collector of eighteenth-century French antiques, she wisely decided to learn everything about French furniture herself. An important figure at the Metropolitan Museum, where she was a trustee and head of the acquisitions committee, she had developed an attachment to Susan, had become Susan's social mentor, as it were, and was passing on to Susan her encyclopedic knowledge of things French.

Susan, as a result, had become an unregenerate francophile. The rooms in her Fifth Avenue apartment were referred to as the *boudoir*, the *salon*, and so forth. The butler was instructed to answer the phone by saying, for example, "Madame is in the *fumoir*." The society crowd found this all pretty rich. "Everything has become '*Oui, oui*,'" they told each other at Mortimer's.

As such joking indicated, Susan Gutfreund found it hard to get respect. Her problem was that she had failed to validate herself through the usual channels. Studying French, decorating her apartment, and giving parties proved insufficient. She wasn't noticeably involved in charities. She didn't have a career. Though *W* considered her a role model for Nouvelle Society, she had violated the canon of conspicuous leisure, which required her to legitimize her ostentatious displays by pretending, from time to time, to do something useful. By neglecting this social ritual she incited, to use Veblen's phrase, "the odiousness and aesthetic impossibility of what is obviously futile."

HAMARTIA

When a company is crowned "The King of Wall Street" one can be certain that the wheel is about to turn. And it did for Salomon and John Gutfreund. While the investment bank continued to expand madly in 1986, increasing the size of its workforce by 1,000 in that year alone, its stock began to fall. From a high of 59 in April 1986, it dropped to 39 by the end of the year. Costs had skyrocketed while a suddenly quiet bond market cut into earnings. Also, corporations were increasingly demanding that their investment banks provide the sort of controversial junk bond financing and "bridge loans" that Salomon had traditionally avoided.

These problems created a venomous dispute that divided the firm. A group of younger partners, led by Tom Strauss and William Voute, a vice-chairman, argued strenuously that the firm ought to push into these risky new financial arenas. That was the current trend, and, as traders never tired of saying, the trend is your friend. Older partners such as the well-known economist Henry Kaufman resisted the move. Junk bonds, they felt, were creating a vast mountain of debt that would one day crush the economy.

With the firm's earnings falling, however, the junk bond proponents prevailed. Kaufman was so disgusted by the decision that he resigned from the executive committee. Only one opponent of the new financing methods remained on that committee: Lewis Ranieri, the rumpled head of mortgage-backed securities who was also Tom Strauss' main contender to succeed Gutfreund as chairman. As 1987 began Ranieri continued to oppose junk bonds and merchant banking, in which a firm invests its own money in a client's deal. This angered the advocates of change, but

Ranieri's power—his department contributed more than a third of the company's revenues—made him invulnerable.

In the spring Gutfreund began to realize he had seriously overexpanded in London. Thinking like a trader, Gutfreund had positioned himself to take advantage of a trend, but "globalization" had failed to produce the revenues he had expected. As a result, the huge and vainglorious London trading floor had become killingly expensive to run. So, again thinking like a trader, Gutfreund moved to cut his losses. Wholesale firings began in London.

The London debacle led Gutfreund to conclude that the entire firm, which had grown from 2,000 to 6,000 employees in five years, was as bloated as a pig's bladder. During the first half of 1987, the company's profits continued to plunge. To stem losses, Gutfreund instituted company-wide budgeting for the first time ever. The move gave Tom Strauss administrative authority over all the firm's independent dukedoms. Predictably, it was resisted by Lewis Ranieri. He had run his department with total autonomy. It had its own corporate finance people, its own trading desk, its own recruiting. Had Ranieri's operation actually been an independent investment bank, it would have been the fourth largest on Wall Street. Ranieri, whom his friends called "Lewi," was a forceful, volatile character. He kept a ceremonial sword in his office, and one day, overcome with emotion during a meeting, he raised the sword and then slammed it down on his desk. He was not a man his colleagues enjoyed opposing.

Given Ranieri's track record, firing him was almost unthinkable. But in the spring, lower interest rates played havoc with the mortgage-securities market, which was Ranieri's forte. And his weakened position provided Gutfreund and Strauss with an opportunity.

One morning in July, Gutfreund called Ranieri uptown to a meeting in the offices of Martin Lipton, the prominent securities lawyer who frequently advised Salomon. When Ranieri arrived, Gutfreund demanded his resignation. Ranieri was shocked by the move, all the more so because Gutfreund— his mentor—failed to specify to Ranieri's satisfaction why he wanted him out. According to one joke that circulated on Wall Street, Gutfreund told Ranieri he wasn't a team player, and Ranieri answered, "What team?"

"There are separatist movements at the firm," Gutfreund explained to a reporter after firing Ranieri. "I guess this restructuring came about because we decided that if we didn't force the firm together, it would grow further and further apart."

Wall Street was as shocked by the decision as Ranieri had been. Ranieri was the firm's most talented individual, its hottest star, the man responsible for producing upward of 40 percent of its revenues. He was what people on Wall Street referred to as a "moneymaker." Gutfreund had fired him in order to pave the way for the ascension of the somewhat colorless Tom Strauss, an administrator.

Around the time Ranieri was fired, the crowd at Mortimer's began to wonder where Susan Gutfreund was. Not long before this, they hadn't been able to open up the gossip columns in the *New York Post*, the *Daily News*, or *Women's Wear Daily* without seeing some mention of Susan Gutfreund, often accompanied by a photograph—though, it went without saying, rarely one in which she faced the camera. By the summer of 1987, however, she seemed to have dropped from sight.

Susan was spending much of her time in Paris with her two-year-old son, John Peter, and his nanny. The Gutfreunds had bought a beautiful eighteenth-century mansion on rue de Grenelle. The house was divided by a courtyard. The Gutfreunds lived on one side, the designer Givenchy on the other. Like the Gutfreunds' Fifth Avenue apartment, the Paris mansion was being decorated by Henri Samuel.

Susan found Paris so civilized. Then too, John Gutfreund was sensing that the problems at Salomon were more serious than people generally realized. There were signs that the magnificent feast on Wall Street was coming to an end. It was one thing for Susan Gutfreund to flaunt her wealth at balls and auctions when Salomon was at its peak. It was another thing altogether to do so when the company's profits had plunged. Susan was keeping a lower profile.

But she still managed to have fun. She was introduced to French society. She took up with the Paris *haute bourgeoisie*, like Victoire and Jacqueline de Ribes, and became particularly close to the Rothschilds. When she returned to Manhattan she enthused breathlessly about her new friends. But for those on Susan's social circuit, Paris and the Parisians whom she had discovered were all pretty familiar, even something of a yawn. Billy Norwich, the *Daily News* columnist, reported that at a gathering in Paris one "social arbiter" told Susan to "shut up" and stop talking about all of these people that "we've known for years."

To spend time with his wife and son, Gutfreund began taking the Concorde to Paris on the weekends. Perhaps those trips fatigued him. Perhaps he was distracted by the political infighting at the firm and the "strategic review" he had undertaken of all its operations. Whatever the case, he neglected another looming problem. Salomon had an unhappy shareholder.

When Phibro acquired Salomon Brothers, Minorco, an investment company controlled by Harry Oppenheimer, the South African magnate, was Phibro's largest shareholder. Oppenheimer had kept that stake during the Phibro-Salomon merger, and though he had sold off some of his holdings since then, he still owned 14 percent of Salomon, Inc.

In April Oppenheimer, through his investment banker Felix Rohatyn, of Lazard Frères, indicated to Gutfreund that he wanted to sell his block. The Oppenheimer fortune was founded on minerals. When Gutfreund had scaled back Phibro's commodities unit, the logic of Oppenheimer's stake in Salomon had diminished. As long as Salomon's stock was high it remained a smart investment. But Salomon's stock was falling.

Gutfreund, however, was unwilling to pay the price Oppenheimer wanted for the block. Nor did he find another friendly buyer. In August Salomon's stock fell even further when the company was caught with large inventories of bonds that suddenly declined in value. Oppenheimer's dissatisfaction increased, but Gutfreund still failed to act. Every investment banker on Wall Street, it seemed, knew that the Oppenheimer block was looking for a home. Salomon's largest shareholder wanted to get out of the stock—a situation fraught with danger—but to the amazement of investment bankers at other firms, Gutfreund did nothing about it. He failed to focus on the problem.

Unsurprisingly, Oppenheimer began looking for buyers elsewhere. In mid-September Rohatyn had lunch with Bruce Wasserstein, the legendary co-head of mergers and acquisitions at First Boston (who was discussed in Chapter 2), and he told him that the Oppenheimers wanted to sell their stake in Salomon. This was a little awkward, to say the least, for Rohatyn. After all, having inveighed long and loud against hostile takeovers, he now found himself in the ironic position of putting his friend John Gutfreund's company in play. But one must serve one's clients.

Wasserstein conveyed the information to Ronald Perelman, the corporate raider and chairman of Revlon. Perelman expressed an interest in acquiring the stock. The following Wednesday, Gutfreund was driven up to the Revlon offices in the GM Building, where he met with Perelman and Donald Drapkin, Revlon's vice-chairman. They offered to buy the Oppenheimer shares and asked Gutfreund for two seats on the board. It was an extremely disturbing development for Gutfreund. Perelman said he was attracted to Salomon by Gutfreund's talent and promised to support the firm's management if he bought the stock, but Gutfreund did not accept that. "Believing Mr. Perelman has no hostile intentions is like believing the tooth fairy exists," he said later.* Gutfreund was convinced Perelman wanted to seize control of Salomon. To prevent him from doing so would require the most Machiavellian cunning Gutfreund had ever shown.

The Jewish holiday Yom Kippur began that evening. Because Perelman was a devout Jew, the two sides scheduled their next meeting for the following Saturday night, when the holiday was over. While Perelman was at the synagogue, Gutfreund kept busy. He contacted Warren Buffet, the Nebraska investor who owned big blocks of stock in Capitol Cities/ABC and the Washington Post Company, and offered to sell him a large stake in Salomon at very generous terms. (A few weeks earlier, Buffet, who had known Gutfreund since the early seventies, had learned that the Oppenheimer block was up for sale, and he had telephoned Salomon's chairman to discuss the possibility of buying a major interest in the company.) They came to a tentative agreement.

After temple on Saturday, Gutfreund walked over to Perelman's East Side townhouse. At a brief meeting, he told him that Salomon's executives wouldn't support Perelman's investment. By the end of the weekend, Gutfreund had arranged to buy the Oppenheimer block for $38 a share—which amounted to a $6 premium over Salomon's stock price at the time—and then to sell what amounted to a 12 percent stake in Salomon to Buffet, for $700 million plus $63 million a year in essentially tax-free dividends.

---

*That remark had an intriguing echo of Susan's comment that living in New York was "like a fairy tale."

When Perelman learned about Salomon's deal with Buffet on Monday morning, he called Gutfreund and offered a higher price than the one Buffet was paying. Salomon, after an emergency board meeting, rejected that offer. Perelman then informed the firm that he was going to ask for government clearance to buy as much as 25 percent of Salomon on the open market. He was, in effect, declaring his intentions to attempt a hostile takeover.

A story began to circulate on Wall Street that Perelman wanted to acquire Salomon and then bring in Bruce Wasserstein to run it. In yet another of the internecine political battles that were always being waged inside investment banks, Wasserstein was fighting with First Boston's chief executive officer Peter Buchanan over control of their firm. But Wasserstein was getting nowhere and he wanted to leave First Boston to run his own company. According to the story, Wasserstein told Perelman that if he were in place at Salomon he could generate $100 million a year in investment banking fees—Salomon's traditional weak point. In addition, he could increase Salomon's earnings by another $100 million a year if he cut overhead. With those two circumstances, the firm would immediately have a strong rebound in pretax earnings. Perelman's allies, however, claimed that this story was concocted as part of a propaganda campaign by Gutfreund to discredit the Revlon chairman.

In any event, many of Salomon's insiders were said to be outraged by the deal Gutfreund struck with Buffet. They felt it was executed in secrecy and haste, and they feared that the dividend payments to Buffet could affect their yearly bonuses. Salomon shareholders were furious as well. Nineteen different lawsuits were filed by investors against the company's board of directors in the wake of the Buffet deal. Gutfreund had succeeded in retaining control of Salomon, but at some expense to his reputation.

* * *

Gutfreund had just been completing the strategic review of Salomon's operations when the skirmish with Perelman took place. The review showed that because of new tax laws and competition from commercial banks, profits had steadily eroded at Salomon's municipal bond and commercial paper departments. Both of them were now losing money. Gutfreund decided to do away with the two departments overnight. In a single blow, the move would eliminate 12 percent of the staff. Equally important, it would demonstrate decisiveness. But it, too, backfired.

First of all, news of the firings leaked out ahead of schedule. Employees reading the *New York Times* on Friday learned that their jobs would not be there on Monday. Those to be fired arrived at the firm that morning to find empty packing boxes by their desks. They were then called en masse into a conference room and informed over a speakerphone that their department no longer existed.

It was hard to feel too much sorrow for those who were dismissed. Making an average of $125,000 a year, they included many young MBAs who had been hired during fat times and were unceremoniously tossed overboard at the first sign of trouble. Still, some of the people had only joined the firm the previous week; one man had gotten married over the weekend.

Many of the people who remained considered Gutfreund's decisions strategically unwise. Trading municipal bonds had been one of the firm's basic businesses. To some former senior members of Salomon, like William Simon, Gutfreund seemed to have lost his nerve. Salomon was supposed to ride out hard times, not fold at the first sign of distress. After all, back in the late seventies, when volatile interest rates tore apart the mortgage-backed securities market that Salomon had just started, did the firm close its department? No, it hunkered down until the early eighties when interest rates stabilized, and at that point the firm was in a position to clean up. What had happened to Salomon's legendary fighting spirit? "When I was running muni bonds, I wanted *more* competition," William Simon told me. "I welcomed it."

The scale of the firings paralyzed Salomon employees. Morale disintegrated even further in the wake of Black Monday. Salomon was not hurt as badly by the market crash as firms like E. F. Hutton and L. F. Rothschild, which were so crippled they had to be sold. Nonetheless, it lost $75 million in October. That set the stage for another humiliating setback: Salomon's decision to withdraw from the Coliseum project. All fall Gutfreund had insisted he was totally committed to the project, regardless of any short-term fluctuations in business. On that assumption, Mort Zuckerman had proceeded to spend more than $35 million, fabricating steel, quarrying stone, and commissioning final architectural plans. When Salomon reversed course and pulled out of the project, the firm had to pay Zuckerman a kill fee said to be in the range of $55 million.

In the space of five years, Salomon had grown from a bond house to a full-fledged investment bank, yet the executives that ran it had remained essentially traders in their outlook and attitudes. Their horizon was short. The trend was their friend, and whether it was globalization or junk bonds or real estate investments, they aggressively muscled in, using the clout of their huge capital base to dominate the game. That was, as the ancient Greeks used to say, their *hamartia*, or fatal flaw. When the trend turned against them, they had to reverse direction suddenly; in the end they fared worse than the firms that were following strategies they had thought through independently.

Gutfreund defied predictions, made after the crash, that he would be ousted from the firm by its other executives. Many of the firm's senior members, however, left in the months that followed. During that period Gutfreund continued to scale back Salomon's trading operations and to expand the role of investment banking.

But Gutfreund was severely diminished by the events of 1987. Neither he nor the firm would again appear as proud and as confident and as arrogant as they had in those heady days in the mid-eighties, when they seemed to stand astride the world and others looked on in awe of their power and ruthlessness. Some things, though, never change. Two months after the crash, Susan Gutfreund appeared at Marie-Heléne de Rothschild's costume ball in Paris wearing an extravagant Christian Lacroix gown and a towering feather headdress. A short while after that, John Fairchild spotted her at Kennedy Airport waiting to board the Concorde. With her were her son, his nanny, a private secretary, and a personal travel agent. It's so expensive to be rich.

7

THE FUTURE OF
THE MONEY CULTURE

"A TERRIBLE PLACE TO WORK"

The tip of lower Manhattan is one of the most historically resonant locations in the United States. Dutch traders inhabited it in 1615. The settlement grew as the Hudson Valley was explored. In 1652 the settlers built a wall around their village, and the street that ran parallel to the inside of the wall became known as Wall Street. The town had expanded about 2,000 feet farther north when the first Continental Congress was convened in Federal Hall at the intersection of Wall and Broad streets. George Washington lived not far away on Cherry Street. The wall no longer exists, and the few townhouses and tenements and soot-blackened churches that remain from that period are so familiar to the people who work on Wall Street today that they are effectively invisible.

There has never been much veneration of the past in New York. In a city of immigrants, who have no connection to that past, and commerce, which is usually unable to exploit the past, such sentimental notions stand no chance against the drive to realize enormous profits by tearing down old buildings and putting up new ones. But while all but the most trifling vestiges of old New York have been eradicated, the earlier city continues to make its presence felt in the curving and narrow streets of the financial district. These little streets have funny archaic names like Water Street and Beaver Street and Pine Street and Broad Street and Exchange Place and, of course, Wall Street itself. Some are barely wide enough to accommodate a delivery truck. They are lined, however, with mammoth skyscrapers—limestone Art Deco extravagances, hulking granite edifices, modernist towers of steel and glass, and, most recently, postmodern buildings with bright ornamental facades.

Their abutment on the old streets creates deep narrow canyons. It is an extraordinary sight to stand at the windows in a corner office high up in one of these buildings at five o'clock in the afternoon and watch hundreds of thousands of people suddenly fill the tiny twisting streets. It is as if the sluice gates on some huge dam had been opened. The crowds pour out of the doors and alleys, past knots of clerks smoking dope, and when they reach the streets themselves, they form into a sort of rushing fleshy stream. As more people spill from the buildings and the crowds increase, they assume the irresistible driving force of a flash flood churning down a dry riverbed. This was the central psychological experience for successful New Yorkers in the eighties. It was not so much a case of being on the fast track as it was of being in the midst of a headlong torrent that swept them along so quickly the riverbanks were a blur.

One day in 1985, just after the market's closing bell, I went around to the office of a successful stock broker at a firm then known as L. F. Rothschild, Unterberg, Towbin, which was located in the upper reaches of one of those Wall Street towers. The broker sat in a small glass-walled office off the large bullpen where the less senior brokers plied their trade at open desks facing a large electronic ticker. His office was hardly a haven from that sink of noise and frenzy. Few people are afforded the luxury of privacy on Wall Street, where it tends to be viewed with some suspicion, and squeezed in with the broker were two female assistants. On his desk sat piles of research material, stacks of prospectuses, and three large Rolodex cylinders that he referred to as his "book" of clients.

Despite the thundering pace of the great bull market, the broker was morose. Excruciating tensions existed at L. F. Rothschild, which would be virtually wiped out in the crash two years later. Like most Wall Street firms, it represented the merger of two other firms. It had been, like most of them, a marriage of convenience. The two factions never really got along. Ironically enough, their differences had been exacerbated by the bull market. Surging stock prices had increased profits in the trading division, which had then attempted to seize control over the investment banking division. In response, the investment bankers had clandestinely plotted to sell the firm. The traders had discovered this plan and were trying to oust the investment banking cabal. It was a miserable situation. People at the firm were forced to choose sides and thus inevitably to make enemies.

As he described this mess, the broker grew more and more despondent. It came time for him to catch his train. We left his office and plunged into the fleshy torrent. The broker continued to talk. In addition to the death struggle between the traders and the investment bankers, he said, the firm was firing many of its retail brokers. The firm had been pushing the stocks of new small companies, which it liked to refer to as "emerging growth companies." The stocks of some of these small companies had performed so well that other investment banks had shouldered their way into this particular niche of the underwriting business. As it became more competitive, some new issues were overpriced and some small companies were persuaded by investment banks to issue stock when in fact the move was premature. Several of these stocks were spectacular disasters, which soured the new-issues market at large by scaring investors away from the stocks of all young, small companies. As a result, many of the brokers at L. F. Rothschild had "burned their books." That is, they had lost every single one of their clients because the price of the stocks they had encouraged them to buy had fallen. The firm's management was not about to carry brokers who weren't producing, thus the layoffs. The whole business had made the broker extremely depressed.

As we reached the twin towers of the World Trade Center and the elevators down to the trains to New Jersey, the broker stopped. Fighting for his footing in the flood of people that rushed around him into the big hole down to the trains, he said, "Wall Street is a terrible place to work. I hate it. I would kill my son before I allowed him to work here."

THE CRASH

Well before the closing bell on October 19, 1987, which was already being called Black Monday, a veritable mob had gathered outside the glass doors of the members' entrance to the New York Stock Exchange. More than 1,000 strong, the crowd clogged the sidewalk and spilled out into Broad Street. It included young British men serving internships at American brokerages, investment bankers wearing gilded horned-rims, television crews hump-backed with camera equipment, gangly Dutch tourists, Japanese businessmen, and girls with frosted hair and skintight acid-washed jeans.

People spanning the entire ethnic, economic, and social spectrum had converged on the Stock Exchange, tying up

traffic on Broad Street, because business had become theater in the eighties, and Black Monday seemed the denouement. Inside on the Exchange, the market was falling faster
and farther than it ever had in history—dropping, in fact,
like a meteor into the void. In the final hour of trading
alone, the Dow plummeted at a rate of 3.5 points per
minute with 1.7 million shares a minute changing hands.
Throughout the city, from Water Street to Park Avenue
Plaza, from Harry's Bar to the "21" Club, investors and
bystanders stared with rapt fascination at computer screens
as the numbers melted away.

As the crowd roiled and seethed around the members'
entrance, a wraithlike man with a drooping moustache
appeared on its fringes.

"The end is near!" he began to yell. "It's all over for the
yuppies! Down with MBAs! It's all over! The Reagan revolution is over! Down with the yuppies!"

A heavy man in a suit and tie had just come out of the
Exchange. In a trader's bull-horn voice he brayed back the
popular T-shirt slogan, "Whoever dies with the most toys
wins!"

"Down with MBAs!"

"Whoever dies with the most toys wins!"

"How many toys do you have now?" someone in the
crowd asked the heavy man.

"None."

"Down with MBAs!" the wraithlike man shrieked in
triumph. "It's all over for the yuppies!"

Black Monday was undeniably a historic moment. It
drew people to the Exchange the way a solar eclipse or
some stunning planetary conjunction would compel ancient
tribes to gather at the temple. It also inevitably brought out
the lunatic fringe. In fact, during the week of the crash the
corner of Broad and Wall—the very heart of the financial

district—became a sort of combination carnival and tent revival, replete with gaping onlookers, hawkers, charlatans, quacks, pickpockets, cultists, prophets, holy-rolling hymnal groups, and comedians. And why had they all come? To witness the Fall of the Yuppie.

From 1982 to 1988 one out of four new jobs in the private sector in New York City had been in the financial services industry. The total personnel of all member firms of the New York Stock Exchange grew during that period by approximately 150,000. Members of other exchanges, such as the American Stock Exchange and the commodities exchanges, expanded as well. Research boutiques and money management firms also flourished. Many of the new jobs at these firms were lower-paid clerical and administrative positions. But, while no precise numbers are available, tens of thousands of MBAs were hired by brokerages and investment banks in the years since the bull market got under way.

That generation of young professionals—who made staggering and unprecedented sums of money while still in their twenties—represented a sort of cultural and economic avant-garde in the eighties. Together with the hordes of new lawyers and accountants who service Wall Street firms, they were a primary force in the creation of the money culture. They were behind everything from the surge in value of American antiques and the proliferation of expensive restaurants to the rising price of housing in cities like New York, Boston, and San Francisco. In the process they became—as much as corporate raiders or inside traders or junk bonds—an emblem of the era.

Because most of these people began work after the commencement of the bull market, they had never lived through a significant downturn. With such an eventuality little more than an abstraction, they consumed—borrowing money for lavish apartments, beach houses, and foreign cars—as if they would always receive the salaries and bonuses that flowed their way during the boom. In the wake of the crash it appeared to many that all that would change. The importance of these young professionals to their firms had never been tested in a slow market, when the brokerages and investment banks that had expanded to such vast proportions would find they must slash operating costs drastically to remain afloat. During the boom years, when firms like Salomon were making more than $500 million a year, they could afford to pay new MBAs $150,000 a year. But the poor conditions in the bond markets as well as the stock market, together with the capital requirements of merchant banking, placed severe strains on the capital of Wall Street firms. To cut costs, the executives who ran the firms began sacrificing young MBAs as if they were so much cannon fodder. By the spring of 1988, 15,000 to 30,000 people had lost jobs in the securities industry.

That accelerated the widespread if superficial re-evaluation of the money culture that began when the young investment banker Dennis Levine was arrested for insider trading in 1986, which led to the downfall of Ivan Boesky and the decision by Drexel Burnham Lambert to plead guilty to insider trading, cut its ties with Michael Milken, and pay a $650 million fine. Business schools were urged to require courses on ethics. Investment banks announced the adoption of sterner policies on conflicts of interest. It seemed to many people that the priorities and attitudes that gave the eighties their momentum had run their course. They believed that the preoccupation with what Arthur Schlesinger called "private interest" was beginning to wane, as was the unbridled optimism that had governed much of the country for much of the decade.

Stock market analyst Robert Prechter had kept close track of the emergence of the country's optimistic mood, as expressed not only in stock prices but also in popular culture. And in the wake of the stock market's October 19 crash—an isolated incident that affected the lives of only a relative handful of Americans—he too saw signs that the mood of the nation itself was shifting. "It is clear that extremes in popular cultural trends coincide with extremes in stock prices, since they peak and trough coincidentally in their reflection of the popular mood," he wrote in 1985. "The stock market is literally a drawing of how the scales of mass mood are tipping. A decline indicates an increasing 'negative' mood on balance, and an advance indicates an increasing 'positive' mood on balance."

Certainly, popular culture in 1987 mirrored in many ways the giddy speculative fever that brought about the stock market's astonishing pre-crash run-up. The parallels in the fashion industry were particularly remarkable. It has often been observed that hemlines and stock prices have kept pace throughout the twentieth century. They both rose in the twenties and sixties and both fell in the thirties and seventies. Miniskirts began appearing again in late 1986, but they did not catch on until the following year. Designers, together with John Fairchild and his fashion publications, began promoting miniskirts heavily in the fall of 1987.

That same year, the feverish exfoliations of the new French designer Christian Lacroix reached the United States. It was Lacroix who popularized the pouf. Perhaps the most astonishing and outrageous dress created in the twentieth century, the pouf was a brilliantly colored, bell-shaped dress that could be as wide as four feet and was festooned with bows and ribbons. It cost $10,000 and up. It was confining and utterly impractical, and the woman who wore it had to negotiate a ballroom with the care a ferry pilot took crossing a busy harbor. Naturally, the pouf became de rigueur for the thin wives of the new tycoons in 1986. The *New York Times* actually ran an article on how to pack a pouf for air travel. The writer prefaced the article by saying that, of course, women flying in private jets need not concern themselves with the problem. These exorbitant, clumsy dresses, which perfectly illustrated Veblen's thesis that the role of the wife is to consume vicariously for her husband, captured the heedlessness of the country prior to the crash. In the wake of the crash, sales of miniskirts plummeted and the full-blown pouf all but disappeared.

It goes without saying that any shift in national mood takes place fitfully and unevenly. Prechter, with hindsight, has argued that even as the stock market roared through 1987 the public had already begun subliminally to express fearful and negative emotions. Popular music reflected the new concerns. Prechter has maintained that popular music moves "in lock step" with the Dow Jones Industrial Average. He has described the Beach Boys—with their fun-fun-fun lyrics and irresistible dance beat—as a bull market band. The group's first hit song, "Surfin'," took off in 1962, the year the bull market of the sixties began. Their last big hit song, "Good Vibrations," was released in 1966, the year the market reached its peak. Soon after, heavy-metal rock bands began to appear, anticipating the surge in pessimism and anger in the late sixties and the decline in stock prices that began in 1968.

Popular music in the eighties, Prechter has observed, went through a similar cycle. Early in the decade, upbeat performers like Phil Collins and groups like Men At Work began to eclipse downbeat bands such as Pink Floyd, whose album *Dark Side of the Moon* had floated on and off the charts throughout the seventies. But in the late eighties a new type of music began to appear. Seven months before the crash, Jon Pareles, a music critic for the *New York Times*, wrote an article called "Glum Rock," which discussed a number of new groups whose songs dwelt on feelings of gloom, ennui, and self-pity. Some of these groups, like Megadeth and Metallica, were proponents of speed metal, a fast, noisy, musically complicated sound with lyrics foretelling death by nuclear war. Other groups, like the Smiths, the Cure, and Depeche Mode, expressed a more general malaise. Life to them was bleak, morose, miserable. Just as in the late sixties, bull market bands with songs about love and fun were giving way to bear market bands that dwelt on violence and alienation.

Nothing, however, seemed more clearly to portray the erosion of eighties optimism than the stock market's crash. While October 19 has now entered history as Black Monday, the market actually came closer to an outright rout the following day. When the stock exchange opened that Tuesday morning, work in all but the trading departments of brokerages and investment banks came to a virtual halt as people gathered at Quotrons to watch the initial surge.

A huge line of spectators waiting to get into the visitors gallery of the New York Stock Exchange spilled out of the building and up the block. They were excited. Without the slightest knowledge of what to expect, they nonetheless anticipated a terrific show. Some wondered when Wall Street's inhabitants would live up to their legend and start leaping from windows.

"Do you think there will be any jumpers?" a woman asked her companion. "Maybe we'll see a jumper."

The two of them looked up at the buildings towering overhead only to see hundreds of office workers at hundreds of sealed windows gazing down at the mob in the street.

Nearby, a young homeless woman with an alert but detached expression sat beside a piece of cardboard on which she had written: MY NAME IS MARIA. I AM 18 YEARS OLD, DEAF & MUTE AND 8 MONTHS PREGNANT. MY MOM DIED IN APRIL. I HAVE TO HELP RAISE MY BROTHER NOW. NOBODY WANTS HIM. I ALSO HAVE A 14 MONTH SET OF TWIN BOYS. I MUST PAY RENT AND BUY FOOD, DO LAUNDRY. I NEED

ALL THE HELP I CAN GET. WELFARE SAID NO. SSI SAID TO WAIT, MY CHECK WILL COME NOV. 1. PLS HELP. THANK YOU.

Across the street, devotees of Lyndon LaRouche had set up a table and were soliciting the crowd in their inimitably aggressive manner. Jeanne Kacprzak, a short woman with curly black hair, was offering people apple cores, saying, "Get your apple cores here! Free apple cores here! Get your apple cores!"

"This is all we've got left," she explained. "In the last depression we sold apples. Now we're so bad off we have to eat apples. So we're selling the apple cores. It's called the IMF diet."

She went on to say that the country had actually been in the midst of a depression for the past eight years, but that the media had conspired to hide the truth from the public. The only way to restore productivity, she continued, was to get rid of the "paper shufflers" on Wall Street. "We have to put all these yuppies back to real work," she said.

Soon the streets around the Exchange were flooded with proselytizers. A man in a jacket and tie appeared with a red megaphone and began to preach to the crowd. "Jesus said, 'What good is it to amass all the riches in the world but lose your soul?'" he told the assembled multitudes. One group was singing Baptist hymns while near them a man with a Karl Marx beard passed out literature denouncing capitalism. All manner of hucksters and barkers appeared as well. One began to sell apples from a box, initially offering them for 10 cents apiece, then slashing them to a nickel when they failed to move. Mitch Simon was doing a brisk trade in a postcard he had made from a photograph of a man about to jump from a tall building. "I sold about sixty yesterday," he said. "They were first two for a dollar, but they sold so quickly I raised the price to a dollar apiece. Comic relief is a real valuable thing, you know."

The press, meanwhile, had undertaken a full-scale stakeout of the story. Television crews had arrived in vans with satellite dishes mounted on their roofs to broadcast live dispatches from the scene. Print reporters, turned away from the full-to-capacity press gallery at the Exchange, began swamping the investment banks with calls. Their assignment was twofold: to explain why stocks had crashed the day before and to assess the market's mood in the wake of that collapse.

But the problem was that the stock market was not an actual entity. The people on the floor of the New York Stock Exchange merely executed trades decided on by hundreds of thousands of investors around the country for hundreds of thousands of different reasons. The phrase "stock market" was simply a metaphor, a convenient code to describe the sum total of the activities of this swarm of investors. Thus, there was no single reason the market collapsed. Rather, there were a thousand reasons—from disappointing U.S. trade statistics to the dropping value of the dollar, from Nancy Reagan's breast cancer and Iran's declaration of war to program trading and the influential Prechter's pronouncement that the Dow was due for a correction. But investors could always find ample reasons to justify either a bullish or a bearish position. The reasons offered up to explain the crash on October 19 were nothing more than convenient catalysts for what seemed to be a massive shift in popular sentiment.

Traders awaited the opening of the Exchange Tuesday morning with dread. Overnight, investment banks and brokerages had been swamped with sell orders. Many were brought about by margin calls on investors who had borrowed money to buy stocks. For a brief period after the market opened at 9:30 no trading took place in some sixty stocks because no buyers could be found. But fears quickly dissipated as corporations began snapping up their own stock to stabilize its price. The market shot up 113 points in the first half hour, and euphoria swept through the floor of the Exchange.

No sooner had corporations helped drive prices up than institutional investors started selling to take profits. Traders were again in a panic. The deluge of sell orders was so gargantuan that the Exchange's computers became temporarily overloaded. Some of the computer screens on the floor of the Exchange went blank, and traders became convinced the system had collapsed. By mid-day, the market had fallen more than 200 points from its high at 10:30.

At noon the trading floor at Drexel Burnham Lambert was utter bedlam. Ed Kantor, the silver-haired man who headed the firm's trading department, was running from station to station, his face grim. The vast U-shaped room was a swirl of paper, cigarette butts, bags of uneaten bagels, tubs of cream cheese and whipped butter. Everywhere stood gesticulating, shrieking traders—the men and women who, with their stylized hysterical gesturing, seemed to form a sort of bas-relief background for much of the action of the eighties. They shrieked at each other, they shrieked at their screens full of declining equity positions, they shrieked at the telephones that went unanswered for crucial seconds while prices dived. But most of all they shrieked at that large abstraction, the market itself. "Stop the selling!" a trader named Frank pleaded to no one in particular as the figures on his Quotron ticked down. "Stop the selling!"

By mid-afternoon, stocks had risen again. Throughout the day the market was lashed by furious trading. After rising 200, it dropped 226, then rose again to close up 102. A staggering 608.1 million shares had exchanged hands without establishing any real direction. The day seemed testament to the frenzy of indecision that had seized Wall Street. As closing time drew near, the crowd again gathered at the Exchange's members' entrance, awaiting some sort of revelation, some signal from the *Zeitgeist*. But the closing bell came and went, and—one by one—steaming, red-faced traders emerged from the glass doors and pushed brusquely through the crowd. It eventually became clear that nothing was going to happen. There would be no oracular utterance, no denouement. So after a while, with their thirst for drama still unslaked, the people in the crowd began to drift uncertainly away, their future as impenetrable as it had been that morning.

THE NINETIES

By the late eighties, the money culture had taken deep root in American society. The philosophy of wealth creation encouraged each person to seek his or her own fortune and let others take care of themselves. Of course, those incapable of taking care of themselves suffered correspondingly. The growing desolation among the nation's poor, the increase in homelessness, and the general rise in frustration and disillusionment that helped bring about the crack plague are all ironic outgrowths of the money culture.

In fact, one of the most far-reaching changes to occur during the eighties was the reversal of the redistribution of wealth that had taken place in the previous fifty years. Those in favor of this shift say it had become necessary again to reward the producers. But it was not the producers who were rewarded so much as the capitalists. The entire takeover and leveraged-buyout phenomenon can be seen as a single giant mechanism to transfer wealth back into the hands of the capitalists. In most takeovers, the new owners of the company assumed heavy debts to finance its purchase from its previous stockholders. To pay off that debt, the new owners cut costs by divestitures and by firing employees and reducing the salaries of those who remained.

This, according to the proponents of takeovers, made companies more efficient.

The point of efficient operations is to enable a company either to reduce the price of its products or to free up money for capital investment and research and development. But the increased cash flow produced at a company that had been taken over did not as a rule go toward those ends. It went instead to service the debt that had been acquired to finance the takeover. In other words, the most obvious effect of a takeover was to transfer money from the company's employees to the individuals on Wall Street who held its stock and junk bonds.

But the eighties did more than just widen the gap between rich and poor. The social conditions that emerged during the decade altered basic American attitudes toward the way money was made and how it was spent. The notion, articulated most vividly by Jerry Falwell, that money has an intrinsic spiritual value, helped make wealth the measure of all things. This standard came to apply even in fields like art. For more than a century the notion that esthetic merit could be determined by commercial success was apostasy. But for artists in the eighties, as Mark Kostabi and his peers demonstrated, the approval of critics was replaced by "the validation of the marketplace." After all, since the bourgeoisie—or collecting class—had lost all resistance to the avant-garde, it had become impossible for the artist to rationalize poor reception to his work on the grounds that the public was too philistine and reactionary to understand him. The only explanation for commercial failure was lack of talent.

If, as Falwell suggested, money was a sign of God's blessing, then it followed that the extent of an individual's wealth was a direct measure of his spiritual standing. The more money one had, the closer one must be to God. In other words—to strip the idea of its religious trappings and put it in the classic nouveau riche formulation—money was a metaphor for status. Indeed, people justified the accumulation of wealth by explaining that they didn't seek money for its own sake but because it demonstrated their success. Throughout the decade, for example, young investment bankers were quoted as saying that the huge sums of money they earned were important mainly as a way of "keeping score" among their peers in the career race. In his ghostwritten autobiography, Donald Trump said he didn't do deals "for the money." He did deals because that's how he got his "kicks." And what provided the kick, of course, was prevailing over an opponent.

Now, as Veblen pointed out, such victories afford little satisfaction unless they become widely known. In other words, the idea of winning—in the sense of defeating a competitor—and of status are inextricably linked. The extravagant parties at the Metropolitan Museum and other philanthropic and cultural institutions were clearly nothing less than elaborate status rituals whereby the nouveaux riches, through thinly veiled acts of conspicuous consumption, established social distinctions based on the wealth they had accumulated as a result of their victories on the corporate battlefield.

But the appetite for recognition and status was not limited merely to the nouveaux riches. The public at large shared it. And though the public could not satisfy it as grandly as could the new tycoons, they could indulge themselves vicariously. That accounted for the success of movies like *Flashdance* and *Top Gun*, where the struggles of the main characters are ultimately rewarded with public admiration and thus enhanced status. (In the climax of *Flashdance*, the main character dazzles the haughty admissions board of an elite ballet school with her dancing skill; in *Top Gun*, the fighter pilot's skill in aerial combat has a similar but even more ecstatic effect on the crew of his aircraft carrier.)

Because money was the direct measure of status in the eighties, net worth came to be, for many people, indistinguishable from self-worth. In 1986 one investment banker I know whose firm had lost money in a downturn that fall complained that lawyers and other investment bankers whose client he was no longer paid him as much deference as they had before. As a result, he said, he felt himself less of a person.

The notion that money in itself is good implies that the act of acquiring money is also good. The money culture of the eighties endorsed a whole new set of attitudes toward the behavior needed to accumulate wealth. For example, the ruthlessness embodied by John Gutfreund came to be seen as a virtue. Such behavior, the argument went, was necessary to revitalize American corporations and restore American productivity. But the money culture endorsed even unproductive activity, such as speculating in takeover stocks, as long as it led to the accumulation of wealth. The creation of tax shelters, to take the most extreme example, yielded nothing productive, even by the standards of Wall Street, which produces no goods but considers trading securities to be socially useful labor because it promotes the efficient flow of capital. Tax shelters simply provided a handful of very wealthy people like Norman Lear with opportunities to avoid the social responsibility of paying taxes.

It seemed as if such activity was so removed from everyday life that it lacked any moral grounding. It was no coincidence that the major financial scandals of the eighties involved, early in the decade, tax shelter scams like the one allegedly run by Charlie Atkins and then, later in the decade, insider trading in takeover stocks. The opportunities— and thus the temptations—were certainly greatest in these fields. But also, both the creation of tax shelters and the speculation in takeover stocks are so divorced from practical human considerations that simply to engage in them is to enter into a moral vacuum.

On December 13, 1987, the *New York Times* ran a front page article headlined "The Plunge: A Stunning Blow to a Gilded, Impudent Age." The consensus of the Wall Street executives and historians interviewed seemed to be that, with the crash the preceding October, the era was drawing to a close. "It will be seen as the end of a period of good, wild times and a return to realities," said financial writer John Brooks, expressing the conventional wisdom.

It was true that the unbridled optimism that first allowed the money culture to flourish had been checked by the crash that October. But the money culture itself may prove more tenacious. Confounding the expectations of many analysts that the crash had inaugurated the onset of a major recession and perhaps even a depression, the stock market began to recover in the latter half of 1988. By January 20, the day George Bush was sworn in as President, the Dow Jones Industrial Average had climbed back to 2235, not so far below the 2246 where it had stood before Black Monday. And while stocks lacked direction, they had certainly not followed the pattern set in the crash of 1929 when, after a brief rally, they began a grim and unstoppable slide.

Without indulging in economic predictions, it seems safe to say that, by surviving the crash, the money culture of the eighties withstood its first serious test. It's interesting to note that the Gilded Age experienced several similar financial panics without coming to a halt. In 1873, for example, the collapse of the stock market during the presidency of Ulysses Grant posed the country with one of the most severe financial crises it had faced up to that time. Prominent financiers were wiped out in that crash, including Jay Cooke, perhaps the most influential investment banker of the era, who had devised ways to sell the bonds that financed the Union's effort in the Civil War. But other titans, such as Jay Gould and Commodore Vanderbilt, survived. So did the speculative mania, driven by the westward expansion, that characterized the era. In fact, in 1883, seven years after losing the presidency to Rutherford Hayes, Grant himself—the eighteenth President, the tactical genius who had won the Civil War—went to work on Wall Street as an investment banker.*

Similarly, the takeover frenzy of the eighties continued unabated despite the insider trading scandal and the crash. In fact, in 1988, the year Drexel Burnham pleaded guilty to insider trading and agreed to pay its $650-million fine, 3,637 mergers and acquisitions were completed, with a total value of $311.4 billion—far and away the biggest year ever for such deals. Among them was Kohlberg Kravis & Roberts' $25-billion leveraged buyout of RJR/Nabisco—the largest takeover in history. Transactions of that size had been unthinkable only a few years earlier. This activity produced a record $1.28 billion in investment banking fees for Wall Street firms, and as a result finance remained an attractive profession for young business school graduates.

Political developments also suggested that the money culture of the eighties would endure. Together with the Iran-Contra scandal, the crash of 1987 seemed to many to provide evidence that the 1988 presidential election belonged to the Democrats. Americans, Democrats believed, were eager to begin once again to redistribute the national wealth. But for all the post-election analysis of Michael Dukakis' personal inadequacies and his mismanaged campaign, the Republican victory was due in no small part to the persistent belief, even in depressed regions of the country like Oklahoma and even among unemployed oil workers, in

---

*Grant, who was plagued by poor judgment after leaving the Army, was swindled by his partner, and in 1884 his firm failed.

Reagan's entrepreneurial ideology, which George Bush promised to maintain. Despite his expressed desire for a "kinder, gentler nation," and for ethical rectitude in government, Bush endorsed, just as staunchly as Reagan did, wealth creation over wealth redistribution.

And so the eighties may be more than—as it is now widely perceived—a short giddy era when the nation lost its senses and turned with almost pagan ecstasy to the worship of money. The decade, instead, may well mark the beginning of a much more long-term shift in public priorities. For the previous fifty years, the country had, with some interruptions, been embarked on an egalitarian course; each succeeding decade further closed the gap between rich and poor. In the thirties, the Roosevelt Administration created social security and laid the foundations for the future welfare state. After World War II, the G.I. Bill enabled working and lower middle class veterans to enroll in college and to buy houses in the suburbs—to assume the privileges of the professional classes. Lyndon Johnson's "war on poverty" and Great Society programs were also dedicated to raising the standard of living of the lower classes.

In the seventies this impulse began to founder, and by the eighties it had been reversed. The grasping materialism of the Gilded Age, which began after the Civil War and replaced the Jeffersonian political idealism that marked the first seventy years of the nation's history, dominated the country from 1865 to 1929—a little more than half a century. It was sustained primarily by the discovery, during the westward expansion and the Machine Age, of new sources of wealth. A fundamental reconstitution of the national economy occurred. And a similar reconstitution seems to be taking place today, as money from Japan and Europe flows in to support U.S. consumption. It has frequently been argued that the Japanese are "taking over" the United States, acquiring the nation's real estate, its corporate stock, its government bonds. But it may well be that the United States is absorbing Japan, just as the carpet-baggers who moved into the South after the Civil War were absorbed into their new surroundings and eventually became an indistinguishable feature of the Southern towns that had at first feared they were being taken over. Thus it may be, if the parallel bears out and if the economic catastrophe predicted by pessimists fails to materialize, that the money culture established in the eighties will continue to drive the country for years to come.

SOURCES

In addition to the people I interviewed, many of whom are listed in the acknowledgments, I relied on many secondary sources. The following is a partial list of those sources.

Chapter 1

Allen, Frederick Lewis. *Only Yesterday: An Informal History of the 1920's.* New York: Harper & Brothers, 1931.

Barnabel, Josh. "Grillwork Missing at Bonwit Building." *New York Times,* June 7, 1980.

Battiata, Mary, *et al.* "The Republicans Hit the Receiving Line, Running." *Washington Post,* January 19, 1981.

————. "Pepping Up the Party Pace." *Washington Post,* January 20, 1981.

Boodman, Sandra. "How Falwell Raises His Millions: The Fund-raising Techniques." *Washington Post,* June 28, 1981.

————. "Falwell's Empire at 25: Signs of Financial Woes." *Washington Post,* June 26, 1981.

Boorstin, Daniel. *The Americans: The National Experience.* New York: Random House, 1965.

Cimons, Marlene. "Hectic Days in D.C. as the Pace Quickens for the Inauguration." *Los Angeles Times,* January 19, 1981.

Clendinen, Dudley. "Rev. Falwell Inspires Evangelical Vote." *New York Times*, August 20, 1980.

Collier, Peter, and David Horowitz. *The Rockefellers: An American Dynasty*. New York: Holt, Rinehart and Winston, 1976.

Duka, John. "A New Opulence Triumphs In Capital." *New York Times*, January 22, 1981.

Eleni. "White Tie, Club Coats In Again." *Washington Star*, January 9, 1981.

FitzGerald, Frances. "A Reporter at Large: A Disciplined Charging Army." *The New Yorker*, May 18, 1981.

Hirshberg, Jennifer. "Throwing a Party for 50,000." *Washington Star*, January 15, 1981.

Josephson, Matthew. *The Robber Barons*. New York: Harcourt Brace Jovanovich, 1934.

Kaufman, Marc, and Tom Crosby. "Nation's Capital Caught Up in the 'Inaugural Madness.'" *Washington Star*, January 19, 1981.

Lasch, Christopher. *The Culture of Narcissism*. New York: W.W. Norton & Company, 1979.

Mayer, Allan J. "A Tide of Born Again Politics." *Newsweek*, September 15, 1980.

McCollum, Charles. "The Nine Lives of the City's Show of Shows." *Washington Star*, January 21, 1981.

McFadden, Robert. "Developer Scraps Bonwit Sculptures." *New York Times*, June 6, 1980.

———. "Designer Astonished by Loss of Bonwit Grillwork." *New York Times*, June 8, 1980.

———. "Builder Says Costs Forced Scrapping of Bonwit Art." *New York Times*, June 9, 1980.

McManus, Otile. "Inauguration Festivities for Reagan." *Boston Globe*, January 20, 1981.

Morgan, Wayne H., ed. *The Gilded Age: a Reappraisal*. Syracuse, New York: Syracuse University Press, 1963.

Murphy, Mary. "The Next Billy Graham." *Esquire*, October 10, 1978.

Nemy, Enid. "The Capital Party Game Is Seeing and Being Seen." *New York Times*, January 19, 1981.

Parrington, Vernon. *Main Currents in American Thought*. New York: Harcourt, Brace and Company, 1930.

Pomberto, Beth Gillin, and Jill Gerston. "Elegance Is Back." *Philadelphia Inquirer*, January 22, 1981.

Prechter, Robert. "Special Report: Popular Culture and the Stock Market." *The Elliott Wave Theorist*. Gainesville, Georgia: August 22, 1985.

———. "Special Report." *The Elliott Wave Theorist*. Gainesville, Georgia: December 28, 1987.

Reed, Rex. "If This Is the Beginning, It's Really the End." *Daily News*, January 23, 1981.

Romano, Lois. "Inaugural Tickets: The Scramble Is On." *Washington Star*, January 8, 1981.

Rosenfeld, Megan. "The Evangelist and His Empire." *Washington Post*, April 28, 1979.

Scheer, Robert. "Q&A: Falwell Doubts There'll Be Any More Witch Hunts." *Los Angeles Times*, March 4, 1981.

———. "The Prophet of 'Worldly Methods.'" *Los Angeles Times*, March 4, 1981.

Schlesinger, Arthur M., Jr. *The Cycles of American History.* Boston: Houghton Mifflin Company, 1986.

Seligsohn, Leo. "The Jerry Falwell Force." *Newsday Magazine*, March 22, 1981.

Sheehy, Gail. *Character: America's Search for Leadership.* New York: Morrow, 1988.

Silverman, Debora. *Selling Culture: Bloomingdale's, Diana Vreeland, and the New Aristocracy of Taste in Reagan's America.* New York: Pantheon Books, 1986.

Smith, Hedrick. "A Hopeful Prologue, a Pledge of Action." *New York Times*, January 21, 1981.

Trump, Donald J., with Tony Schwartz. *Trump: The Art of the Deal.* New York: Random House, 1987.

Veblen, Thorstein. *The Theory of the Leisure Class.* New York: NAL Penguin, 1953. Originally published in 1899.

Watters, Susan. "Washington: Inaugural Fever." *Women's Wear Daily*, January 14, 1981.

Weintraub, Boris. "And Is There Any Room at the Inn?" *Washington Star*, January 8, 1981.

West, Richard. "Mr. Reagan Goes to Washington." *New York*, February 2, 1981.

Wills, Garry. *Reagan's America.* Garden City, New York: Doubleday, 1987.

Woodward, Kenneth L. "A $1 Million Habit." *Newsweek*, September 15, 1980.

Chapter 2

The bulk of the information in this chapter is drawn from the transcripts of the trial: *United States of America* v. *Charles Agee Atkins et al.* in the U.S. District Court, Southern District of New York. Docket Nos. 88-1116, 88-1122, 88-1123.

I am also grateful to Bill Agee for conducting several interviews and for providing research material on the civil lawsuits against Atkins.

Other sources consulted include:

Blumberg, Paul. *Inequality in an Age of Decline*. New York: Oxford University Press, 1980.

Carrington, Tim, and Daniel Hertzberg. "Wall Street Saga: Tax Shelter Promoter Lured Large Investors, Then Soon Lost Favor." *Wall Street Journal*, August 23, 1983.

Cowan, Paul. "The Merger Maestro." *Esquire*, May 1984.

Gerth, Jeff. "Former Oil Official Was Arrested in Stolen-Data Case Linked to Iran." *New York Times*, September 10, 1988.

Scully, John, with John A. Byrne. *Odyssey*. New York: Harper & Row, 1987.

Shanahan, Eileen. "Foreign Subsidiaries Provided Illegal Nixon Gifts, Oilmen Say." *New York Times*, November 15, 1973.

Sobel, Robert. *Panic on Wall Street*. New York: E.P. Dutton, 1988.

Stuart, Reginald. "Ashland Chief Cites Moral Shift in U.S." *New York Times*, August 22, 1975.

Chapter 3

Alpers, Svetlana. *Rembrandt's Enterprise: The Studio and the Market*. Chicago: University of Chicago Press, 1988.

Dowd, Maureen. "Youth, Art, Hype: A Different Bohemia." *New York Times Magazine*, November 17, 1985.

Frank, Peter, and Michael McKenzie. *New, Used & Improved: Art for the Eighties*. New York: Abbeville Press, 1987.

Hirschberg, Lynn. "The Four Brushmen of the Apocalypse." *Esquire*, March 1987.

Kostabi, Mark. *Sadness Because the Video Rental Store Was Closed*. New York: Abbeville Press, 1988.

Kroft, Steve. "Mark Kostabi: The Art of Business." *West 57th Street*. New York: CBS, aired on September 15, 1987.

McGuigan, Cathleen. "New Art, New Money." *New York Times Magazine*, February 10, 1985.

Pye, Michael. "Inside Deals of New York's Smart-Art Barons." *The Listener*, October, 1987.

Schwartz, Gary. *Rembrandt: His Life, His Paintings*. New York: Viking, 1985.

Small, Michael. "Art for Whose Sake?" *People*, July 11, 1988.

Stevens, Mark. "On Art: Retouching Rembrandt." *New Republic*, August 22, 1988.

Chapter 4

Anonymous. "Wedding Royale: Let 'Em Eat Cakes." *Women's Wear Daily*, April 20, 1988.

———. "Mercedes Hooks Her Bass." *Women's Wear Daily*, December 12, 1988.

Churcher, Sharon. "Making It by Doing Good." *New York Times Magazine*, July 3, 1988.

Clews, Henry. *Fifty Years in Wall Street*. New York: Irving Publishing Co., 1908.

Fussell, Paul. *Class*. New York: Summit Books, 1983.

Gallaher, J. G. "Leo X, Pope." *The Catholic Encyclopedia*. New York: McGraw Hill, 1967.

Josephson, Matthew. *The Robber Barons*. New York: Harcourt Brace Jovanovich, 1934.

Kornbluth, Jesse. "The Working Rich." *New York*, November 24, 1986.

Mellow, James. "The Fine Art of Directing the Met Museum." *New York Times Magazine*, November 3, 1985.

Morrisroe, Patricia. "The New Snobbery." *New York*, April 7, 1986.

Parrington, Vernon. *Main Currents in American Thought*. New York: Harcourt, Brace and Company, 1930.

Silverman, Debora. *Selling Culture: Bloomingdale's, Diana Vreeland, and the New Aristocracy of Taste in Reagan's America*. New York: Pantheon Books, 1986.

Stern, Robert A. M., *et al. New York 1900*. New York: Rizzoli International Publications, 1983.

Tomkins, Calvin. *Merchants and Masterpieces: The Story of the Metropolitan Museum of Art*. New York: E.P. Dutton, 1970.

Veblen, Thorstein. *The Theory of the Leisure Class*. New York: NAL Penguin, 1953. Originally published in 1899.

Chapter 5

Chase, Donald. "Producers: Don Simpson and Jerry Bruckheimer." *Millimeter*, December 1985.

Latham, Aaron. "Barry Diller and the Killer Dillers." *Manhattan,inc.*, February 1988.

Litwak, Mark. *Reel Power*. New York: Morrow, 1986.

Orth, Maureen. "The Baby Moguls." *New West*, June 19, 1978.

Pollock, Dale. "Flashfight." *Los Angeles Times*, July 10, 1983.

———. "Hollywood's Hit Men." *Los Angeles Times*. November 18, 1984.

Schatz, Thomas. *The Genius of the System*. New York: Pantheon Books, 1988.

Chapter 6

Anonymous. "Nouvelle Society." *W*, December 29, 1986.

Bianco, Anthony. "The King of Wall Street." *Business Week*, December 9, 1985.

————. "The Decline of the Superstar." *Business Week*, August 17, 1987.

Brown, Tina. "Gayfryd Takes Over." *Vanity Fair*, November 1986.

Dunlap, David. "Biltmore Closes, Surprising Guests." *New York Times*, August 16, 1981.

Leinster, Colin. "The Man Who Seized the Throne at Phibro-Salomon." *Fortune*, December 24, 1984.

McGoldrick, Beth. "Salomon's Power Culture." *Institutional Investor*, March 1986.

Michaelis, David. "The Nutcracker Suit." *Manhattan,inc.*, December 1984.

Niebuhr, Reinhold. *Reinhold Niebuhr on Politics*. Harry Davis, ed. New York: Charles Scribner's Sons. 1955.

Swartz, Steve. "Home to Roost." *Wall Street Journal*, October 2, 1987.

Vogel, Carol. "Susan Gutfreund: High Finances, High Living." *New York Times Magazine*, January 10, 1988.

Chapter 7

Glaberson, William. "Stunning Blow for a Glittering, Impudent Age." *New York Times*, December 13, 1987.

Prechter, Robert. "Special Report: Popular Culture and the Stock Market." *The Elliott Wave Theorist*. Gainesville, Georgia: August 22, 1985.

————. "Special Report." *The Elliott Wave Theorist*. Gainesville, Georgia: December 28, 1987.